DOLLAR POLITICS

CONGRESSIONAL QUARTERLY
1735 K STREET, N.W., WASHINGTON, D.C.

Congressional Quarterly Inc.

Congressional Quarterly Inc., an editorial research service and publishing company, serves clients in the fields of news, education, business and government. It combines specific coverage of Congress, government and politics by Congressional Quarterly with the more general subject range of an affiliated service, Editorial Research Reports.

Congressional Quarterly was founded in 1945 by Nelson and Henrietta Poynter. Its basic periodical publication was and still is the *CQ Weekly Report,* which is mailed to clients every Saturday. A cumulative index is published quarterly.

The CQ *Almanac,* a compendium of legislation for one session of Congress, is published every spring. *Congress and the Nation* is published every four years as a record of government for one presidential term.

Congressional Quarterly also publishes paperback books on public affairs. These include the twice-yearly *Guide to Current American Government* and such recent titles as *The Washington Lobby, Crime and the Law* and *Politics in America.*

CQ Direct Research is a consulting service which performs contract research and maintains a reference library and query desk for the convenience of clients.

Editorial Research Reports covers subjects beyond the specialized scope of Congressional Quarterly. It publishes reference material on foreign affairs, business, education, cultural affairs, national security, science and other topics of news interest. Service to clients includes a 6,000-word report four times a month bound and indexed semi-annually. Editorial Research Reports publishes paperback books in its fields of coverage. Founded in 1923, the service merged with Congressional Quarterly in 1956.

Dollar Politics was prepared by the Congressional Quarterly research staff under the direction of Wayne Kelley, Research Director. The book was edited by Robert A. Diamond, Book Service Editor.

Contributors: Stanley N. Wellborn, Thomas J. Arrandale, Oliver W. Cromwell, Robert E. Cuthriell, Alan Ehrenhalt, John Hamer, Carol Moore, Esther Safran, Wayne Walker. Research assistance: Linda Green, Andrea W. Loewenstein. The cover was designed by Howard Chapman, Art Director.

The data on campaign finances of labor and other groups appearing on pages 73-78 was compiled by the Citizens Research Foundation.

Library of Congress Catalog No. 77-184425
International Standard Book No. 0-87187-026-6

Copyright 1971 by Congressional Quarterly Inc.
1735 K Street, N.W., Washington, D.C. 20006

TABLE OF CONTENTS

Individuals and organizations providing substantial gifts at critical moments can threaten to place a candidate in moral hock.

President's Commission on Campaign Costs, 1962

DOLLAR POLITICS: THE RISING COSTS OF DEMOCRACY

The cost of running for political office in America has climbed to such dizzy heights in recent years that the task of bringing it down to something approaching a reasonable level—and keeping it there—has come to seem almost beyond the bounds of legislative ingenuity. Many observers consider regulation of election campaign financing the most important unsolved problem of democracy.

Mounting campaign costs have increased the reliance of candidates on large contributions by wealthy individuals or interest groups. This, in turn, has nourished the image of the office-holder as indebted to these financial backers rather than being free to follow his conscience or represent the wishes of his constituents.

$400 Million in '72

There are few topics in American politics about which less is known than the cost of election campaigns. But one fact is certain: modern political campaigns for Congress and the Presidency are expensive. The most detailed and reliable figures show that costs are rising with every presidential campaign. *(Graph p. 5)*

The Citizens' Research Foundation (CRF) of Princeton, N.J., founded in 1958, is regarded as the most comprehensive source of itemized campaign contributions and expenditures.

In 1952, the total cost of campaigns for all elective offices in the United States was $140-million, according to CRF estimates. These costs rose to $155-million in 1956, $175-million in 1960, $200-million in 1964, $300-million in 1968 and are projected at $400-million in 1972. The expenses in 1970 will have increased to 185 percent of the 1952 base year; however, after economic and political adjustments, the increase is estimated at about 45 percent over the 20-year period. Cost per vote also increased, from 19 cents in 1952 to 60 cents in 1968. *(Fund-raising p. 3; costs p. 11)*

Increased use of the broadcast media, particularly television, has accented the growing problem of campaign costs. Television and radio, a major source of news for Americans, are ideally suited to large constituencies. Television emerged after 1952 as the dominant form of communications in presidential and many congressional campaigns. The spurt in broadcast time spending testified to the increase in use of television and radio. Total charges for political broadcasts in general elections at all levels of government increased from $9.8-million in 1956 to $59.2-million in 1970.

Congressional Reaction

The rising costs of campaigning created in the late 1960s and early 1970s a favorable climate for the enactment of new legislation to regulate political spending. There was general agreement in both political parties that the existing law, the 1925 Federal Corrupt Practicss

Act, was inadequate to cope with the problems of contemporary political financing. A November 1970 Gallup Poll found that 78 percent of adult Americans favored a law limiting the total amount of money spent in political campaigns; it had become difficult for a political figure to publicly oppose the need for new legislation on political spending.

Partisan politics also worked in favor of new legislation. The Democratic party controlled Congress and was heavily in debt as the 1972 presidential campaign against President Nixon approached. Democrats looked upon campaign finance legislation as one way to narrow the financial odds against them. And although the Republicans were reluctant to lose the advantage that their well-stocked campaign war chest provided, they were also unwilling to come out on the wrong side of the campaign spending issue.

Congress worked on three major campaign spending bills in 1970-1971:

• In 1970, Congress cleared a bill limiting spending for political radio and television broadcasting and repealing the "equal time" provisions of the 1934 Communications Act. President Nixon vetoed the bill, and the Senate failed to override. In a letter to Minority Leader Hugh Scott (R Pa.), Mr. Nixon said he would endorse a "comprehensive election reform bill" in 1971. *(p. 43)*

• In 1971, at the end of the first session of the 92nd Congress, House-Senate conferees had agreed on a compromise campaign spending bill regulating spending on all media—radio-television, printed material and billboards. The bill cleared the Senate before adjournment and was expected to pass the House early in the second session. President Nixon indicated he would sign it. Under the bill presidential candidates in 1972 would be limited to $8.4-million for television spending—an amount less than that spent by the Republicans in 1968. *(1971 spending bill p. 44)*

• Also in 1971, Senate Democrats attached a campaign financing amendment to the Nixon Administration's new economic policy tax bill. The measure would have provided the two major parties in 1972 with a $20-million presidential campaign fund financed out of the U.S. Treasury from tax check-offs by individual taxpayers. House-Senate conferees, faced with a threatened veto by President Nixon, who opposed the amendment, agreed to delay implementation of the plan until after the 1972 election. *(Presidential campaign fund p. 57)*

'Money Monster'

Dollar politics has been an issue in American campaigns as far back as 1832 when the U.S.-chartered but semi-autonomous United States Bank spent heavily to support Henry Clay, Whig candidate for the Presidency against incumbent Andrew Jackson. Clay, believing that he had found an issue for the campaign, pressed for congressional action on a bill to renew the bank's charter.

Clay though that if Jackson vetoed the bill, he would lose Pennsylvania—the bank was located in Philadelphia—and other eastern states in the election. The strategy backfired. Jackson met the challenge with a strong veto message describing the bank as a "money monster" and campaigned against it effectively in the campaign and won the election easily.

Money played an important role in the victory of Republican William McKinley over Populist William Jennings Bryan in the 1896 election. McKinley's campaign was managed by wealthy financier Marcus A. Hanna, whose genius as a fund-raiser has been described by historian Eugene H. Roseboom: "For banks the (campaign finance) assessment was fixed at one-quarter of one percent of their capital. Life insurance companies contributed liberally, as did nearly all the great corporations. The Standard Oil Company gave $250,000 to Hanna's war chest. The audited accounts of the national committee revealed collections of about $3,500,000."

'Getting out the Vote'

Machine Politics. Although corporate money was involved in 19th century political campaigning, the existence of big city political machines reduced the impact of the wealthy contributor's dollar.

The machines mobilized the highly populated urban immigrant centers providing services and patronage for the lower classes in return for straight party ticket voting at the polls. The major campaign activity and power of the machine was "getting out the vote" on election day. It was not uncommon for the machines to pay individuals to vote for machine-supported candidates. Candidates depended on the machine to deliver the vote in much the same way that candidates today are said to depend on their wealthy contributors. Tennessee Democratic Kenneth Douglas McKellar, who served in the Senate from 1917-1953, was described as a "junior partner" of Edward Crump, political boss of Memphis.†

"The Last Hurrah." Machine politics required a large working class electorate rooted to the urban centers. The boss's strength lay in the neighborhood networks and the direct face-to-face communications maintained by the ward heeler with the voters who looked to the machine for influence and favors.

Rising standards of living and education, the exodus to the suburbs and the general mobility of the American electorate led to the decline of machine politics. Mayor James Michael Curley, political boss of Boston from 1900-47, said in November 1948: "The people are better educated in the science of government—politics, if you say—than ever before. Winning elections with only money and machine organization is a thing of the past." Curley, whose stormy career became the basis of a novel, *The Last Hurrah,* had once told the municipal employees of Boston that if President Hoover were re-elected, they could expect a 10-percent cut in salary.

Mass Communications. The machine methods of getting out the vote were inappropriate to political campaigning in an increasingly transient and mobile society where voters changed their occupations and addresses

---

†*V.O. Key Jr., Southern Politics, 1949.*

with greater frequency than in earlier decades. A growing number of voters regarded themselves as independents who would vote for a candidate, not for a straight party ticket. Mobilizing this kind of electorate and delivering its vote has required the expensive techniques of the mass media. *(Broadcast spending p. 19-27)*

The new style of campaigning, geared to the needs of the mass society, has brought to the fore a new group of political experts—pollsters, consultants, direct mail specialists, advertising agencies and television consultants on the selling of candidates. Like the political bosses of the past these specialists earn their reputations by getting out the vote. Unlike the bosses, however, they do not normally or necessarily covet the spoils or responsibilities of political office.

The costly services of these experts has added to the mounting costs of campaign spending on mass media and has provided wealthy candidates and contributors with opportunities to spend large sums on what are considered the most effective campaign methods. *(Wealthy candidates p. 28; richest contributors p. 32; defense contractors' contributions p. 36; effectiveness of spending p. 14, 19-27, 28-31)*

Unenforced Statute

Muckrakers in the early part of the 20th century highlighted the influence on government exerted by big business through unrestrained spending on behalf of favored candidates for public office. Federal attempts to inhibit the influence of political money resulted in the Federal Corrupt Practices Act of 1925, which the 1971 campaign spending bill repealed and replaced. *(Federal Election law p. 15)*

The 1925 Act, which limited both giving and spending, was riddled with loopholes making reported amounts merely indicative of actual spending. The Act did not cover primaries or nominating conventions, nor did it require reports by certain types of political committees. Frequently, congressional candidates reported (to the Clerk of the House and the Secretary of the Senate) that they had received and spent nothing on their campaigns, maintaining the position that the campaign committees established to elect them to office had been working without their "knowledge and consent."

No candidate for the House or the Senate ever was prosecuted under the 1925 Act although it was widely known that most candidates spent above the limits set in the Act and did not report the full extent of their spending. Only two members of Congress—two Senators in 1927—have ever been barred for spending in excess of the Act's limits.

In 1971, in an effort to dramatize the unenforceability of the Act, one losing House candidate in the 1970 election, Dennis J. Morriseau, who had run on the Liberty Union ticket for Vermont's at-large seat, informed the Clerk of the House that he would refuse to comply with the Act's requirement that he file a report of his spending in the 1970 campaign. Morriseau also informed the Justice Department, but he was not prosecuted.

Groups which supported campaign spending legislation in 1971 were hopeful that the new law would be more effective than the 1925 Act, but this would depend on the willingness of politicians to enforce legislation regulating their own behavior.

CAMPAIGN FUND-RAISING: METHODS AND HIGH COSTS

No one knows exactly how much money it takes to get elected. But, as Will Rogers said in less expensive days, "It takes a lot of money to even get beat with."

A Congressional Quarterly survey indicates that it also takes a lot of money to raise money.

Where this money comes from and how it is raised are among the major problems of political life.

In giving as well as spending, the loopholes in the 1925 Corrupt Practices Act are large. *(p. 15)*

Technically, an individual cannot contribute more than $5,000 to any national political group or candidate. However, he can contribute unlimited funds to state, county and local groups which can pass along the money to national committees or candidates in their own name. An individual also can contribute in the name of relatives—wife, children and cousins.

Corporations cannot contribute, but officers may give freely. Unions are prohibited from contributing, but contribute through their political action committees.

There are certain standbys who can be counted on by both parties. Among the Republicans are the Mellons, Rockefellers and Whitneys. Among the Democrats are the Laskers, Kennedys and Harrimans.

Contributions also come from foreigners. A. Onassis contributed a total of $2,000 to the Republican National Committee in 1969 and 1970. A spokesman for the Republican National Committee said "it is probably safe to assume this is Aristotle Onassis." Aristotle Onassis is married to the former Jacqueline Kennedy. Greek ship owner Constantine Diamantis of Piraeus contributed $10,000 to the Republican Party in 1970.

According to data from the Survey Research Center at the University of Michigan, only about 8 percent of the population contributed in 1968. However, 38 percent of those solicited gave.

Both parties rely on big contributors. In every presidential election since 1952, with one exception, the Democratic National Committee has relied on contributors of more than $500 for upwards of 60 percent of their funds. For the same period, again with the exception of one election year, the Republican National Committee got more than 50 percent of their contributions from donations of over $500.

Wealthy candidates and their relatives have become important campaign contributors. According to the National Committee for an Effective Congress, 11 senatorial candidates in 1970 in the seven largest states were millionaires. These were Sen. Lloyd Bentsen (D Texas), Sen. James L. Buckley (Cons-R N.Y.), George Bush (R Texas), Sen. Philip A. Hart (D Mich.), Howard M. Metzenbaum (D Ohio), Richard L. Ottinger (D N.Y.), Lenore Romney (R Mich.), Sen. Hugh Scott (R Pa.), Sen. Adlai E. Stevenson III (D Ill.), Sen. Robert Taft Jr. (R Ohio) and Sen. John V. Tunney (D Calif.).

Other contributors include individuals or groups with a special interest in a given campaign. In 1970, there were 14 new ad hoc peace groups formed to raise funds.

Some contributors are appointed to office. The 1970 campaign contributors included Walter Anneberg, who contributed $2,500 to the senatorial campaigns of J. Glenn Beall Jr. in Maryland and $2,500 to George Murphy in California; Shelby Davis, who contributed $2,500 each to George Bush in Texas and Robert Taft Jr. in Ohio; Kenneth Franzheim II, who gave $2,500 each to Beall, Taft and William C. Cramer in Florida; Kingdon Gould Jr., who gave Beall $1,500; John P. Humes, who gave Beall $2,500; J. Wm. Middendorf II, who gave Beall $1,000 and Bush $500; and John D. J. Moore, who gave Beall $2,500. Anneberg, Davis, Franzheim, Gould, Humes, Middendorf and Moore are respectively ambassadors to Great Britain, Switzerland, New Zealand, Luxembourg, Austria, the Netherlands and Ireland.

Costs of Fund-Raising

As much as two-thirds of every dollar raised is spent by some political committees for soliciting the funds.

The costs of all types of fund-raising are rising, according to Herbert Alexander, director of the Citizens' Research Foundation.

The most profitable form of fund-raising is the $1,000-a-plate political dinner. Overhead on a $1,000-a-plate dinner is approximately 5 percent to 10 percent while it can run as high as 50 percent on a $10-a-plate dinner.

The advent of direct mail advertising and solicitations has had a significant effect on the rising costs of raising political money. The reactions among professionals to this fund-raising method are mixed. The Democrats are just getting into direct mail and Republicans are disappointed in its results for them. Conservatives disagree among themselves on its effectiveness.

According to John T. Calkins, executive director of the National Republican Congressional Committee, costs of mailings are increasing and returns are a little over half of what had been expected. The Democratic National Committee early in 1971 established a new committee specifically designed for direct mail drives.

Charles McManus, president of the Americans for Constitutional Action, is critical of the high cost of using direct mail. He said his committee, by using its own carefully screened lists and running its own fund-raising campaign, is able to raise money at a cost of only about 7.5 percent of the total receipts. In 1970, the committee's receipts totaled $138,475. McManus claimed his costs are "less than eight times the cost of fund-raising by some organizations making indiscriminate use of mass mailings."

In defense of mass mailings Richard Viguerie, a direct mail specialist, told Congressional Quarterly that some small organizations are able to raise funds with low costs—but many of these small organizations will stay small. I'd much rather have a million with $400,000 for costs and $600,000 to candidates than give $100,000 to $150,000 year after year."

Viguerie guarantees results. If not, he takes the loss. In 1969, he conducted a direct mail solicitation for John Marchi in his campaign for mayor of New York City. Marchi was to get 50 cents out of every dollar that came in. While this did not cover Viguerie's early costs, he assumed that most of the contributions would come in three to four days before the election and he would make his profit then. The money did not come. Marchi got approximately $100,000, but Viguerie's $100,000 did not cover the costs of the mailings.

Congressional Quarterly Study. In July and August, 1971, Congressional Quarterly examined records in the House Clerk's office and interviewed officials of several political committees to determine the costs of raising money for various types of groups.

Direct Mail Professional

Direct mail is Richard Viguerie's business. He started his business in January 1964, and since has become the most successful political direct-mail fundraiser.

In mid-1971, he employed 65 persons and owned his own Washington-based computer and printing company.

Of the more than 600,000 pieces of mail done by the Viguerie Company every week, most are designed, written and printed on the premises and then sent to selected individuals from among the several million names on Viguerie's computer tapes.

"I feel like a man who has got a tiger by the tail," Viguerie said.

Discussing unfavorable publicity he received because of the rates charged, Viguerie told Congressional Quarterly that "direct mail has the unfair reputation of being too expensive. When any business opens you don't make money immediately. You have to amortize costs over a period of time."

While Viguerie would not discuss his specific rates, he said that he usually works on the basis of a flat fee which depends on the size of the mailing and the amount of work required in writing the copy. According to Viguerie, "our creative work is the most expensive thing we're selling."

In 1970, the company turned down 40 to 50 congressional candidates and did mailings in about six Senate races. Viguerie guarantees results and prefers to do the entire mailing from creating the concepts to selecting the lists used: "Our customers only have to approve the copy and count the money."

Among Viguerie's clients in 1970 were the Young Americans for Freedom, of which he is a former executive secretary, and the White House, for whom he did a 12,000-piece mailing.

Self-identified as a conservative Republican, Viguerie said he is "ideologically pure." Although he said he has been approached by a number of liberal Democrats, including some current Democratic presidential contenders, he will not work for a Democrat, even a conservative one.

"We're trying to make money but also we're concerned with perpetuating a political philosophy," he said.

The 1970 Campaign Fund, organized to help liberal Democratic senatorial candidates, raised $874,956 in 1970 and gave the candidates they supported 57 cents out of every dollar raised, a check of House records showed. George Agree, an organizer of the group, estimated the percentage of cost to be "in the low 40s." "If we weren't working from scratch and had an established following our costs could have been lower," Agree said. Costs were kept to a minimum by hiring only part-time help so people would work only when there was work to be done. Major costs of the committee were list rentals, printing and postage.

Using the fund's list of contributors and other lists of his own, Sen. George McGovern (D S.D.) has been able to raise funds through direct mail at costs of from 13 percent to 50 percent of receipts, according to Jeffery Smith, a McGovern campaign worker in charge of direct mail solicitation.

The Committee for Ten, organized in 1970 to raise funds for the campaigns of 10 non-incumbent anti-war Democrats, spent 44 percent of every dollar raised on soliciting money, according to House records. Of the total $86,883 raised, $37,934 was spent to cover the costs of solicitations. Out of these expenses, $11,000 went to Washington Information Associates, the organization that set up the committee.

Another new group in 1970, the Conservative Victory Fund, operating out of the offices of the American Conservative Union, contributed 35 percent of its receipts to candidates the committee supported—approximately $150,000 of the $427,000 collected by the committee. According to Mrs. Luana Law, a spokesman of the Conservative Victory Fund, an additional $96,000 was channeled through the fund to candidates and never appeared on the records of committee filed with the House Clerk's office. Including this money channeled through the committee, fund-raising costs were 58 percent of receipts; the fund-raising costs of money that went directly to candidates was 65 percent of receipts.

Rep. John M. Ashbrook (R Ohio), Conservative Victory Fund 1970 chairman, said in a December 1970 interview with *The Cleveland Plain Dealer,* "The criticism of the costs is legitimate. I'm skeptical of the whole fund-raising area."

Records in the House Clerk's office do not list contributions from individuals who may give directly to a candidate as a result of the urging of various political committees. Thus, some committees may be more effective in fund-raising than the reports required by the Corrupt Practices Act indicate.

The Council For A Livable World reported spending $214,626 during the 1970 calendar year, but only about $35,000 of it was in contributions to candidates. The council also reported spending $112,603 in 1969, of which $5,000 was a 1970 campaign contribution.

In accordance with the provisions of the Corrupt Practices Act, the council reports all its expenses in detail, according to a July 27, 1971, letter from national director Thomas A. Halsted. This includes expenditures for salaries, rent, postage and other items.

But Halsted said that the reports to the House Clerk's office do not reflect the full scope of the council's campaign spending activities because "we also urged our membership to contribute directly to a number of candidates." He added that "these contributions, made at our urging, totaled $272,500; added to our own $39,500, the council's true input to 1969-1970 campaign spending was therefore $312,000."

Probably the highest fund-raising costs were reported in 1968 by the United Republicans of America. The committee distributed less than 10 percent of the $473,453 raised to candidates. The committee did not file a complete report for 1970.

Direct Mail Solicitation

One Senator reported that he received a letter soliciting campaign funds addressed to "Honorabl" at the "Sen Ofc Boulevard" and still another letter that used his name repeatedly—but began "Although we have never met...."

Millions of letters soliciting funds are sent out by computers in an election year. With the increasing need for large sums of money and the use of computer techniques by direct mail professionals, mass mail solicitation has become the most important means of fund-raising in a number of major political campaigns.

According to direct mail specialist Viguerie, "direct mail comes close to being a science. We know the importance of the color of envelopes, length of letters, personalized variables in letters, because we've tested all of these variables. The results are analyzed...and the success of each variation is measured.

"It's exciting what can be done," Viguerie said, "but you seldom find a client who is interested in using all of this information in a sophisticated manner." Most users of direct mail are interested in geographic and financial breakdowns—for example, all of the contributors in a given state who have contributed $10 or more to a conservative cause.

The collection of personal data by direct mail list brokers has raised questions similar to those concerning credit data banks. Lists include information on what publications an individual reads, what charities he contributes to, what candidates he is supporting financially and his stands on political issues. And the lists are available for sale by the list brokers.

For candidates and political committees, direct mail broadens the political base of support. Olga Gechas, director of the Democratic National Committee Direct Mail Committee, said that contributions in response to this type of solicitation "give more stability to the party's fund-raising than large givers and dinners. When there is a bad year economically or the market falls large givers don't contribute. Sometimes they become disenchanted with a candidate or have a disagreement with a party official. These givers provide a limited base of support."

Direct mail works against the traditional premise that in order to finance large campaigns a candidate has to rely on big business, labor and large contributors. A small contribution goes to a candidate or committee with a personal commitment by the donor. It comes from people who expect nothing in return.

Names In Computers

Direct mail experts estimate conservatively that there are more than 500 million names on computers. An official of the Direct Mail Advertising Association said that "people's names get on lists because people exist....Only

Campaign Spending

Indexes of Direct Campaign Expenditures by National-Level Committees, Number of Votes Cast, and Consumer Prices

▬▬ EXPENDITURES
||||| VOTES CAST
— CONSUMER PRICE INDEX

1912 = 100

1912 '16 '20 '24 '28 '32 '36 '40 '44 '48 '52 '56 '60 '64 1968

Sources: Citizens' Research Foundation, Elections Research Center, Bureau of Labor Statistics and The Twentieth Century Fund.

COPYRIGHT 1971 CONGRESSIONAL QUARTERLY

Chapman

hermits could avoid getting on lists but then they'll probably get on somebody's list of hermits."

Buying and selling political mailing lists has become a successful business. Periodicals and book clubs sell lists to all comers. Viguerie sells lists of anything from "active Americans" to "retired military" to conservative Republicans. The United Nations International Childrens Emergency Fund (UNICEF) has sold its lists to the Democratic National Committee and the 1970 Campaign Fund. The Internal Revenue Service sells aggregate income statistics about taxpayers broken down by zip code. This is valuable to identify high-income communities for fund-raising.

Direct mail lists are sold or rented on a per name basis. Because list brokers combine lists there is the continuing problem of duplication. The same name can

Republican Fund-Raising

Republican National Committee estimates of receipts in 1970 from the following sources and activities:

Direct mail appeal to small contributors	$3,200,000
Appeals in newsletters of Republican Congressional Campaign Committees and other special mail appeals	2,600,000
Memberships in Republican Victory Associates ($500 or more) and in Republican National Associates ($1,000 or more)	2,000,000
March 1970 dinner ($1,000 a plate)	2,000,000
Private luncheons sponsored by Republican Boosters	1,300,000
National Committee's fee (10 percent) for local fund-raising appearances by Vice President Agnew and Cabinet officers	350,000

appear with slight variations in spelling, initials, married name and different addresses. In 1970, there were reports of individuals receiving as many as 15 letters in a given week from the same candidate or organization.

"I tell my clients either they want a small stack of complaint letters and a small stack of checks or they'll get a large stack of complaints and a large stack of checks," Viguerie said.

Republicans vs. Democrats

Direct mail has been used successfully by Republicans for about eight years and only sporadically by the Democrats during that period. In 1971, the Democratic National Committee organized a separate direct mail committee, with an independent budget, in hopes of broadening the national party's bases of support.

Calkins, executive director of the National Republican Congressional Committee, told Congressional Quarterly that he no longer finds direct mail as successful as it was for Republicans in the 1964 Goldwater campaign. Increasing cost of printing and postage makes it "not the most efficient means of fund-raising." The committee's mailing program for the first six months of 1971, according to Calkins, is only 55 percent as effective as it should be.

Comparing the use of direct mail by both national parties, Viguerie said, "Republicans are in the 19th century in their use of direct mail and the Democrats have been in the Middle Ages." However, he added that after looking at the new concepts, quality and techniques, Democrats are beginning to use "the Democrats may leap over the Republicans into the 20th century in making intelligent use of direct mail."

The Democratic direct mail committee is not making any money yet. Profit is being reinvested to help develop the program. In 1971, the mailings are doing a little better than breaking even.

In 1970, the Democratic National Committee mailed 3 million fund-raising letters. In 1971, they plan to send out 4 million to 5 million pieces and will boost the volume to 15 million pieces of mail during the 1972 campaign.

In the 1960s, the committee relied on door-to-door solicitation to reach small contributors in a "Dollars for Democrats" campaign. In 1971, many people refused to open their door for this type of solicitation.

In addition, "It isn't profitable to get a dollar from every Democrat anymore—it takes much more than that

for a fund-raising campaign to break even," according to Miss Gechas, director of the Democratic National Committee Direct Mail Committee. With an 0.8-percent return on mailings and an average contribution of $10, the committee just breaks even. At present, the return rate on these solicitations varies from near zero to 8 percent depending on the timing, letter and list used. The committee is testing a number of different techniques—taking samples of various lists and trying various approaches to samples from the same list.

McGovern's Campaign

One Democratic presidential hopeful, McGovern, is using direct mail solicitation as his primary source for fund-raising. So far, his results are good, according to campaign aides.

McGovern has collected and computerized the names of individuals who have visited his office or written him and others with whom he has had contact. In addition, McGovern has the list of contributors to the 1970 Campaign Fund. In 1970, McGovern wrote a cover letter and lent seed money to the fund with the understanding that he would regulate the distribution of the list. The committee raised $874,956, more money than any previous attempt by one organization for liberal Democrats.

McGovern's first mailer of 250,000 raised more than $300,000 from approximately 15,000 contributors, according to Jeffrey Smith, who was in charge of the McGovern mail campaign. This was a notable success—at a cost of $39,000 the overhead on the mailer was only 13 percent of the money ultimately raised.

According to Smith, a follow-up letter asking contributors to pledge $10 per month to the McGovern Presidential Club brought pledges from 1,500 within a few days. Smith anticipates a total of between 2,000 to 3,000 pledges.

By early 1972, the McGovern committee hopes to have identified 100,000 contributors and to have $1,000,000 in profits ready for use in the primaries, most of the money coming from mailings.

The committee has doubled its money on all of its mailers, Smith said, with costs always staying below 50 percent of the amount raised. The last mailing of 100,000 raised $85,000 at a cost of $39,000 or a 45-percent overhead. The return on the solicitation was a respectable 4 percent.

Emotional Giving

"It doesn't make any difference whether it's ban the bomb or bomb the bastards," said Robert Strauss, Democratic National Committee treasurer, "people contribute in response to emotional appeals."

Fund-raising records were set in 1968 by two candidates who were ideological opposites. Former Sen. Eugene J. McCarthy (D Minn. 1959-1970), Democratic antiwar candidate, was able to draw upon a small number of very large contributors. George C. Wallace, American Independent Party candidate, had a "level of grass roots participation never before reached by the major parties in this country," according to Herbert Alexander in *Financing the 1968 Campaign*.

According to Alexander: During the pre-convention period in 1968, McCarthy was able to raise $2.5-million from about 50 large contributors. Of the reported 424 contributors of more than $10,000 in 1968, 100 contributed to McCarthy's campaign.

Wallace, on the other hand, was able to attract an estimated 750,000 small contributors, Alexander said. The last election in which there was this level of grass roots support was in the campaign of conservative Republican presidential candidate Goldwater in 1964. Goldwater's pre-convention campaign drew 300,000 contributors, a figure that was unprecedented at that time.

Viguerie attributed Wallace's and McCarthy's success to the fact that they asked for funds from previously untapped sources. "They asked for money. They didn't know that it couldn't be done so they did it. It's a myth that money is unavailable to these types of candidates."

Not only have candidates who arouse emotional appeals fared well, but so have political committees. The 14 ad hoc peace groups, most of them new in 1970, raised more than $600,000. The money was used to support peace-oriented candidates.

Strauss of the Democratic National Committee told *Congressional Quarterly* that "emotional appeals are the most effective in raising money; that's why McCarthy, Wallace and Agnew are such effective fund-raisers—each has their own peculiar emotional appeal."

Strauss added that this explains why the Democratic National Committee has trouble raising funds. "The national committee appears to many to be an inanimate, headless and soulless body." The Democratic National Committee tested a variety of media appeals in four cities and found that this was not an effective fund-raising technique. According to Strauss, the committee could not arouse the same emotional reaction a candidate could. After the convention, when there is a specific candidate, the committee's fund-raising attempts are much more successful.

In 1971, the Democrats have had the most success with a negative emotional appeal—directed against President Nixon. The spring 1971 issue of the *National Democrat* advised party supporters, "Don't wait till '72 to vote against Richard Nixon: Become a DNC Participating Member." The letter bringing the best response in the direct mail solicitation, according to Olga Gechas, reads: "There are two reasons to contribute to the Democratic National Committee, one is Nixon, the other is Agnew." The letter has been so effective, according to Miss Gechas, the Republicans are quoting it. "It must be hurting them," she said.

Fund-Raising Dinners

Dinners are the most effective means of fund-raising, according to spokesmen of both major parties. This classic method of increasing political coffers is used by almost every candidate. They range from $5,000-a-person cocktail parties for the major party candidates to 89 cents-a-plate fund-raising dinners for tongue-in-cheek candidate Pat Paulsen at a New York Automat and a Los Angeles cafeteria in 1968.

During the 1968 campaign, the Citizens' Research Foundation was able to account for at least $43.1-million collected from these events—$21.5-million raised by Republicans, $17.9-million raised by Democrats and $3.6-million raised by the American Independent Party.

Like all other types of fund-raising, the costs of dinners are increasing. However, the costs are considered minimal

Expenditures of Party Committees, 1970

	Republican	Democratic
National Committee	2,980,308	$1,617,593
Senate Campaign Committee	928,843	568,067
House Campaign Committee	2,444,807	360,471
Other nationwide committees	4,515,339	1,144,622
Total	$10,869,297	$3,690,753

compared to the costs of other means of fund-raising, according to Strauss. "For us it's only the cost of the dinner. We don't take on any extra people, no advance men, no extra long-distance telephone lines and we don't do any additional entertaining before the dinner."

While fund-raising dinners have been commonplace since the 1930s, the approach to them has changed. Previously, a prospective donor was invited to a dinner and there subjected to partisan appeals for a contribution or pledge; his gift is now assured in advance by the sale of tickets of admission.

President Eisenhower on Jan. 20, 1956, spoke on closed-circuit TV to 53 banquets held simultaneously in 37 states. Ticket sales netted between $4-million and $5-million for the Republican party.

In the 1960s techniques for political dinners were developed further. President Kennedy's Inaugural Eve Gala in Washington, D.C., grossed $1,250,000. Events which Kennedy attended between his inauguration on Jan. 20, 1961, and the final dinner in Houston the night before his assassination on Nov. 22, 1963, raised more than $10-million for the Democratic party. In the administrations of Presidents Kennedy and Lyndon B. Johnson, those who paid $1,000 a plate at major political dinners were known as members of the President's Club.

In 1965, the Republican Senatorial Campaign Committee drew 800 guests at a $500-a-plate dinner honoring Sen. Everett M. Dirksen (R Ill. 1951-69), Senate Minority Leader. Net proceeds amounted to $380,000, enough to cover the committee's operations for a year.

Vice President Spiro T. Agnew has become a key Republican fund-raiser. Since entering office he has helped raise approximately $5-million for the Republican party according to the Republican National Committee.

For the invitees the costs of fund-raising dinners has increased considerably. Rep. Charles E. Bennett (D Fla.) on Dec. 1, 1970, told the House Committee on Standards of Official Conduct: "The cost of political filet mignon has jumped from a $100-a-plate donation only five years ago to currently $1,000 for Republicans and $500 for Democrats."

Among the favorite invitees to fund-raisers are Washington lobbyists and representatives of trade associations, as well as friendly corporation executives and labor union officials. For these people it is another form of political contribution that can be counted above the maximum $5,000 allowed for an individual to contribute to a candidate. These parties are so numerous that one Washington-based lobbyist reported more than 200 requests for political contributions in the first nine months of 1970.

Corporations and Campaigns

The Tillman Act of Jan. 26, 1907, banned corporate gifts of money to candidates for federal elective offices or to committees supporting the candidates. The ban was incorporated in the Federal Corrupt Practices Act of Feb. 28, 1925, which broadened the prohibition to cover contributions of "anything of value." Former President Eisenhower pointed out in the *Reader's Digest*, January 1968, that corporations nevertheless "apply a variety of subterfuges: they lend office equipment and the services of their public relations experts and lawyers; they make it easy, through bonuses and expense accounts, for executives to contribute substantial sums; and they buy advertising space at ridiculously high rates in political pamphlets and program brochures."

Prosecution of Corporations. In the 62 years following enactment of the 1907 law on campaign financing, the Department of Justice prosecuted only three business concerns for violation of the ban on political gifts by corporations. Then, in the period from May 1969 to January 1970, the Department pressed charges against 14 companies, mostly in California, for violations of the Federal Corrupt Practices Act allegedly committed during the 1968 campaign. The National Brewing Company of Baltimore and six California companies pleaded guilty and were fined. Others pleaded "no contest" and were fined. One pleaded not guilty and was acquitted. American President Lines and Pacific Far East Lines, both of San Francisco, were fined $50,000 each; other corporations involved were fined smaller amounts. Newsmen made repeated but unsuccessful efforts to learn the names of the candidates, including incumbent members of Congress, who had received the illegal contributions.

Indirect Contributions. To get around the prohibition on political contributions by corporations, the National Association of Manufacturers in 1963 founded the Business-Industry Political Action Committee on the model of the AFL-CIO's Committee on Political Education. BIPAC solicited contributions from individuals in the business world and spent $203,283 in 1964, $294,000 in 1966, $478,675 in 1968, and $498,904 in 1970 in support of the business-oriented candidates for Congress. Almost 95 percent of the candidates that BIPAC supported in 1968 were Republicans.

Contributing Businessmen

An article in the *Washington Post*, Dec. 6, 1970, pointed out that "Businessmen's contributions of $5,000 and more seemed to fall like confetti into the coffers of Lloyd M. Bentsen Jr. (Democrat), a Houston banking, insurance and mutual funds multimillionaire..., and Republican Rep. George Bush, a Houston oil millionaire who lost to Bentsen in the Nov. 3 general election." Oilmen accounted for 46 percent of individual contributions of $5,000 or more, and bankers, mutual fund managers, and others in the financial world for an additional 19 percent, in the campaigns of various Texas candidates in 1970. The list of those surveyed included several who ran for the governorship, five candidates for the U.S. Senate, and one candidate for the U.S. House of Representatives.

Six candidates in the 1970 congressional primaries in North Carolina, Pennsylvania and Texas received money from an organized group of businessmen, the Business-Industry Political Action Committee, set up in 1963 by the National Association of Manufacturers. When all six candidates were victorious, the committee's June 1970 newsletter crowed: "BIPAC Bats 1,000 Pct." Edward I. Maher, editor of the newsletter, said his organization avoided direct lobbying. "If you get the right group down there, you don't have to lobby."

BIPAC reported at the end of 1970 that it had received $302,554 during the year. Its expenditures, totaling $539,157, went mostly for donations to the campaigns of Republicans and of southern and conservative Democrats. Among the directors of BIPAC were Robert B. Anderson, Secretary of the Treasury in President Eisenhower's second term; Arthur H. Motley, president of Parade Publications; and H. C. Lumb, vice president of the Republic Steel Corporation.

The Chamber of Commerce of the United States published in 1968 a booklet for the guidance of businessmen wanting to swell the campaign funds of selected candidates for public office without violating the legal ban on political contributions by corporations, a ban in effect since 1907. The booklet said, among other things, that a political action committee set up by a corporation or a trade association should be located elsewhere than in the corporation's or trade association's offices. Brushing aside this advice, the General Foods Corp. provided space in its main office at 250 North St. in White Plains, N.Y., for a political action group, the North Street Good Government Group, made up of the corporation's executives. The group contributed funds in 1970 to three key members of the House Committee on Agriculture. Similarly, the Lone Star Cement Corp.'s headquarters in Greenwich, Conn., were the headquarters also of the Lone Star Executive Voluntary Political Fund, which gave financial help in 1970 to members of the Senate and House Committees on Public Works.

Bankers as Contributors

Another group of capitalists, the Bankers' Political Action Committee, undertook to raise more than $200,000 for congressional, gubernatorial and other 1970 elections. "The candidates who will receive help from BankPAC," according to the *American Banker*, Oct. 22, 1970, "will be selected candidates of the House Banking and Currency, Ways and Means and Rules Committees and the Senate Banking and Currency and Finance Committees." BankPAC's report of Oct. 29 to the Clerk of the House said the committee had disbursed $55,000 to incumbents of both parties seeking re-election, including 21 members of the House Banking and Currency Committee.

Rep. Wright Patman (D Texas), chairman of the Banking and Currency Committee, received no contribution from BankPAC. For many years, he had been a leading critic of the country's major banks. On Oct. 29, Patman asked the Department of Justice to investigate bankers' campaign contributions. Referring to the Federal Corrupt Practices Act of 1925, which incorporated a 1907 provision prohibiting gifts by national banks to political campaigns, he said that BankPAC and similar groups had been "set up in a manner designed to skirt the edges of this statute."

News stories published on the Sunday before the election said that BankPAC had made contributions to the campaigns of various House members running for re-election. Two of the candidates who were defeated, William O. Cowger (R Ky.) and Chester Mize (R Kan.), said the stories had alienated voters. One who survived, Lawrence G. Williams (R Pa.), said he had never asked for, never received, and would have "rejected as unwanted" the $1,500 contribution to him which BankPAC had listed in its reports. The committee reported, Jan. 1, 1971, that $33,500 in contributions had been returned by the recipients.

BankPAC allegedly delayed disbursal of $46,050 until just before the election, so that the contributions making up that sum would not become publicly known until after the election. These contributions were made Oct. 30, the day after the last pre-election report was required. The $46,050 was contributed to nine members of the House Rules Committee (six Democrats, three Republicans), eight members of the House Committee on Ways and Means (five Democrats, three Republicans), the Senate and House Minority Leaders, and others. BankPAC's report of Jan. 1, 1971, brought the Oct. 30 contributions to light.

Receipts of BankPAC in 1970 totaled $205,428; expenditures, $101,100. The committee's largest contributions, $5,000 each, went to two Senators, Harry F. Byrd (Ind. Va.), a member of the Finance Committee, and Harrison A. Williams Jr. (D N.J.), a member of the Banking and Currency Committee. Byrd ran and won as an independent. Williams was re-elected. BankPAC's box score in the elections was perfect in the Senate, where it supported five winners (three Democrats and two Republicans), and almost perfect in the House, where 19 of the 21 candidates it supported (11 Democrats, 10 Republicans) were victorious.

The House Special Committee to Investigate Campaign Expenditures, headed by Rep. Thomas P. O'Neill Jr. (D Mass.), looked into BankPAC's activities in the 1970 election, especially its contributions sent to candidates who might not have wanted them and could have been harmed by them. The committee's report of Jan. 11, 1971, referred to "the explosive situation" created by "the naive belief" of BankPAC that all of its donations would be accepted. The report recommended that the 92d Congress (1971-72) consider legislation to deal with possibly unwanted contributions.

Labor and Campaign Contributions

The War Labor Disputes Act of June 25, 1943 (Smith-Connally Act), put labor unions on a par with corporations as to political contributions. One section of the act applied to unions, for the duration of the war, the prohibition enacted in 1907 against campaign contributions by corporations. The Labor-Management Relations (Taft-Hartley) Act of June 23, 1947, made the ban permanent.

Taft-Hartley proscribed all contributions and expenditures by labor unions for candidates for public office, whether the money came from dues or from voluntary donations by members. However, during consideration of the bill in the Senate, Taft said, June 5, 1947: "The prohibition is against labor unions using their members' dues for political purposes." The courts, heeding that statement, have sanctioned political expenditures by unions if the funds are contributed voluntarily by members.

Supreme Court Decisions. Interpretation of the ban on union campaign expenditures came to the fore when the *CIO News,* a weekly publication of the Congress of Industrial Organizations, in its issue of July 14, 1947, urged members to vote for a particular candidate for Congress in a special election. Federal authorities obtained an indictment of the CIO on a charge that it had violated the Taft-Hartley ban. The U.S. District Court for the District of Columbia dismissed the case on the ground that the ban was incompatible with the First Amendment to the Constitution.

When the case, *United States v. CIO,* was appealed, the Supreme Court took into account on the one hand a statement by Senator Taft, during debate on the bill, that endorsement of a candidate in a union publication, "if it were supported by...union dues,...would be a violation of the law" and, on the other hand, the fact that the *CIO News* was circulated primarily among members of the union.

Justice Stanley F. Reed, delivering the five-to-four opinion of the Court on June 21, 1948, stressed the point that the periodical had no general public circulation. The Court said: "If...(the law) were construed to prohibit the publication, by corporations and unions in the regular course of conducting their affairs, of periodicals advising their members, stockholders, or customers of danger or advantage to their interests from the adoption of measures, or the election to office of men espousing such measures, the gravest doubt would arise in our minds as to its constitutionality" (335 U.S. 106).

Taft-Hartley again required interpretation in connection with the 1954 congressional elections. During the campaign, the United Automobile Workers sponsored and paid for television broadcasts in Detroit which urged the election of named candidates for the Senate and the House. The main issue raised here was whether the broadcasts were intentionally aimed at the public in general or could be taken as an effective way to reach the union's members. However, the union lawyers also raised the question whether the Act invaded constitutional rights of expression.

Both questions were prominent during the argument of the case, *United States v. U.A.W.,* when it reached the Supreme Court on appeal. The Court's majority, six members, refused to rule on the constitutional issue; but three dissenters—Chief Justice Earl Warren and Justices Hugo L. Black and William O. Douglas—asserted that the law was unconstitutional "as construed and applied" in the U.A.W. case. Justice Felix Frankfurter, delivering the majority opinion, March 11, 1957, said that if the government could prove to the satisfaction of a jury, that a union had spent members' dues, or a corporation had spent stockholders' funds, to influence votes of the general public, violation of the law would have occurred, and the constitutional issue would have to be decided (352 U.S. 567). The case was remanded to the U.S. District Court for the Eastern District of Michigan, where a jury found the union not guilty.

Other Cases. Two methods of easing the impact of Taft-Hartley on labor unions were upheld by the courts in 1960-61. George P. Macdonald described the first method in the April 1969 issue of *Prospectus; A Journal of Law Reform:* "A union member simply signs a card designating part of his dues as voluntarily given.... Since that portion of the dues is then construed as a voluntary contribution, it may be directly contributed to Federal candidates." The U.S. District Court for the Eastern District of Missouri ruled in 1960 that this device did not constitute a violation of the Taft-Hartley Act.

In the second case, a union with several locals held a plebiscite among its members on whether to use union dues to finance partisan political activities. A majority voted in the affirmative, and the union executives considered the vote as transforming the money involved into "voluntary funds." The presiding judge of the U.S. District Court for the District of Alaska said in a decision in 1961 on the legality of this maneuver: "Each union decided by a vote of its membership...first, whether they would contribute and second, how much. Surely, that is voluntary; and that, I think, is the crux of the situation here."

Three officials of the Plumbers and Pipefitters Union, Local 562, St. Louis, were indicted May 9, 1968, on charges of conspiring to make political contributions in the 1964 and 1966 elections in violation of the Taft-Hartley ban. The three were found guilty Sept. 27, 1968, and fined $1,000 each and sentenced to one year in jail. In a similar case, the Seafarers International Union and eight of its officials and employees were indicted in New York City, June 30, 1970. Allegedly illegal contributions of $40,000 to Republican and Democratic campaign committees were cited in the indictment as part of a conspiracy involving campaign donations of $750,000 over a period of years. The contributions were funneled through the Seafarers Political Activity Donation Committee which, the indictment said, existed only on paper.

COPE's Role

When the AFL and the CIO merged in December 1955, the Committee on Political Education was formed as an amalgamation of the AFL's Labor League for Political Education and the C.I.O.'s Political Action Committee. COPE's funds, coming directly from the treasuries of the AFL-CIO and its affiliated unions, are used for such nonpartisan activities as voter registration drives, publication of candidates' voting records, and exhibits on campaign issues. Funds made available to COPE through voluntary gifts of union members are spent, legally, to support particular candidates. However, even COPE's political education activities often designedly help one candidate more than his rival or rivals, as in get-out-the-vote drives in districts where pro-labor voters predominate.

COPE in 1964 said that of the candidates it had supported in 1960, 57 percent had been elected; in 1962, 60 percent; and in 1964, 68 percent. In 1966, COPE and other labor groups reportedly contributed more than $1 million to candidates for the Senate and the House, with a high percentage of success.

Loans and Debts

Sen. Hugh Scott raised the question of the legality of post-election settlement of campaign debts by corporations. On the Senate floor July 23, 1971, Scott said,

"If the candidate charges communications or transportation services used in his campaign and fails to pay the bill, he has, in effect, received an involuntary campaign contribution."

The Corrupt Practices Act forbids corporations from making loans or contributions to candidates or committees. However, this has not been interpreted to include credit extended by telephone, telegraph and air carrier companies.

Scott asked the General Accounting Office for a study of outstanding debts and negotiated settlements related to political campaigns. According to the study, $2.1-million has been incurred in airline bills and approximately $400,000 in telephone bills. The American Telephone & Telegraph Company classified $76,892 of political campaign debts for the years 1968, 1969 and 1970 as "written off as uncollectible." More than half of this amount, $48,399, was owed by the McCarthy campaign to the Indiana branch of the company. American Airlines, as of April 1971, had $1,377,834 in debts incurred by political candidates—ranging from $426,833 incurred by the Democratic National Committee to $69,386 incurred by Nixon campaign committees.

Political Investment

In 1971, in the case of New Orleans philanthropist Edith R. Stern, the U.S. Court of Appeals in New Orleans ruled that a political contribution could be considered an investment.

Mrs. Stern argued that $61,000 spent on behalf of two Louisiana reform slates were not gifts but donations made "to protect my property and personal interests by promoting efficiency in government." She paid the $35,908 required by the Internal Revenue Service for gift taxes and then filed a successful suit for recovery.

Mrs. Stern was reported to be the first and only giver to have informed the Internal Revenue Service and the courts that a campaign expenditure was an economic investment.

A 1959 IRS regulation said that all gifts to candidates or parties are "not allowable as deductible contributions for gift-tax purposes."

The code required that an individual pay gift taxes on donations exceeding $3,000 to one recipient in any calendar year, except that a sum in excess of $3,000 may be applied toward a lifetime exclusion of $30,000. Many contributors avoid the gift taxes by making gifts of less than $3,000 to multiple committees. For example, in 1970 various members of the Pew family of Philadelphia (J. Howard Pew is chairman of the Sun Oil Company) contributed more than $40,000 to various Republican committees. All contributions were less than $3,000.

For other contributors the tax costs were significant. Mrs. John D. Rockefeller paid gift taxes of $854,483.44 on her contributions totaling $1,432,625 to the 1968 presidential campaign of her stepson, New York Gov. Nelson A. Rockefeller (R).

Writing the decision for the court in the case of Mrs. Stern, Judge Homer Thornberry said that her dealings with the candidates were "at arm's length, and free of any donative intent." In a footnote he added that her expenditure was "an economic investment."

EXPENDITURES: MORE SPECIALIZATION, MORE DOLLARS

The increasing complexity and expense of campaigning are forcing American politicians to look more closely at where and how their money is spent.

Democratic and Republican spending in the 1968 general election campaign for the presidency was $35.2-million, some 38.6 percent higher than a 1964 total of $25.4-million, according to Herbert Alexander, director of the Citizens' Research Foundation, Princeton, N.J. Alexander estimated Republican spending at $24.9-million in 1968 and $14.4-million in 1964 and Democratic spending at $10.3-million in 1968 and almost $11-million in 1964.

The outlook for 1972 is for even higher spending, unless legislation before the 92nd Congress clears in time for the election. *(Action on the 1971 campaign spending bill, p. 44)*

Competition for the campaign dollar is becoming more competitive among the growing legions of such specialists as political consultants, pollsters, advertising men and television time-buyers. Even the time-tested vote-getter of door-to-door canvassing has been complicated by feeding its results into computer data banks.

Pre-Nomination Expenses

The most comprehensive estimates of campaign spending generally date only from the primaries, but it has been argued that campaigns and their attendant expenses begin several years before the nomination contests. For example, Richard M. Nixon's extensive travel in 1966 on behalf of Republican congressional candidates made him a major presidential contender after the Republicans' impressive election results that year. The 30,000-mile tour, including the salary and expenses of one assistant, cost $90,000. The money was raised independently of the campaigns.

Mr. Nixon's first campaign planning session for his 1968 presidential race was held in early January 1967. "Nineteen months and more than $10-million later, Richard Nixon was the Republican nominee for President," wrote Alexander in his book *Financing the 1968 Election.*

Ronald Reagan's 1967-68 nationwide speaking tours contributed to his later candidacy for the Republican presidential nomination, Alexander wrote, yet at the time they were also legitimate activities of the incumbent Governor of California. Incumbent Representatives and Senators, in effect, run for office throughout their terms, while enjoying the use of the frank, the impact of *Congressional Record* reprints, their travel allowances and other benefits. "It is virtually impossible," Alexander concluded, "to separate any politician's activities into those which are part of his present position from those which may be pointed toward a future position or campaign."

Pre-nomination and post-nomination campaign organizations are often almost identical. The number of workers increases as election day nears. So do expenses. But the campaign managers, press secretary, policy advisers, pollsters, advance men, schedulers and speechwriters, researchers and political intelligence staff have been hired months earlier.

Campaign offices often open in presidential primary states months before an election. Mr. Nixon opened a New Hampshire headquarters six months before the state's 1968 primary. Rep. Paul N. McCloskey Jr. (R Calif.), who said he would challenge the President in the 1972 primaries, opened his New Hampshire office in August 1971, and Sen. George McGovern (D S.D.), the only announced presidential candidate, opened his office there in February.

Primaries. Mr. Nixon spent $500,000 in the 1968 Wisconsin primary. Staff costs totaled $28,168, and media costs were $320,211. He spent an additional $1.3-million in his other four major primary efforts and also ran in five lesser contests.

Alexander reported that the six Democratic contenders incurred costs of $25-million in their 1968 primary races, but deficits and debt settlements probably reduced the total actually spent to about $21-million.

Wealthy candidates in the 1970 primaries spent $1 to $11 for each vote received. Rep. Richard L. Ottinger (D N.Y. 1965-71) estimated that he spent $1.8-million in his Senate campaign, including $1-million for televised advertisements projecting him as a man of experience in a state where almost two-thirds of the voters did not know who he was. *(Story on wealthy candidates, p. 30)*

Convention Costs. National convention expenses were $796,263 for the Republicans in 1968, according to Alexander, and included $1,973 for signs, $25,976 for the orchestra and $16,886 for decorations.

The Democrats spent $1,746,301 at their convention, according to Alexander. They listed their largest expenditure, $811,841, as "uncategorized costs," but noted that $360,485 had been spent on equipment rental.

Campaign Expenses

Political Consultants. A well-heeled non-incumbent candidate in a typical campaign for an important political office may enlist the services of a professional political consultant, a computer firm, a pollster, an advertising agency, a film-maker, a speechwriter, a television and radio time-buyer, a direct mail organization and possibly an accounting firm.

The cost of such services for a tight House race easily could run to more than $100,000 per candidate—exclusive of television time expenses.

The political consultant may visit his candidate's state or district only occasionally, preferring instead to closet himself with poll results, computer breakdowns of voting patterns and demographic profiles. He prefers to plan a campaign as early before the primary as possible. He generally prefers newcomers for whom he can build an image. He is expensive. Some consultants command $500 a day for their full-time personal services. One firm requires about $80,000 for an average House campaign; the firm claims it must clear $1,200 a day to meet salary and travel expenses.

A well-versed campaign consultant must be qualified to work in public opinion surveys, electronic data processing, fund-raising, budgeting, media, research, public relations and press services, advertising and volunteer recruitment. Some participate in policy decisions as well.

No organization has the talent or resources to take on all these jobs at once, but some offer prospective clients a "package" of related services. This practice assures that one firm will be responsible for victory or defeat. Some experienced politicians, however, still prefer to draw on a variety of experienced individuals and firms for their campaigns.

Other firms, such as Matt Reese and Associates, of Washington, act only as consultants for work contracted out to other individuals or agencies. Reese has charged as much as $25,000 for a plan detailing a timed approach to campaign management and control, staff, county organizations, finance, communications, party contact, scheduling and advance management, advisory committees, other special committees and the specific "Citizens for John Doe" committee. Reese will also prepare campaign budgets.

Polls. William R. Hamilton and Staff is a division of a Washington public opinion and marketing research firm, Independent Research Associates Inc., one of dozens of such firms that play an increasingly important part in campaigns. "In the past," says a Hamilton booklet, "candidates have gone through entire campaigns without polls; in today's politics, however, the chances are about five to one that the opposition is making his campaign decisions based on knowledge of how the voters feel about the candidates and issues."

Hamilton, whose firm has done more than 125 studies for political, governmental and commercial clients since its founding in 1963, recommends a basic, in-depth poll prior to any major campaign activity. Trained resident interviewers in randomly selected urban blocks or rural areas of a particular constituency interview five to eight probable voters in each area. The interviewer spends about 45 minutes to an hour with each voter.

When campaign funds are "extremely scarce," Hamilton recommends a telephone poll in place of an in-the-home poll. He also offers "telephone panel-backs," or follow-up polls, and scout studies—quick spot studies—of a particular group of voters.

Hamilton claims that polls' total costs vary only plus or minus 15 percent. What do vary are costs per interview and the amount of information and analysis provided. The cost of Hamilton's statewide personal interview poll of 300 to 800 probable voters ranges from $5,000 to $10,000. Telephone polls are usually about 50 to 60 percent of the costs of a personal interview polls, he said, or $2,500 to $5,000. Telephone follow-ups can range from $750 to $2,500.

The sample size for congressional or metropolitan area constituencies is usually 200 to 400, depending on the size and complexity of the area, says Hamilton. A personal interview poll, Hamilton says, should cost between $3,000 and $5,000. The basic telephone poll costs between $2,000 and $3,500, and the telephone follow-ups are slightly less than for statewide studies.

Scout studies vary, depending on the type of voter desired in the sample. Hamilton says the costs should range from $250 to $1,000.

"Remember," he says in his booklet, "that while polling initially costs money—without directly bringing either money or votes into a campaign—its value in ultimately reducing the cost-per-vote in an election can be many times its original cost."

"There is a curious aspect to the heavy use of polling in Nixon's (1968) campaign," Alexander reported. "As eager as Nixon and his staff were to know what the polls revealed about what people thought, everybody was anxious to make it clear that Nixon would not tailor his politics to fit what the research said people wanted—and, indeed, there is evidence that he did not do so.

"Nixon—and many other politicians—pay out much money for polls, and then respond as much to unscientific and intuitive judgments as to the polls themselves."

Alexander estimates that the total for polling for all candidates at all levels in 1968 was about $6-million, $1-million more than the 1964 estimate. The $6-million broke down to 1,200 polls at an average cost of $5,000, he said. As for the three major presidential contenders, Alexander wrote, Mr. Nixon spent $384,000; Humphrey, $262,000, and Wallace, $37,000.

Broadcasting. According to Federal Communications Commission (FCC) reports, candidates in 1970 spent $59.2-million, including commissions, on broadcasting—the highest figure yet for a non-presidential election year. That figure represented an increase of $29.2-million, or 97.3 percent, over 1966, the last non-presidential year. That year, primary and general election candidates spent $30-million, including commissions. *(Broadcast spending, p. 19; 1971 legislation on broadcast costs, p. 44)*

In the 1968 presidential year, Roger Ailes of REA Productions Inc. in New York, one of Richard Nixon's top television producers, was quoted as saying, "This is the beginning of a whole new concept. This is it. This is the way they'll be elected forevermore. The next guys will have to be performers."

But the majority of candidates handled by top media consultants in 1970 lost, and Robert Ailes, another REA Productions official, said, "There were no races where media management made the difference. The ones that were going to win in this election year won without any help."

Michael Rowan said he believes that "image" campaigns never work at all. "I'm not interested in that image projection garbage," he said, "because people know it's a put-on...McGinnis (Joe McGinnis, author of *The Selling of the President, 1968*, which chronicled Mr. Nixon's television campaign) can point to the screen and say, 'Look, they're manipulating the voter,' and I can say, 'So what? It isn't doing anything.' It didn't do anything for Nixon—if he'd lost any more in the Gallup Poll during the last 15 weeks of the campaign, he'd have lost the election.

"Those guys tested for recall and they tested for theme," Rowan continued, "but they didn't go one step further and ask how the people felt about the spots—and the answer was, they didn't like them."

There are campaigns where television is not much of a factor, either because of the location of media markets or the area's political makeup. For example, only a rare congressional candidate from Manhattan could afford substantial television time at New York City rates. Candidates from New Jersey have the same problem, because that state has no television stations of its own and depends on New York facilities.

In some rural areas, said a Senate aide, "people know and want to see the guy, not a face on the tube. Our TV is largely just short spots. We have some billboards, and we have hand cards—which the Senator hands out himself." Such a campaign still depends largely on the candidate's personal appearances.

Print Advertising. "Television has done to print what the jet plane did to railroads," Michael Rowan said. "You could run a political campaign without print, but there are certain things you want to use it for—information too complex for electronic media, information that needs a fuller explanation. The big thing with print, after all, is identification. The last thing you're going to see in the campaign is a name on a ballot. We usually take the district's ballot logo and use it on the screen or in our printed stuff. It's usually a poor design, but the voter is familiar with it."

A slight identification can be the turning point in local and state races, according to Reese. "One advantage in a lesser campaign is that nobody much cares who wins, unless he has some personal reason," Reese said. "A slight identification or superficial contact is enough to get someone to vote for the candidate. That's easy for the consultant, because he can see that you do have that letter in your mailbox."

"I have this feeling about print stuff, though," Rowan said, "that people aren't going to read anything unless there's a reason—they get too much mail. That's where you wind up—as another thing through a mail slot. On TV, you're the only one there."

Agencies determine the execution of posters, billboards, brochures, newspaper and magazine ads and handouts. While some politicians discredit the effectiveness of newspaper ads (Rep. Charles E. Bennett (D Fla.) told the House Committee on Standards of Official Conduct that he bought newspaper advertising only "so they won't get mad at me"), the medium consumed 10 to 15 percent of the total budget of a modern statewide campaign in 1970.

Billboards are bought by market, rather than by state, and by what are called "showings," according to Jack Bowen of a Washington advertising agency, Bailey, Deardourff and Bowen. A showing is a projection of the percentage of people in an area who will see a billboard message at least once during a week. Billboards are bought in advance, by the month.

In the New York metropolitan area, Bowen said, a billboard for one month at a 100 showing would total 232 different boards costing $34,160. At a 75 showing, or 174 boards, the cost would be $25,620.

In the Billings, Mont., area, a 100 showing, or 14 boards, would cost $1,050; a 75 showing, or 11 boards, $825. In Atlanta, Ga., a 100 showing, or 80 boards, would cost $8,630; a 75 showing, or 60 boards, would cost $6,480.

Persons buying billboards for a presidential campaign, Bowen said, usually buy within a selected list of 50 to 100 top markets.

Besides the agency fee, campaigns must pay for the advertising itself. For example, about $130,000 was spent for one two-page Nixon ad in *Life* magazine in 1968, according to Alexander.

Ad agencies also oversee campaign paraphernalia. Feely and Wheeler, a New York advertising agency, handled the following list for Mr. Nixon's 1968 campaign: 20.5 million buttons, 9 million bumper strips, 560,000 balloons, 400,000 posters and placards, 28,000 straw skimmers, 30,000 brochures, 3.5 million speeches and position papers and 12,000 paper dresses and jewelry. The total cost was $1,124,626 but did not include two books, *Nixon Speaks Out* and *Nixon on the Issues*, published by campaign committees, Alexander wrote.

As for the Democrats, Alexander wrote, "Even such staples as buttons and bumper stickers were in chronically short supply...O'Brien (Lawrence F. O'Brien, Democratic national chairman) could not scrape up $100,000 to buy the first order (of designs which had been ready for weeks) until Sept. 23."

Staff and Office Expenses. Although headquarters and staff generally account for less than 20 to 30 percent of most campaign budgets, a long-time aide to a western Senator refused to estimate a probable cost for his boss' next campaign. "It depends on who you find," he said, "a retiree who will work for just about expenses or someone you hire away from a full-time job. Staff costs are among the imponderables."

At campaign headquarters, costs continue through election day for items such as rent, supplies, utilities and salaries of some employees. There are expenses for transporting voters to the polls if not enough persons volunteer for such duty. And poll-watchers may have to be paid.

Volunteer workers' services, though nominally free, are costly to administer. Indirect expenses include recruitment drives, maintenance of headquarters, transportation of canvassers and "socials" to sustain enthusiasm and other items.

Speechwriting and Research. Speechwriters and researchers are usually included on the campaign staff, but occasionally freelance writers are hired. Commercial research firms and clipping services are often contracted to provide extensive background information and continuous updating on candidate publicity.

Professional gag men have been retained by parties or candidates at least as far back as the Herbert Hoover-Al Smith campaign, but these have been partisan volunteers whose activities were kept as secret as possible. Today the candidate's joke writers have been openly credited with making or breaking several campaigns.

Jim Atkins, a Washington public relations man who has supplied 20 campaigns, including three presidential races, with humorous lines, charges "$100 a campaign, no matter what the campaign, for whatever I happen to turn out." When asked if this was a high sum when no work is absolutely guaranteed, he replied, "Look at the 1960 slogan against Nixon: 'Would you buy a used car from this man?' How much was that worth?"

Atkins thinks it may have cost Mr. Nixon the election, as might Alice Roosevelt Longworth's remark about Republican Thomas E. Dewey. "He looks," she said, "like the figure of a bridegroom on a wedding cake."

Travel. Stated campaign travel costs may be considerably inflated, according to Alexander, since as much as half the total is reimbursed by the organizations of reporters traveling with candidates. Most of this reimbursed transportation is for flying on a plane provided by the campaign or in the candidate's plane, but some ground transportation, such as press buses, may also be paid for.

As figures from Mr. Nixon's 1968 general election campaign show, substantial portions of travel costs can be recouped when the candidate and his staff fly with enough reporters. A reported $1,837,416 was spent on Mr. Nixon's tour, according to Alexander, and $492,000 was reimbursed from media travelers.

Travel accommodations vary widely among candidates. George C. Wallace, the American Independent party candidate for President, began his 1968 campaign with a DC-7, Alexander reported, which was either loaned by or rented from Henry Seale, a Texas oil millionaire. Later Wallace added a DC-3 and two Electra prop-jets. According to Wallace's final report, at least $1,235,000 had been spent on planes, rental cars, hotels and so on.

Mr. Nixon's campaign reported spending $1,345,416 for travel, after media reimbursements, compared with Humphrey's report of $875,600. "The Humphrey style of travel was definitely tourist class compared to that of the luxurious and efficient Nixon entourage," Alexander reported; Humphrey and his staff lurched along in chartered buses. Nixon's group flew.

"Freebies." Some candidates receive goods and services without charge from their supporters. For instance, a friend may lend his private plane to a candidate or may lend a building rent-free for an office. Incumbents have certain financial advantages, too, such as computerized mail files of correspondence during their tenures.

Furthermore, when campaign totals are given, they represent committed costs, not actual expenditures. Some of the debts from the Kennedy, McCarthy and Humphrey campaigns of 1968 were settled for less than their full amount. For instance, wrote Alexander, the Kennedy campaign left a $3.5-million debt, but efforts were made to settle accounts at an average of about 33 cents on the dollar. If all outstanding Kennedy campaign debts were settled at that rate, Alexander continued, the total real cost of the campaign would be about 25 percent less than the listed, committed cost.

Is Spending Effective?

Election day 1970 brought bad news to some of the campaign's heaviest spenders, including Democratic Senate candidates Howard W. Metzenbaum (Ohio), Ottinger and Republican Senate candidates George Bush (Texas), William C. Cramer (Fla.), Tom Kleppe (N.D.) and George Murphy (Calif.).

Educator Alexander Heard had asserted in 1960 that "The old notion that the side with more money will for that reason win, or will usually do so, is *not* correct."

But big campaign spenders say they can point to better-than-random correlation between financial outlay and victory. Other political consultants analyze the situation this way:

• The majority of voters have made up their minds about the candidate they will vote for by the start of the campaign. Unswayed by bids for their favor during the campaign, they will vote for their pre-chosen candidate.

• About 10 to 15 percent of the electorate, the voters who are "independent and susceptible" when the campaign begins, often hold the balance of power.

• The candidate with the most money cannot be sure of winning to his side enough of the undecided voters to give him a victory, but the candidate with less money may be unable to present his case adequately to the crucial group of undecided voters.

A lot of money helps, and "spending is as effective as ever, but it's wasted on 50 percent of the bases in any political campaign," said John Calkins of the Republican Congressional Campaign Committee.

The point of all the pre-primary polls and voting research, say the consultants, is to find the 50 percent that is not wasted. The consultants discount a direct correlation between the amount of spending and the chances for success. They emphasize that what counts is where the money is spent.

That means a budget, said Matt Reese—something that "is almost never done—a budget that has options to it in case the money isn't collected. See, you can get locked into a campaign—like buying billboards that you have to buy in April, and then you have no money for TV and radio; when you get bumper strips and have no money for election day. You've got to put everything in the campaign in relation to every other thing—early in the campaign....

"You can lose a campaign on media alone when you spend so much on paid communication that you starve free communication—that's your public relations—or your campaign organization. I recommend 60 percent to 40 percent toward media, but we usually don't have that....I only lost one campaign in a bangup way, and that was because there was no budget. We had no media support whatsoever.

"There are two ways to get out the vote," Reese said. "One is persuasion; the other is organization. Either one is enough if it works completely, but only the most naive ignore one or the other."

Setting resource allocation ("And that isn't only money," said Reese. "It's time, talent and organization, too") depends largely on the nature of the area the candidate hopes to represent.

Another contingency is connecting the technique to the candidate. "Billboards are mainly for name recognition," said Jim Johnson, a political coordinator for the presidential campaign of Sen. Edmund S. Muskie (D Maine). "They're good in a district race, when you can put them up on all the main arteries and everybody who drives past can see your name. But Muskie has a 90 percent name recognition in the country."

Alexander Heard distinguished between primaries and other nominating steps.

"Money," he wrote, "probably has its greatest impact...in the shadow land...where it is decided who will be a candidate...and who will not." The effect of money in politics is far more certain there, he said, than in determining the outcome of elections.

Reese threw in a qualification: "Well, when the primary is tantamount to the election, such as the primary for the Governor of Lousiana, primaries are very important. Anyway, spending money early is the best way to prevent opposition from developing. Mandel (Marvin Mandel, the Democrat who won in the 1970 Maryland gubernatorial election) showed so much strength at the beginning—he had radio and TV spots in June, probably; he dried up sources of money for other candidates, he got to the politicians. He shut off the opposition's resources."

FEDERAL ELECTIONS LAWS: A HISTORY OF LOOPHOLES

More than a century of legislative attempts to regulate campaign financing in the United States has resulted in much controversy and minimal control. As an anonymous article in the April 1967 *University of Pennsylvania Law Review* stated: "Campaign finance laws are typical of attempts by politicians to regulate their own affairs; and, although the statutes create the impression that regulation has been attempted, they all too often embody carefully drafted loopholes which drain them of any substance."

Legislation on campaign spending in the United States has had three aims: (1) to limit and regulate donations made to candidates and their campaign committees; (2) to limit and regulate disbursements made by candidates and their committees, and (3) to inform voters of the amounts and sources of the donations and the amounts, purposes and payees of the disbursements. Disclosure, it was felt, would reveal which candidates, if any, were unduly indebted to interest groups, in time to forewarn the voters.

The first provision of federal law on campaign financing was incorporated in an Act of March 2, 1867, making naval appropriations for the fiscal year 1868. The final section of the Act read: "And be it further enacted, That no officer or employee of the government shall require or request any workingman in any navy yard to contribute or pay any money for political purposes, nor shall any workingman be removed or discharged for political opinion; and any officer or employee of the government who shall offend against the provisions of this section shall be dismissed the service of the United States."

Reports circulated in the following year that at least 75 percent of the money raised by the Republican Congressional Committee came from federal officeholders. Continuing agitation on this and other aspects of the spoils system in federal employment led to adoption of the Civil Service Reform Act of Jan. 16, 1883, which authorized establishment of Civil Service rules. One of the rules stated "That no person in the public service is for that reason under any obligation to contribute to any political fund...and that he will not be removed or otherwise prejudiced for refusing to do so." The law made it a crime for any federal employee to solicit campaign funds from another federal employee. This law is still on the books (U.S. Code, 1964 Edition, Title 18, Section 602).

Corrupt Practices Laws

Muckrakers in the early part of the 20th century highlighted the influence on government exerted by big business through unrestrained spending on behalf of favored candidates. After the 1904 elections, a move for federal legislation took shape in the National Publicity Law Association, headed by former Rep. Perry Belmont (D N.Y. 1881-88).

President Theodore Roosevelt, in his annual State of the Union message on Dec. 5, 1905, proposed that: "All contributions by corporations to any political committee or for any political purpose should be forbidden by law." Roosevelt repeated the proposal in his message of Dec. 3, 1906, suggesting that it be the first item of congressional business.

In response to the President's urging, Congress by the Act of Jan. 26, 1907 (Tillman Act), made it unlawful for a corporation or a national bank to make "a money contribution in connection with any election" of candidates for federal office. Further regulation of campaign financing was provided by an Act of June 25, 1910. The new law required every political committee "which shall in two or more states influence the result or attempt to influence the result of an election at which Representatives in Congress are to be elected" to file with the Clerk of the House of Representatives, within 30 days after the election, the name and address of each contributor of $100 or more, the name and address of each recipient of $10 or more from the committee, and the total amounts that the committee received and disbursed. Individuals who engaged in similar activities outside the framework of committees were also required to submit such reports.

An act of Aug. 19, 1911, extended the filing requirements to committees influencing senatorial elections and to require filing of financial reports by candidates for the office of either Senator or Representative. In addition, it required statements to be filed both before and after an election. The most important innovation of the 1911 act was the limitation of the amount that a candidate might spend toward his nomination and election: a candidate for the Senate, no more than $10,000 or, if less, the maximum amount permitted in his state; for the House, no more than $5,000 or, if less, the maximum amount permitted in his state.

The basic campaign financing law in effect through 1971 was the Federal Corrupt Practices Act of Feb. 28, 1925, which regulated campaign spending and disclosure of receipts and expenditures by congressional candidates. This Act limited its restrictions to election campaigns, since at the time it was passed the question of whether Congress had power to regulate primary elections was unsettled.

The 1925 Act increased the amounts that legally could be spent by candidates. Unless a state law prescribed a smaller amount, the Act set the limit of campaign expenditures at: (1) $10,000 for a Senate candidate and $2,500 for a House candidate; or (2) an amount equal to three cents for each vote cast in the last preceding election for the office sought, but not more than $25,000 for the Senate and $5,000 for the House.

The 1925 Act incorporated the existing prohibition of campaign contributions by corporations or national banks, the ban on solicitation of political contributions from federal employees by candidates or other federal employees and the requirement that reports be filed on campaign finances. It prohibited giving or offering money to anyone in exchange for his vote. In amending the provisions of the Act of 1907 on contributions, the new law substituted for the word "money" the expression "a gift, subscription, loan, advance, or deposit of money, or anything of value."

Hatch Act

On Aug. 2, 1939, the Clean Politics Act, commonly called the Hatch Act—after Sen. Carl A. Hatch (D N.M. 1933-49)—was enacted. It affected campaign financing in only a secondary way, by prohibiting active participation in national politics by federal employees and the use of relief funds for political purposes.

An amendment to the Hatch Act, approved July 19, 1940, made three significant additions to legislation on campaign financing. It forbade individuals or business concerns doing work for the federal government under contract to contribute to any political committee or candidate. It asserted the right of Congress to regulate primary elections for the nomination of candidates for federal offices and made it unlawful for anyone to contribute more than $5,000 "during any calendar year, or in connection with any campaign for nomination or election, to or on behalf of any candidate for an elective federal office." However, the Act specifically exempted from this limitation "contributions made to or by a state or local committee." The 1940 amendment also placed a ceiling of $3-million in a calendar year on expenditures by a political committee operating in two or more states. Wartime legislation in 1943 temporarily, and the Taft-Hartley Act of 1947 permanently forbade labor unions to contribute to political campaigns.

Subsidized Campaigning. Proponents of governmental subsidization of election campaigns appeared to have won a major victory in 1966. An act approved Nov. 13 of that year authorized any individual paying federal income tax to direct that $1 of the tax due in any year be paid into a Presidential Election Campaign Fund. The fund, to be set up in the U.S. Treasury, was to disburse its receipts, on a proportional basis, among political parties whose presidential candidates had received 5 million or more votes in the preceding presidential election.

However, an act of June 13 of the following year provided that "Funds which become available under the Presidential Election Campaign Fund Act of 1966 shall be appropriated and disbursed only after the adoption by law of guidelines governing their distribution." As Congress never adopted any guidelines, the 1966 act became a dead letter. *(1971 effort p. 57)*

Primary Campaigns

Application of federal laws on campaign financing to primary elections was first made in 1911. The act of 1911 limiting campaign expenditures in congressional elections covered primaries as well as general elections. However, the Supreme Court in the Newberry case of 1921 struck down the application of the law to primaries, on the ground that the power the Constitution gave Congress to regulate the "manner of holding election" did not extend to party primaries and conventions. The Federal

Corrupt Practices Act of 1925 exempted primaries from its operation.

The Hatch Act amendments of 1940, as noted, made primaries again subject to federal restrictions on campaign contributions despite the Newberry decision. This new legislation was upheld in 1941, when the Supreme Court handed down its decision in *United States v. Classic et al.,* which reversed the Newberry decision. The *Classic* decision was confirmed by the Supreme Court in 1944 in *Smith v. Allwright.* When the Taft-Hartley Act was adopted in 1947, its prohibition of political contributions by corporations, national banks and labor organizations was phrased so as to cover primaries as well as general elections.

Enforcement Efforts

The Senate in 1927 barred Senator-elect William S. Vare (R Pa.) from taking his seat after reports indicated that his campaign had cost $785,000. In the same year, the Senate refused to seat Senator-elect Frank L. Smith (R Ill.). More than 80 percent of Smith's campaign fund had come from three men who had a direct interest in a decision of the Illinois Commerce Commission, of which Smith continued to be a member throughout the campaign. One of the three donors was Samuel Insull, owner of a controlling interest in a network of utility companies.

In 1934, a case reached the Supreme Court which required the Court to rule on, among other things, the constitutionality of the requirement in the 1925 Act that lists and amounts of campaign contributions and expenditures be filed publicly. The case, *Burroughs and Cannon v. United States,* involved primarily the applicability of the Act to the election of presidential electors. Justice George Sutherland on Jan. 8, 1934, delivered the opinion of the Court. Applicability of the Act to presidential campaigns was upheld. The decision included the following statement on disclosure: "Congress reached the conclusion that public disclosure of political contributions, together with the names of contributors and other details, would tend to prevent the corrupt use of money to affect elections. The verity of this conclusion reasonably cannot be denied."

In the six decades from 1907 to 1968, the Tillman Act and later legislation on campaign financing was largely ignored. Alexander Heard wrote in *The Costs of Democracy* in 1960 that the prohibition in the Federal Corrupt Practices Act of direct purchases of goods or advertising for the benefit of a candidate was "manifestly violated right and left"; that the prohibition of campaign contributions by federal contractors "goes ignored"; and that the prohibition of loans to candidates by banks was "disregarded." Then, in the closing years of the 1960s, Washington's attitude toward enforcement of the Federal Corrupt Practices Act seemed to change. The Nixon Administration successfully pressed charges in 1969 against corporations (mostly in California) that had contributed campaign money in 1968.

Another form of violation, failure to report or false reporting under the Corrupt Practices Act, was ignored until 1968, despite the fact that newsmen repeatedly uncovered instances of failure to file reports or the filing of incomplete reports. Attorney General Herbert Brownell in 1954 stated as the position of the Department of Justice that the initiative in such cases rested with the Secretary of the Senate and the Clerk of the House.

Public interest in this form of violation grew during the 1960s. When 54 House candidates in the 1962 election failed to file financial reports, Congressional Quarterly asked the Department of Justice whether it would prosecute the delinquents. The Department on Nov. 19, 1963, replied that its policy remained as before—"not to institute investigations into possible violations in the absence of a request from the Clerk of the House of Representatives or the Secretary of the Senate."

The situation changed in 1967 when W. Pat Jennings, a former member of the House of Representatives (D Va., 1955-66), was elected Clerk of the House. In 1968, he broke precedent by sending to the Department of Justice a list of 21 fund-raising committees (20 Republican, one Democratic) with a notation that their treasurers had not complied with "the time requirement as set forth in the Federal Corrupt Practices Act."

The Department of Justice, however, declined to press charges against the committees. In explanation, it said the violators had not been adequately warned of possible prosecution.

Jennings continued his one-man crusade in 1969. In January of that year, he sent to the Justice Department a list of 107 candidates in the 1968 congressional elections who had failed to file the required financial reports or had missed the post-election deadline of Dec. 5, 1968, for filing final reports. The names of the 107 delinquents were not released, and the Department of Justice did not institute proceedings against them. Reportedly, no incumbents were among the 107 candidates involved.

Assistant Attorney General Will Wilson, in a letter of May 1970 to members of Congress who had inquired, said that fair play required the Department of Justice to notify candidates and committees in advance of the possibility of prosecution. This requirement was soon fulfilled. A Department of Justice spokesman on July 16, 1970, said the Criminal Division considered that by then those involved had been sufficiently warned of the possibility of prosecution. He indicated that the Department of Justice was ready to undertake prosecutions, provided that in the Department's judgment its own investigations of certified violations warranted court action. However, nothing happened.

Jennings sent a list of delinquents to the Attorney General early in 1971. In mid-February, a Justice Department spokesman first said, "We don't know what we're going to do" about these cases and later added that no prosecutions were contemplated since the 1970 warning had applied to "campaign committees, not candidates," whereas Jennings' list was a list of candidates.

State Laws

New York State in 1883 enacted a law prohibiting solicitation of campaign contributions from state employees and in 1890 required candidates to file sworn financial statements. California in 1893 limited the total amount of money that could be spent on behalf of a candidate and established a list of legitimate campaign expenses. By 1905, some type of regulation of campaign finances was in effect in 14 states. However, Justice Felix Frankfurter, delivering the opinion of the Supreme Court, March 11, 1957, in *United States v. U.A.W.*, said:

"These state publicity laws either became dead letters or were found to be futile."

Florida in 1951 adopted a law on campaign financing which often is cited as a model. It requires each candidate to appoint a campaign treasurer and to designate a single bank as the campaign depository. Contributions to the campaign must be deposited within 24 hours of receipt, with deposit slips showing the names and addresses of donors and the amounts contributed by each. Candidates are required to publish periodic reports of campaign expenditures during the campaign, every week in the case of candidates for the U.S. Senate and the governorship and every month in the case of candidates for all other offices.

By 1971, eight states regulated campaign financing by imposing limits on spending by candidates and political committees and by requiring candidates and committees to report receipts and expenditures. Twelve states made some, but not all, of the foregoing requirements. Twenty-one other states had less comprehensive regulations. Nine states—Alaska, Delaware, Georgia, Illinois, Louisiana, Maine, Nevada, Pennsylvania, Rhode Island—had no regulations. Prosecutions for violation of state laws on campaign financing have been rare.

Loopholes in the Legislation

Most of the laws concerning campaign financing in the United States have been filled with loopholes. Louise Overacker wrote in *Presidential Campaign Funds* in 1946: "The Hatch Act limitations were included in an act which purported to 'Prohibit Pernicious Political Practices.' One might...parody it to read: 'An Act to *Promote* Pernicious Political Activities.' It defeats its own purpose by encouraging decentralization, evasion and concealment."

Rep. James C. Wright Jr. (D Texas), testifying July 21, 1966, before the Subcommittee on Elections of the House Administration Committee, said that legislation on campaign financing was "intentionally evaded by almost every candidate." He added: "I dare say there is not a member of Congress, myself included, who has not knowingly evaded its purpose in one way or another."

An anonymous article in the April 1967 *University of Pennsylvania Law Review* described the "regulation of political finance today" as "more loophole than legislation." This description was echoed in a message which President Johnson sent to Congress May 25, 1967, proposing election reforms. The message said of the Federal Corrupt Practices Act and the Hatch Act: "Inadequate in their scope when enacted, they are now obsolete. More loophole than law, they invite evasion and circumvention."

The citizens' lobby Common Cause took legal action on Jan. 11, 1971, to plug loopholes in the Corrupt Practices Act by filing suit in the U.S. District Court for the District of Columbia against the Democratic and Republican National Committees and the Conservative Party of New York State, which had successfully supported candidates for federal offices in the November 1970 elections. The suit asked the court to declare illegal, and order a stop to, the giving of large sums by an individual in the names of his wife and children and the setting up of more than one political committee for a single candidate.

Donors' Loopholes. The Federal Corrupt Practices Act requires the treasurer of a political committee active in two or more states to report at specified times the name and address of every donor of $100 or more to a campaign. To evade such recording, a donor can give less than $100 to each of numerous committees supporting the candidate of his choice. A Senate subcommittee in 1956 checked the contributions of sums between $50 and $99.99 to one committee. It found that, of 97 contributions in that range, 88 were over $99, including 57 that were exactly $99.99.

Technically, an individual cannot contribute more than $5,000 to any national committee or candidate. However, he can contribute unlimited funds to state, county and local groups which pass along the money in their name.

Members of the same family can legally contribute up to $5,000 each. A wealthy donor wanting to give more than $5,000 to a candidate or a political committee can privately subsidize gifts by his relatives. Each such subsidized gift can amount to $5,000. In this way, the donor can arrange for his brothers, sisters, uncles, aunts, wife and children to present $5,000 gifts to the favored candidate or committee.

Corporations can skirt the prohibition of contributions to a political campaign by giving bonuses or salary increases to executives in the expectation that the executives as individuals will make corresponding political contributions of the kind the corporation favors.

Corporations can lend billboards, office furniture, equipment, mailing lists and airplanes to candidates or political committees. If a loan of this kind is deemed a violation of the letter of the law, the corporation can rent these items to a candidate or committee, instead of lending them, and then write off the rental fee as uncollectible.

Labor unions can contribute to a candidate or political committee funds collected from members apart from dues. They can use such funds also for nonpartisan registration and voting drives even if the drives are confined to precincts loaded with voters who favor pro-union candidates. They can emphasize the pro-union or anti-union views of candidates in publications impartially presenting voting records and published statements of candidates.

Candidates' Loopholes

Federal or state limitations on the amount of money a candidate may knowingly receive or spend are easily evaded. Former President Eisenhower, in a 1968 *Reader's Digest* article, wrote: "Another gaping loophole in the 1925 law results from the phrase referring to the candidates' 'knowledge or consent.' A congressional candidate simply makes sure that he 'knows nothing' about the activities created by his backers. One committee, for example, may pay for the use of 100 billboards, but the candidate—and this must be quite a feat—never 'sees' them as he campaigns through his district."

The loophole opened by the law's phrase "knowledge or consent" enables numerous candidates to report that they received and spent not one cent on their campaigns. In 1964, four Senators reported that

their campaign books showed zero receipts and zero expenditures. They were Vance Hartke (D Ind.), Roman L. Hruska (R Neb.), Edmund S. Muskie (D Maine) and John C. Stennis (D Miss.).

Four years later, when Sen. George McGovern (D S.D.) reported no receipts or expenditures, his executive assistant, George V. Cunningham, said: "We are very careful to make sure that Sen. McGovern never sees the campaign receipts." Two new Senators elected in 1968— William B. Saxbe (R Ohio) and Richard S. Schweiker (R Pa.)—reported general-election expenditures of $769,614 and $664,614, respectively, to their state authorities but expenditures of only $20,962 and $5,736, respectively, to the Secretary of the Senate.

The credibility gap fostered by the "knowledge or consent" loophole is further widened by the fact that the Federal Corrupt Practices Act applies only to political committees operating in two or more states. If a committee operates in one state only and is not a subdivision of a national committee, the law does not apply. If a committee operates in the District of Columbia only, receiving funds there and mailing checks to candidates in a single state, the law does not cover it. Rep. Thomas P. O'Neill Jr. (D Mass.), chairman of the House Special Committee to Investigate Campaign Expenditures, used a District of Columbia committee as the recipient of contributions for his 1970 campaign.

Limits on the expenditures that a political committee may make are evaded by establishing more than one committee and apportioning receipts and expenditures among them so that no one committee exceeds the limit. Since the law limits annual spending by a political committee to $3-million, the major parties form committees under various names, each of which is free to spend up to $3-million.

State Law Loopholes

A law on campaign finances adopted in Massachusetts in 1962 was hailed as uncommonly tough. It limited the number of committees supporting a candidate to three. The law also required that each committee have a bank account, that the bank report money deposited in the account or paid out from it, and that names and addresses of doners of more than $25, and the addresses of persons whose bills were paid, be made public. Despite the supposed stringency of the law, when Edward M. Kennedy in 1964 reported expenditures of $100,292.45 for his successful bid for the Democratic nomination for the U.S. Senate, newspapers estimated that his staff, billboard, television and other expenses amounted to 10 times that sum.

Some state laws exempt from the ceilings and reporting requirements money spent directly on publicity, such as the costs of television and radio spots, advertisements in newspapers and handbills and booklets. Exemptions apply in other states to renting of halls for meetings, hiring of publicity agents and conveyance of voters to and from the polls. Some states require reports from candidates but not committees, or reports on receipts but not expenditures. Places where reports are to be filed, such as the headquarters of the candidate's party, or the place "where the candidate resides," often constitute obstruction rather than promotion of disclosure.

RADIO-TELEVISION SPENDING: NO ELECTION GUARANTEE

Heavy spending for political broadcasts did not guarantee election success for either Republican or Democratic candidates for Congress or Governor in 1970.

Incumbency appeared to be a more important factor in winning than a flood of dollars for radio and television, according to an analysis of the Federal Communications Commission's June 1971 "Survey of Political Broadcasting" covering the 1970 elections.

The FCC report shows that Republicans outspent Democrats on general election broadcasts for campaigns at all levels with total outlays of $16,531,867 compared to $14,257,198 for Democrats.

Republican Senate candidates spent $4.4-million on broadcasts for their general election campaigns compared to $4.2-million spent by Democratic candidates. But Republicans won only 11 of the 35 contested Senate seats. Democrats took 22, one was won by a Conservative and one by an independent.

Republicans also outspent Democrats $5-million to $3.7-million on political ads in general election gubernatorial contests. Yet the Republicans won only 13 governorships compared to 22 for the Democrats.

In House general election campaigns, Republicans spent $2.1-million on broadcast advertising, and Democrats spent $1.8-million. But Democrats won 255 House seats, and Republicans won 180 seats.

This is not to imply, however, that there is no correlation between broadcast spending and political success. Party labels aside, a majority of those candidates who spent more than their general election opponents in 1970 won their races, as the following chart shows. The second chart shows the success of incumbents.

CANDIDATES OUTSPENDING OPPONENTS

	Winners		Losers	
Governor	19	54.3%	16	45.7%
Senate	20	57.1	15	42.9
House*	229	64.7	125	35.3

The FCC survey reported broadcast spending in only 354 House races in 1970.

CANDIDATES WHO WERE INCUMBENTS

	Winners		Losers	
Governor	17	70.8%	7	29.2%
Senate	24	80.0	6	20.0
House	379	96.7	13	3.3

In primary campaigns, Democratic candidates more than doubled Republican expenditures for political broadcasting. The Democrats spent a total of $11,708,776 compared to $5,129,913 spent by Republicans.

Over-all Spending. A total of $50,292,164 was spent by all candidates in 1970. The Democrats topped the Republicans by more than $4-million.

In totals for both primary and general election campaigns, Democrats spent $25,965,974 while Republicans spent $21,661,780. In addition, candidates from other parties spent $2,664,410.

The FCC's figures for 1970 do not include, as they have in past years, the 15-percent commissions paid to advertising agencies which arrange political broadcasts. If commissions are added, the 1970 spending total becomes $59.2-million. *(Chart, p. 27)*

The 350-page survey was submitted to Congress by FCC Chairman Dean Burch on June 16 when he testified before the House Subcommittee on Communications and Power.

Based on a nationwide survey of television and radio station receipts, the report provides the most detailed information on political broadcast spending since the FCC began compiling such figures in 1960. A total of 696 television stations, nearly 100 percent, and 4,027 radio stations, or 94 percent, responded to the FCC survey.

For the first time, the report lists expenditures by individual candidates for Senator, Representative, Governor and lieutenant governor. Spending on announcements and program time in both primary and general election campaigns is revealed, as well as the number of minutes of free time granted candidates by local stations.

The details on radio and television spending constitute perhaps the most comprehensive information available on the actual costs of statewide campaigns for Senator and Governor. The federal campaign reporting laws applying to candidates for Congress are so full of loopholes many candidates report nothing, or only a fraction of their actual political outlays. Primaries are not covered by federal law. *(Reports by Senate candidates, chart p. 62; analysis of campaign spending laws, p. 15)*

In many Senate races, radio and television costs are the most expensive part of the campaign.

Breakdown of Figures. The report showed that more money was spent by gubernatorial candidates than for any other office. Including primary and general elections, gubernatorial candidates spent $13,950,572 of the $50.3-million total.

Candidates for all other state and local offices spent a total of $15,553,176. Senatorial candidates spent $13,631,960 while candidates for the House of Representatives spent $5,185,388. Candidates for lieutenant governor spent $1,971,068.

Of the $50.3-million, $47.9-million was spent on spot announcements of 60 seconds or less while only $2.4-million was for program time of longer duration, the report revealed.

Most of the paid program time was on radio rather than television. In the general election, Democratic candidates purchased 1,212 hours of non-network radio program time at a total cost of $89,768. Republicans spent $69,157 for 901 hours.

Republican candidates bought more non-network television program time, however, spending $574,139 for 613 hours compared to 469 hours for $460,507 by Democrats.

The FCC's figures on network television expenditures show that Republicans outspent Democrats in the general election, buying 85 minutes for $161,259 compared to 50 minutes for $111,258 by the Democrats. Republicans also spent $5,562 for six minutes in primary campaigns.

On network radio, both parties bought a total of 45 minutes. However, Democrats spent $16,083 compared to only $10,084 by Republicans. In addition, Republicans purchased $12,357 worth of spot announcements on network radio, compared to none by Democrats.

Free Time. Sustaining, or free, broadcast time was granted candidates by 396 different television and 1,341 radio stations. Free time generally was provided to opposing candidates in approximately equivalent amounts in accordance with Section 315 (a) of the Communications Act of 1934, the so-called "equal time" provision.

In Senate elections, Republicans were granted 8,363 minutes of free non-network television time compared to 8,120 minutes for Democrats. Republican candidates also got more free non-network radio time than Democratic opponents, 25,743 minutes to 18,774 minutes.

In House general election races, Democrats got slightly more free television time, 12,107 minutes compared to 11,711 for Republicans. But GOP candidates again were given more free radio time, 42,194 minutes to 34,536 for Democrats.

In general election campaigns, Democrats running for Governor appeared on television for a total of 8,907 free minutes, while Republicans got 13,900 minutes. On radio, Democrats had 27,368 minutes without charge, while Republican candidates had 20,823.

Network television stations granted a total of 596 free broadcast minutes during 1970 general elections and 520 minutes during primaries. However, much of this time was on interview programs such as *Meet the Press, Face the Nation* and *Issues and Answers*, which are not subject to the equal time provision.

Democrats were granted 380 free minutes in general campaigns while GOP candidates got 216 minutes. In primaries, Democrats got 384 network minutes compared to 136 for Republicans.

The largest amount of free network time in the general election went to Gov. Ronald Reagan (R Calif.), who got 54 minutes compared to 39 for his Democratic opponent, Jess Unruh.

Adlai E. Stevenson III (D Ill.) got 40 minutes while his Republican opponent Ralph T. Smith was given 32 free minutes.

In Ohio, Robert Taft Jr. (R) appeared free of charge for 24 minutes while Howard Metzenbaum (D) got 22 minutes.

And in New York, James L. Buckley (Cons-R) got 14 minutes compared to 20 minutes for Charles E. Goodell (R) and 14 minutes for Richard L. Ottinger (D).

Background

Broadcast spending in U.S. elections has increased markedly since 1960, the first year figures were tabulated by the FCC. *(Chart, p. 27)*

The 1970 total of $50.3-million (or $59.2-million including commissions) was the highest yet for a non-presidential election year—representing an increase of $23.1-million, or 85 percent, over 1966, the last non-presidential year. A total of $27.2-million (or $30-million with commissions) was spent in 1966 by candidates in both primary and general campaigns.

In 1968, congressional and gubernatorial spending totaled $40.2-million, not including presidential spending of $18.7-million.

The formula of large television and radio expenditures on a carefully prepared "image" campaign appeared to be due new evaluation after the 1970 elections.

In the 1968 presidential year, Roger Ailes of REA Productions Inc. in New York, and one of Richard Nixon's top television producers, was quoted as saying: "This is the beginning of a whole new concept. This is it. This is the way they'll be elected forevermore. The next guys will have to be performers."

But the majority of candidates handled by top media consultants in 1970 lost.

After the 1970 elections, Robert Ailes, another REA Productions official, said: "There were no races where media management made the difference. The ones that were going to win in this election year won without any help."

During and after the 1970 campaigns, considerable reaction against the deluge of electronic electioneering came from political commentators, the public and even some politicians.

"A two-dimensional, 18-inch-high candidate," said Sen. Gaylord Nelson (D Wis.) in Senate debate, "presented with all the candor of a laundry product or a dancing dog act does little to assure a concerned public of the relevance and responsiveness of the political process in this country."

Frank Reynolds of the American Broadcasting Company and Nicholas Johnson of the FCC, among others, suggested that political spot commercials should be banned.

Media Studies. One difficulty in assessing the effectiveness of political broadcast advertising is that no one really knows what the public thinks about the massive media campaigns or whether voting behavior is influenced.

Very little evidence has been gathered through research by social scientists in the field. Many persons presume that in politics name recognition automatically means votes, "image" ads are better than "issues" ads, spot announcements reach the widest audience and the more ads the better.

However, there is no proof that these presumptions are correct, and some recent research tends to indicate that they may be misleading.

One project on the 1970 elections was conducted by a group of researchers in Wisconsin and Colorado. Lawrence Bowen, Charles K. Atkin and Kenneth G. Sheinkopf, all of the Mass Communications Research Center at the University of Wisconsin, and Oguz B. Nayman of Colorado State University, presented their findings in a paper entitled "How Voters React to Electronic Political Advertising." The paper was read at the annual conference of the American Association for Public Opinion Research in Pasadena, Calif., in May 1971.

The research team conducted pre-election telephone interviews with 512 voters in Wisconsin and Colorado to assess their reactions to televised political advertising aired during the 1970 gubernatorial campaigns. They found that voters tended to see a greater number of ads for the candidate who was advertised most heavily, but they gave closer attention to those ads that entertained them or fulfilled their needs for information.

Viewers tended to learn more about their favored candidate than his opponent. But only one-third of the partisan respondents reported that their preferred candidate's ads strengthened their intention to vote for him. Almost as many indicated that the opposing candidate's ads produced a negative reaction.

These results suggested that a limited number of high-quality, substantively informative broadcast advertisements may be more effective than a saturation presentation of superficial image-oriented spot announcements.

Another study of the 1970 elections was conducted by Decision Making Information (DMI), a Los Angeles political consulting firm, under a research grant from the American Medical Political Action Committee.

DMI conducted post-election surveys of 4,520 voters in 10 states in the four days immediately following the November 1970 elections.

The survey showed that 72 percent of those questioned recalled seeing a political advertisement on television during the campaigns, but only 41 percent remembered radio ads.

Voters were then asked to identify the most important things they had learned about the candidates during the campaigns and to name the source of that information.

Although nearly three out of four could recall television ads, only 25 percent said it was the source of their most important information. Only 2 percent of the sample recalled important candidate information from radio.

Voters were asked if they received their most important information in an advertising format or a news format. A total of 39 percent said newscasts or news articles were their most important source, 32 percent named advertising and 22 percent claimed to have received it from both news and advertising.

Vincent P. Barabba, chairman of the board of Decision Making Information, told a March 1971 seminar of the American Association of Political Consultants:

"In my judgment, mass media have been misused in political campaigns—perhaps to the same extent that they have been misused in commercial business campaigns and certainly with at least the same frequency. There are some good examples of effective mass media utilization...but they are more likely to be exceptions than the rule."

Barabba also said, "The campaign consultant of the 1970s will help determine the minimum amount of campaign funds required for the campaign to reach its maximum vote potential."

Proposed Legislation. The Federal Election Campaign Act of 1971 (S 382—S Rept 92-229), reported June 21 by the Senate Rules and Administration Committee, would place a limit of 5 cents on broadcast spending and 5 cents on non-broadcast media spending multiplied by the voting age population. Any unspent portions of funds authorized for one type of media could be spent on the other, which in effect would allow total broadcast spending as high as 10 cents times the voting age population.

In a Gallup Poll conducted after the elections in November 1970, 78 percent of those polled said they would favor a law which would limit the total amount a candidate could spend in his campaign. Only 15 percent were opposed and 7 percent had no opinion.

Senate Spending

The 1970 Senate elections produced some of the most controversial and costly media campaigns in history. Candidates in many states saturated prime time television and radio with spot announcements designed to discredit their opponents and build favorable images for themselves. *(Chart, p. 24)*

Broadcast expenditures in Senate elections totaled $9.3-million in 1970 general election campaigns and $4.4-million in primary races.

Republicans narrowly outspent Democrats in the general election, $4.4-million to $4.2-million. In primaries, Democratic contenders spent nearly $1-million more than Republican candidates, $2.6-million to $1.7-million.

Candidates from other parties spent $672,735 in general and $1,342 in primary campaigns, the FCC reported.

Although winners outspent losers in 20 of the 35 Senate general elections, few absolute conclusions can be drawn about the effectiveness of broadcast spending.

In about half of the 20 races won by top spenders, two candidates' expenditures were so nearly equal that the difference in spending could not account for victory. And in 15 races candidates lost despite outspending their opponents by amounts ranging up to $218,000.

Many factors other than broadcast advertising helped determine the outcome of these elections. Incumbency, for example, was a factor in 30 Senate races, and incumbents won in 24 of them.

Non-Incumbent Contests. Theoretically, the best test cases for the efficacy of media campaigns would be the five elections in which there were no incumbents. But the results of higher spending in these races were mixed.

In Delaware, Rep. William V. Roth Jr. (R) spent $13,775 in winning easily over Jacob W. Zimmerman (D), who spent $12,341, for the seat vacated by retiring Sen. John J. Williams, a four-term Republican. Roth's previous experience in the House was an obvious advantage in this election.

But in Florida, Rep. William C. Cramer (R) spent $145,484 in the general election, only to lose to State Sen. Lawton Chiles (D) who spent only $49,489. The contest was for the seat vacated by retiring Sen. Spessard L. Holland (D).

Chiles put slightly more than half of his broadcast funds into radio. He was one of the few candidates in the nation to spend more money on radio than on television. Chiles also utilized the media in other ways, such as a newsmaking 1,000-mile hike across the state to dramatize his lack of funds for television.

The retirement of Sen. Eugene J. McCarthy (D) in Minnesota led to a race between former Vice President Hubert H. Humphrey and Republican Rep. Clark MacGregor. MacGregor outspent Humphrey, $172,011 to $164,636. But Humphrey still won back a seat in the Senate where he served from 1949 to 1965.

In Ohio, Rep. Robert Taft Jr. (R) resisted a strong challenge by wealthy businessman Howard Metzenbaum (D), who spent $242,246 in a losing general election battle for the seat being vacated by retiring Sen. Stephen M.

Young (D). Taft, whose family name already was a household word in Ohio, spent $223,035 in the hard-fought contest.

Finally, in Texas, former Rep. Lloyd M. Bentsen Jr. (D 1948-55) defeated Rep. George Bush (R) for the seat held by Ralph W. Yarborough (D). Bentsen won over Yarborough in the primary. Bush outspent Bentsen in the campaign, $293,142 to $174,991. However, Bentsen had spent $218,603 in the primary, compared to $128,405 by Yarborough, in a media campaign which made his name well-recognized throughout the state.

Other Costly Races. Several other Senate general election campaigns were noteworthy for high expenditures which produced varying results.

In California, the Democratic challenger, Rep. John V. Tunney spent $472,987, with about $50,000 going to radio time, to defeat incumbent Sen. George Murphy (R), who spent $400,731, including more than $75,000 on radio.

In Illinois, Adlai E. Stevenson III, son of the late Democratic presidential candidate, outspent and defeated Senate appointee Ralph T. Smith (R). Stevenson spent $261,573 compared to Smith's $252,206. The Democratic challenger outspent the incumbent Smith on radio broadcasts, $40,352 to $9,720.

An expensive media blitz in Indiana by Republican Rep. Richard Roudebush failed to unseat Democratic incumbent Vance Hartke. Roudebush spent $364,825 compared to Hartke's $214,130.

In Missouri, State Attorney General John Danforth (R) spent $228,475 in an unsuccessful attempt to capture the Senate seat held by Stuart Symington (D), who spent $199,170.

One of the widest spending margins was in New Jersey, where Republican Nelson Gross lost despite spending $391,462, or more than twice the $173,057 spent by Democratic incumbent Harrison A. Williams Jr..

But the nation's most expensive general election campaign was in New York, where the three-way race between Republican incumbent Charles E. Goodell, Rep. Richard L. Ottinger (D) and Conservative James L. Buckley resulted in massive media expenditures on all sides.

Wealthy plywood heir Ottinger spent the most, $641,151, compared to $569,443 by Goodell and $516,472 by Buckley, the ultimate victor.

Finally, Republican incumbent and Minority Leader Hugh Scott spent $267,270 in a narrow victory over his Democratic challenger William G. Sesler, who spent only $25,374. Despite spending more than 10 times as much as Sesler, Scott won by only 220,000 votes out of 3.6 million.

Senate Primaries. Bitter intraparty rivalries in several primary elections led to heavy expenditures, including the highest total outlay by any Senate candidate in the nation for a single campaign, primary or general.

California industrialist Norton Simon (R) spent $800,823, including more than $251,000 on radio ads alone, in an unsuccessful effort to defeat incumbent Sen. George Murphy.

In the California Democratic primary, Tunney spent $83,238 to win the nomination over Rep. George E. Brown, who spent $51,004.

Ottinger spent $734,490 to win the New York Democratic primary over Rep. Richard McCarthy ($2,100),

Theodore C. Sorensen ($85,204) and Paul O'Dwyer ($25,974). This campaign was one of the most well-publicized in the nation, with accusations that the wealthy Ottinger was buying the right to oppose Goodell. During this campaign, candidate McCarthy performed such stunts as scuba diving in the polluted Hudson River and soaring over Central Park in a hot-air balloon. He was quoted as saying, "If I had Ottinger's money, I wouldn't have to do these things."

In Ohio, former astronaut John Glenn spent $31,081 in losing the Democratic primary to Metzenbaum, who spent $265,381. Taft spent $151,346 in the Republican primary to defeat Gov. James Rhodes, who spent $92,191.

Gubernatorial Spending

Some of the most expensive races in the nation were those for statehouses, in which candidates for Governor and lieutenant governor spent a total of almost $16-million.

Republicans outspent Democrats in general election gubernatorial campaigns, $5-million to $3.7-million. But Democrats spent more in primary contests, $3.8-million to $1.2-million. Other party candidates spent about $104,000 in general and $4,000 in primary campaigns. *(Chart, p. 26)*

Of 35 general election gubernatorial races, only 19 were won by the candidate who outspent his opponents on radio and television.

Incumbents won 17 of 24 contests and lost seven. But four of the seven incumbents who were defeated outspent their opponents on broadcasting.

In Arkansas, Gov. Winthrop Rockefeller (R) spent a total of $334,097 in primary and general campaigns but failed to hold the statehouse in the face of a challenge by Democrat Dale Bumpers, who spent $194,007.

Idaho's Gov. Don Samuelson (R) spent $38,825 in a losing battle with Democrat Cecil D. Andrus, who spent $35,505.

Despite expenditures of $30,548 by Nebraska Gov. Norbert T. Tiemann (R), the incumbent, he lost to Democrat J.J. Exon, whose outlays totaled $20,128.

In South Dakota, Gov. Frank L. Farrar (R) was beaten by Richard F. Kneip (D), who spent only $21,602 compared to $47,995 by Farrar.

Non-Incumbent Contests. In the 11 contests which had no incumbents, the effectiveness of high broadcast spending also was inconclusive. The top spenders lost in six races and won in five.

In Alabama, former Gov. George C. Wallace (D) spent a total of $437,283 in winning a third term and a chance to keep his presidential aspirations alive. However, Wallace was outspent in the Democratic primary by Gov. Albert Brewer, who spent $431,093 compared to $396,073 by Wallace.

In Connecticut, Rep. Thomas J. Meskill (R) defeated Rep. Emilio Q. Daddario (D) in a close race. Meskill's broadcast spending total of $94,717 was highest in the state, but Daddario actually outspent Meskill in the general election, $78,972 to $71,072.

In Georgia's Democratic primary, former Gov. Carl Sanders spent $290,207 in losing to peanut farmer Jimmy Carter, who spent only $170,238. Carter then spent another $102,280 and won the governorship against Republican Hal Suit, who spent $63,850.

In Minnesota, State Sen. Wendell R. Anderson (D) beat Attorney General Douglas M. Head (R) in the general election, although Anderson was outspent by Head, $158,797 to $176,379, respectively.

In Nevada, Mike O'Callaghan (D) won despite being outspent by Las Vegas businessman and Lt. Gov. Ed Fike. Fike spent $80,785 compared to $70,879 by O'Callaghan.

New Mexico's gubernatorial race was won by rancher Bruce King (D), who spent only $26,302 in defeating his Republican opponent Pete V. Domenici, an Albuquerque attorney whose broadcast spending totaled $47,826.

Former Rep. John J. Gilligan (D) spent $507,539 in winning Ohio's governorship in a contest with state auditor Roger Cloud (R), who spent $283,932, including more than $86,000 in the Republican primary.

In Pennsylvania, millionaire industrialist Milton J. Shapp (D) spent $175,947 in a close primary race, then spent another $428,435 in defeating Lt. Gov. Raymond J. Broderick (R). Broderick actually outspent Shapp in the general election by more than $55,000, however.

South Carolina's Lt. Gov. John C. West (D) was outspent by more than $10,000 by Rep. Albert W. Watson (R), but still won the election. West spent $106,298 compared to $116,358 by Watson.

In Tennessee, Memphis dentist Winfield Dunn (R) spent $197,106 in the general election campaign and defeated businessman John Jay Hooker (D), who spent $130,071. However, Hooker spent nearly that much in the Democratic primary race, so his total spending of $259,404 was greater than Dunn's $223,338.

Wisconsin's gubernatorial race was a close one between Lt. Gov. Jack B. Olson (R), who spent $161,236 in losing, and Democrat Patrick J. Lucey, who spent $160,205. Lucey spent $40,894 in the Democratic primary, however, making his total outlay of $201,099 greater than that of Olson, who spent only $189 in the Republican primary.

In Florida, the highest broadcast expenditures were in the primary elections. State Sen. Reubin Askew won an upset victory over Earl Faircloth in the Democratic primary, although Faircloth outspent Askew, $121,119 to $95,211.

In the Republican primary, millionaire Jack Eckerd spent $191,580 in an unsuccessful attempt to defeat incumbent Gov. Claude Kirk. Askew, who defeated Kirk in the general election, also outspent him, $75,460 to $66,980.

New York produced the nation's most expensive broadcast campaign. Republican Gov. Nelson A. Rockefeller spent $1,188,069, all but $5,892 in the general election. Democratic challenger Arthur J. Goldberg, former Supreme Court Justice and United Nations ambassador, spent $364,527 in the general campaign. Goldberg spent $50,474 in the Democratic primary in holding off a bid for the nomination by Howard Samuels, who spent $240,502.

House Spending

Elections for the House of Representatives also resulted in heavy broadcast spending in many states. Again, results were mixed and high expenditures did not guarantee success for candidates of either party.

The FCC survey reported broadcast spending in 354 of the 435 House races. Of these contests, 229 were won by candidates who outspent their opponents on broadcast advertising. However, many of them were incumbents.

Republicans outspent Democrats in general elections, $2.1-million to $1.8-million. But Democrats spent more than Republicans in primaries, $771,000 to $523,000.

In 31 House contests, expenditures in excess of $20,000 were reported by at least one of the opposing candidates. However, in only 12 of these races did the candidate who spent the most on radio and television win.

In Alaska, Democrat Nick Begich spent $21,297 in defeating his Republican opponent, Frank H. Murkowski, an Anchorage banker, who spent $13,731 in the contest for Alaska's at-large House seat.

In California's 6th District, William S. Mailliard (R) spent $18,220 but was outspent by his Democratic opponent, Russell R. Miller, who spent $25,055. Incumbent Maillard was re-elected. This was the only House race in California in which either candidate spent more than $20,000 on broadcast advertising.

In Colorado's 1st District, Democrat Craig Barnes, a Denver attorney, spent $25,848 in an unsuccessful attempt to defeat James D. (Mike) McKevitt (R), who spent $14,941.

Georgia's 5th District was the scene of a successful re-election campaign by Republican Rep. Fletcher Thompson, who spent $20,423 in defeating black challenger Andrew Young (D), a former aide to the late Rev. Martin Luther King. Young spent $14,863 in his losing effort.

One of the widest margins in House broadcast spending between winner and loser occurred in the 23rd District of Illinois, where conservative author Phyllis Schlafly (R) spent $44,196 in a vain attempt to unseat Democratic incumbent George E. Shipley, who invested only $3,508 in broadcast campaigning.

The state of Indiana was the setting for three of the most costly House races in the nation. In the 3rd District, Rep. John Brademas (D) held off an expensive media blitz by Don M. Newman (R), a pharmacist. Newman spent $29,541 compared to $27,684 by Brademas.

In Indiana's 8th District, incumbent Roger H. Zion (R) was outspent by Democratic attorney J. David Huber, who spent $21,238 compared to Zion's $15,099. Nonetheless, Zion won re-election to a third term.

And in the 11th Indiana District, Danny L. Burton (R), a state senator and insurance executive, spent $30,489 but failed to unseat incumbent Andrew Jacobs Jr. (D), who spent $22,595.

In Iowa, Democratic state representative Edward Mezvinsky spent $23,275 on electronic electioneering in an unsuccessful attempt to unseat veteran Republican Rep. Fred Schwengel, who spent $16,253.

Two races in Kansas saw candidates spend more than $20,000 on radio and television ads. In the 2nd District, Dr. William R. Roy (D) spent $22,897 in unseating three-term Republican incumbent Chester L. Mize, who spent only $9,031. But in the 3rd District, Lt. Gov. James H. DeCoursey Jr. (D) spent $33,738 but lost to Rep. Larry Winn Jr. (R), whose outlays totaled $17,382.

Maryland's 5th District election was a close contest between incumbent Lawrence J. Hogan (R), running for a second term, and State Sen. Royal Hart (D). Hogan spent $20,557 in defeating Hart, who spent $12,227.

(Continued on p. 25)

1970 Senate Races: Spending Reports by Candidates and FCC

(Asterisk indicates incumbent. Winner in **bold face** type.)

Candidate[1]	Reported To Senate[2]	Reported to FCC[3] Primary	General	Total
ALASKA				
Kay (D)	$ 5,000	$ 12,372	$ 34,435	$ 46,807
*Stevens (R)	21,735	4,279	18,020	22,299
ARIZONA				
Grossman (D)	180,778	25,836	85,388	111,224
Kruglick (D)		10,462		10,462
*Fannin (R)	6,698	1,208	86,190	87,398
CALIFORNIA				
Brown (D)		51,004		51,004
Tunney (D)	0	83,238	472,987	556,225
*Murphy (R)	1,631,402	71,007	400,731	471,738
Simon (R)		800,823		800,823
CONNECTICUT				
*Dodd (D)	0	1,924	49,602	51,526
Donahue (D)		102,281		102,281
Duffey (D)	0	40,856	88,782	129,638
Marcus (D)		46,285		46,285
Weicker (R)	0	49,813	80,954	130,767
DELAWARE				
Zimmerman (D)	1,875		12,341	12,341
Roth (R)	4,690		13,775	13,775
FLORIDA				
Bryant (D)		66,729		66,729
Chiles (D)	16,966	34,003	49,489	83,492
Schultz (D)		101,229		101,229
Carswell (R)		61,819		61,819
Cramer (R)	333,986	70,580	145,484	216,064
HAWAII				
Heftel (D)	5886	16,140	65,747	81,887
*Fong (R)	0	35,847	37,463	73,310
ILLINOIS				
Stevenson (D)	35,120	0	261,573	261,573
*Smith (R)	0	89,061	252,206	341,267
INDIANA[4]				
*Hartke (D)	0	212	214,130	214,342
Roudebush (R)	0	150	364,825	364,975
MAINE				
*Muskie (D)	205,871	0	31,605	31,605
Bishop (R)	47,820	0	8,593	8,593
MARYLAND				
Finch (D)		18,801		18,801
Mahoney (D)		23,775		23,775
*Tydings (D)	9,000	44,260	93,561	137,821
Beall (R)	457,188	80	115,995	116,075
MASSACHUSETTS				
*Kennedy (D)	583,394	18,448	152,065	170,513
Spaulding (R)	879	26,653	14,984	41,637
MICHIGAN				
*Hart (D)	829	0	143,893	143,893
Huber (R)		25,104		25,104
Romney (R)	0	63,481	44,978	108,459
MINNESOTA				
Humphrey (D)	150	32,022	164,636	196,658
MacGregor (R)	1,626	24,381	172,011	196,392
MISSISSIPPI				
*Stennis (D)	3,196	299	1,624	1,923
MISSOURI				
*Symington (D)	97,252	407	199,170	199,577
Danforth (R)	234,144	4,182	228,475	232,657
MONTANA				
*Mansfield (D)	3,275	0	11,439	11,439
Wallace (R)	0		10,728	10,728
NEBRASKA				
Morrison (D)	30,440	0	20,674	20,674
*Hruska (R)	180,756	54	25,093	25,147
NEVADA				
*Cannon (D)	3,941	16,385	74,309	90,694
Raggio (R)	3,897	6,110	82,991	89,101
NEW JERSEY				
Guarini (D)		53,096		53,096
*Williams (D)	106,503	17,603	173,057	190,660
Gross (R)	23,860	85	391,462	391,547
NEW MEXICO				
*Montoya (D)	0	5,683	23,628	29,311
Cargo (R)		10,195		10,195
Carter (R)	0	8,346	37,354	45,700
NEW YORK				
O'Dwyer (D)		25,974		25,974
Ottinger (D)	65,204	734,490	641,151	1,375,641
Sorenson (D)		85,204		85,204
*Goodell (R)	185,541	863	569,443	570,306
Buckley (C)	1,141,378	40	516,472	516,512
NORTH DAKOTA				
*Burdick (D)	300	68	44,877	44,945
Kleppe (R)	1,150	2,000	71,561	73,561
OHIO				
Glenn (D)		31,081		31,081
Metzenbaum (D)	300	265,381	242,246	507,627
Rhodes (R)		92,191		92,191
Taft (R)	1,500	151,346	223,035	374,381
PENNSYLVANIA				
Reece (D)		10,829		10,829
Sesler (D)	16,511	19,468	25,374	44,842
*Scott (R)	1,603	0	267,270	267,270
RHODE ISLAND				
*Pastore (D)	0	2,829	24,247	27,076
McLaughlin (R)	0	0	6,263	6,263
TENNESSEE				
Crockett (D)		31,929		31,929
*Gore (D)	28,717	70,445	144,191	214,636
Brock (R)	3,483	41,551	167,910	209,461
Ritter (R)		19,303		19,303
TEXAS				
Bentsen (D)	0	218,603	174,991	393,594
*Yarborough (D)		128,405		128,405
Bush (R)	8,193	65,622	293,142	358,764
UTAH				
*Moss (D)	9,547	9,202	115,786	124,988
Burton (R)	12,516	1,007	91,736	92,743
VERMONT				
Hoff (D)	203,626	5,390	73,631	79,021
*Prouty (R)	6,693	238	56,248	56,486
VIRGINIA				
DuVal (D)		36,563		36,563
Rawlings (D)	136,197	4,519	24,409	28,928
Garland (R)	101,496	526	31,114	31,640
*Byrd (Ind.)	384,580	1,202	90,231	91,433
WASHINGTON				
*Jackson (D)	138,829	47,354	42,736	90,090
Elicker (R)	24,960	0	0	0
WEST VIRGINIA				
*Byrd (D)	300	315	8,615	8,930
Dodson (R)	3,254	0	1,702	1,702
WISCONSIN				
*Proxmire (D)	372,934	0	191,783	191,783
Erickson (R)	0	17	79,596	79,613
WYOMING				
*McGee (D)	169,087	9,273	47,968	57,241
Wold (R)	12,419	383	39,010	39,393

1. Candidates who spent less than $10,000 are not included unless they were major party nominees.

2. Federal law requires all candidates for the U.S. Senate to report general election spending to the Secretary of the Senate. In practice, most candidates omit the substantial amounts spent on their behalf by political committees.

3. The FCC reduced all figures in these columns by 15 percent in order to subtract agency commissions. To obtain actual spending, divide the net figures by 85 percent.

4. The election was challenged and is pending in federal court.

(Continued from p. 23)

Minnesota had expenditures of more than $20,000 by candidates in two districts, the 3rd and the 7th. Republican Bill Frenzel spent $25,849, far more than his Democratic opponent George Rice, a former television commentator who spent only $3,708. Frenzel won the 3rd District seat. In the 7th District, two Scandinavian farmers each spent more than $20,000 in a close contest. Bob Bergland (D) spent $23,624 in defeating six-term incumbent Odin Langen (R), who spent $21,665.

Campaigns for Montana's two seats in the House also resulted in high expenditures on broadcasting. In the 1st District, Missoula Mayor Richard G. Shoup (R) spent $12,574 and defeated incumbent Arnold Olsen (D), who spent $20,595. In the 2nd District, Rep. John Melcher (D) spent $20,795 in fighting off a challenge by Jack Rehberg (R), who spent $16,080.

New York congressional contests resulted in some of the highest expenditures in the nation. The highest outlay by a single House candidate for broadcast spending was in New York's 1st District, where radio station owner Malcolm E. Smith Jr. (R) spent $58,117, all of it on radio announcements, in a vain attempt to unseat five-term incumbent Otis G. Pike (D), who spent only $6,382, also on radio ads.

In New York's 17th District, Democratic incumbent Edward I. Koch spent $14,531 in maintaining his House seat against a strong challenge by Peter J. Sprague (R), a Manhattan business executive who spent $29,160.

In the 29th District, veteran incumbent Samuel S. Stratton (D) spent only $9,565 in a victory over Republican Rep. Daniel E. Button, who spent $20,271 in a costly losing effort.

In the 35th District, Rep. James M. Hanley was outspent by former Police Chief John F. O'Connor (R), who spent $21,178 to Hanley's $7,562. Hanley successfully held his House seat.

An expensive campaign in New York's 39th District saw Buffalo attorney Thomas P. Flaherty (D) outspend former professional football player Jack Kemp (R), $35,732 to $32,698. Nonetheless, Kemp won the seat.

In North Carolina's 10th District, incumbent James T. Broyhill (R) spent $22,954 in defeating former Rep. Basil L. Whitener (D 1957-69), who spent $9,251.

Two races in Ohio led to candidates' expenditures of more than $20,000. In the 12th District, James W. Goodrich (D) spent $22,811 in an unsuccessful attempt to unseat Republican incumbent Samuel L. Devine, who spent only $8,920. In the 23rd District, Republican William E. Minshall, the incumbent, spent an overwhelming $31,248 in defeating Democratic challenger Ronald M. Mottl, who spent only $2,293.

Oklahoma also had two costly races, in both of which incumbents were re-elected despite higher spending by challengers. In the 1st District, veteran incumbent Page Belcher (R) spent $20,290 in holding off an attempt to unseat him by James R. Jones (D), a Tulsa attorney who spent $20,684. In the 4th District, Democratic incumbent Tom Steed was outspent but still defeated Jay G. Wilkinson (R), a former aide to President Nixon. Wilkinson spent $32,997 compared to $22,228 by Steed.

In Texas, there were four races in which candidates spent more than $20,000. The higher spenders won in two of these races.

In the 3rd District, incumbent James M. Collins (R) spent $22,945 in a successful re-election campaign despite the fact that his Democratic challenger, Dallas Judge John Mead, spent nothing on broadcasting advertising. In the 7th District, Republican Bill Archer spent $48,311 in defeating Jim Greenwood (D), who spent only $15,383.

In the 21st District of Texas, San Antonio businessman Richardson B. Gill (R) spent $25,116 in an unsuccessful effort to unseat Democratic incumbent O. C. Fisher, who spent $12,681. And in the 22nd District, Arthur Busch (R), a Houston college professor, spent $37,607 but failed to defeat incumbent Bob Casey (D), who spent $13,952.

Finally, in Wisconsin's 7th District, Democratic Rep. David R. Obey, who surprised observers in 1969 by winning the seat held for 20 years by Republican Melvin R. Laird, now Defense Secretary, spent $30,237 in defeating Andre E. Le Tendre (R), who spent $14,196.

Primary Spending. In 17 primary elections for congressional nominations, spending in excess of $10,000 was reported by one or more candidates. In 12 of these races, the higher spender won.

In Alaska's Republican primary, State Sen. C.R. Lewis of Anchorage, a member of the John Birch Society, spent $17,423 in an unsuccessful effort to win the nomination over Frank H. Murkowski, who spent $8,522.

In California's 11th District, Rep. Paul N. McCloskey Jr. spent $17,814 and won the Republican primary against Forden "Skip" Athearn, a Hillsborough attorney who spent nothing on broadcast advertising.

In Colorado's 1st District, Craig Barnes spent $16,267 in winning the Democratic primary over incumbent Byron G. Rogers, who spent only $4,524.

The Democratic primary in Georgia's 2nd District saw a crowded contest between ultimate winner Dawson Mathis, who spent $10,704, Harry L. Wingate ($10,550), Fred B. Hand Jr. ($9,173) and Thomas C. Chatmon ($907).

In Georgia's 5th District, Andrew Young spent $14,138 to win the Democratic nomination over Wyman C. Lowe ($929), Lonnie King ($166) and Ray Gurley, who spent nothing on broadcast advertising.

Another costly race was that for the House seat in Iowa's 1st District, where expenditures of more than $15,000 were reported in both Democratic and Republican primaries. In the Democratic contest, Edward Mezvinsky spent $15,961 in winning the nomination over William Albrecht, who spent $6,026, and William A. Strout, who spent $1,759. In the Republican primary, State Sen. David M. Stanley spent $29,366 in an unsuccessful attempt to unseat Rep. Fred Schwengel, who spent $7,474.

In Louisiana's 3rd District, Rep. Patrick J. Caffery spent $16,100 in winning the Democratic primary over Jules G. Mollere, who spent $15,432, and Warren J. Moity, who spent $1,000.

In the race for the Republican nomination in Massachusetts' 12th District, William D. Weeks spent $21,992 but failed to defeat incumbent Rep. Hastings Keith, who spent only $2,816.

In Maryland's 8th District Democratic primary, three candidates spent more than $15,000. They were Thomas B. Allen, $35,503; Leonard S. Blondes, $17,357; and Thomas Hale Boggs Jr., $15,897. The nomination went to Boggs.

In the 7th District of North Carolina, incumbent Rep. Alton Lennon (D) spent $15,205 in his successful attempt to win the nomination over challenger Charles G. Rose, who spent $8,138.

(Continued on p. 27)

1970 Governors' Races: TV and Radio Spending

(Asterisk indicates incumbent. Winner in **bold face** type.)

Candidate 1	Television and Radio Spending Reported to FCC 2			Candidate 1	Television and Radio Spending Reported to FCC 2		
	Primary	General	Total		Primary	General	Total
ALABAMA				**MICHIGAN**			
Wallace (D)	$ 396,073	$ 41,210	$ 437,283	Levin (D)	68,587	189,323	257,910
*Brewer (D)	431,093		431,093	Ferency (D)	10,100		10,100
Carter (D)	37,116		37,116	Parris (D)	26,588		26,588
Woods (D)	69,672		69,672	*Milliken (R)	787	256,299	257,086
ALASKA				**MINNESOTA**			
Egan (D)	40,283	33,798	74,081	**Anderson (D)**	25	158,797	158,822
Carr (D)	66,500		66,500	Head (R)	22	176,379	176,401
*Miller (R)	21,495	25,806	47,301	**NEBRASKA**			
Pollock (R)	26,568		26,568	**Exon (D)**	6,722	13,406	20,128
ARIZONA				*Tiemann (R)	12,115	18,433	30,548
Castro (D)	4,550	25,235	29,785	**NEVADA**			
Nader (D)	23,674		23,674	**O'Callaghan (D)**	15,346	55,533	70,879
*Williams (R)	471	39,684	40,155	Thornley (D)	10,795		10,795
ARKANSAS				Fike (R)	13,310	67,475	80,785
Bumpers (D)	76,282	117,725	194,007	Springer (Ind.)	425	14,997	15,422
Compton (D)	10,937		10,937	**NEW HAMPSHIRE**			
Faubus (D)	49,743		49,743	Crowley (D)	4,085	8,274	12,359
McClerkin (D)	29,969		29,969	*Peterson (R)	9,142	7,851	16,993
Wells (D)	11,387		11,387	Thomson (ANH)	9,880	8,685	18,565
*Rockefeller (R)	25,737	308,360	334,097	**NEW MEXICO**			
Carruth (AI)	93	12,266	12,359	**King (D)**	8,378	17,924	26,302
CALIFORNIA				Daniels (D)	20,711		20,711
Unruh (D)	9,233	221,703	230,936	Domenici (R)	9,281	38,545	47,826
Yorty (D)	39,687		39,687	**NEW YORK**			
*Reagan (R)	54,450	380,919	435,369	Goldberg (D)	50,474	364,527	415,001
COLORADO				Morgenthau (D)	40,182		40,182
Hogan (D)	70	44,641	44,711	Samuels (D)	240,502		240,502
*Love (R)	53	28,536	28,589	*Rockefeller (R)	5,892	1,182,177	1,188,069
CONNECTICUT				**OHIO**			
Daddario (D)	11,689	78,972	90,661	**Gilligan (D)**	150	507,389	507,539
Meskill (R)	23,645	71,072	94,717	Cloud (D)	86,730	197,202	283,932
Barnes (R)	76,515		76,515	Brown (R)	50,363		50,363
FLORIDA				Lukens (R)	59,207		59,207
Askew (D)	95,211	75,460	170,671	**OKLAHOMA**			
Faircloth (D)	121,119		121,119	**Hall (D)**	41,320	45,263	86,583
Hall (D)	27,670		27,670	Baggett (D)	42,051		42,051
Mathews (D)	49,712		49,712	Cannon (D)	16,823		16,823
*Kirk (R)	19,520	66,980	86,500	*Bartlett (R)	216	62,268	62,584
Bafalis (R)	23,665		23,665	Little (A)	1,632	30,780	32,412
Eckerd (R)	191,580		191,580	**OREGON**			
GEORGIA				Straub (D)	0	33,000	33,000
Carter (D)	170,238	102,280	272,518	*McCall (R)	11,950	61,782	73,732
Sanders (D)	290,207		290,207	**PENNSYLVANIA**			
Suit (R)	15,683	63,850	79,533	**Shapp (D)**	175,947	428,435	604,382
Bentley (R)	44,449		44,449	Casey (D)	164,901		164,901
HAWAII				Broderick (R)	61,205	483,609	544,814
*Burns (D)	86,012	19,582	105,594	**RHODE ISLAND**			
Gill (D)	49,494		49,494	*Licht (D)	4,819	133,784	138,603
King (R)	35,941	34,017	69,958	DeSimone (R)	0	90,736	90,736
Porteus (R)	17,306		17,306	**SOUTH CAROLINA**			
IDAHO				**West (D)**	118	106,180	106,298
Andrus (D)	11,762	23,743	35,505	Watson (R)	184	116,174	116,358
Ravenscroft (D)	13,866		13,866	**SOUTH DAKOTA**			
*Samuelson (R)	9,808	29,017	38,825	**Kneip (D)**	722	20,880	21,602
Smith (R)	12,930		12,930	*Farrar (R)	8,060	39,935	47,995
IOWA				**TENNESSEE**			
Fulton (D)	2,083	32,904	34,987	Hooker (D)	129,333	130,071	259,404
*Ray (R)	127	53,673	53,800	Snodgrass (D)	92,075		92,075
KANSAS				Taylor (D)	20,324		20,324
*Docking (D)	0	101,782	101,782	**Dunn (R)**	26,232	197,106	223,338
Frizzell (R)	32,959	90,086	123,045	Jarman (R)	29,046		29,046
Harman (R)	24,436		24,436	Jenkins (R)	52,928		52,928
MAINE				Robertson (R)	18,506		18,506
*Curtis (D)	22	34,183	34,205	**TEXAS**			
Erwin (R)	5,287	32,300	37,587	*Smith (D)	2,392	147,217	149,609
MARYLAND				Eggers (R)	14,533	181,164	195,697
*Mandel (D)	79,748	108,813	188,561	**VERMONT**			
Blair (R)	3,971	28,376	32,347	O'Brien (D)	5,713	26,793	32,506
MASSACHUSETTS				*Davis (R)	234	69,012	69,246
White (D)	97,317	196,133	293,450	**WISCONSIN**			
Bellotti (D)	54,960		54,960	**Lucey (D)**	40,894	160,205	201,099
Donahue (D)	60,887		60,887	Olson (R)	189	161,236	161,425
O'Donnell (D)	16,913		16,913	**WYOMING**			
*Sargent (R)	20,233	293,224	313,457	Rooney (D)	28	1,834	1,862
				*Hathaway (R)	0	10,968	10,968

1. *Candidates who spent less than $10,000 are not included unless they were major party nominees.*

2. *The FCC reduced all figures in these columns by 15 percent in order to subtract agency commissions. To obtain actual spending, divide the net figures by 85 percent.*

Non-Presidential Radio and TV Spending*

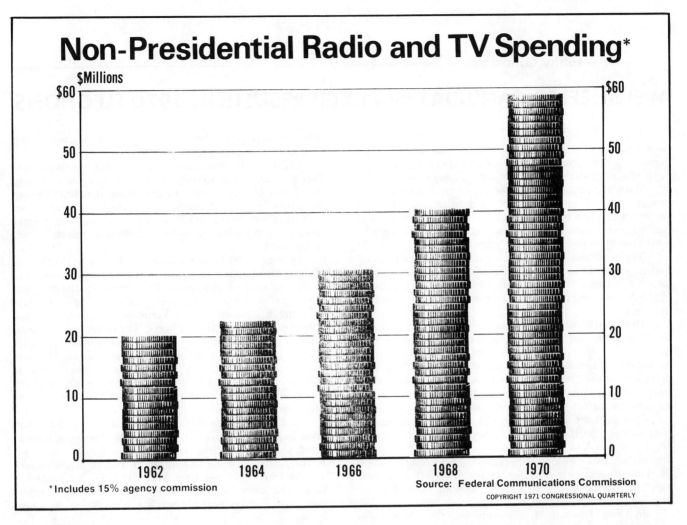

$Millions

*Includes 15% agency commission

Source: Federal Communications Commission

(Continued from p. 25)

Ohio's 19th District Democratic primary election, which had 15 candidates, was won by Charles J. Carney, who spent $4,992 on broadcast advertising. Other high spenders were Richard P. McLaughlin, $11,051; Gary J. Thompson, $6,671; and John M. Hudzik, $3,744.

In Pennsylvania's 17th District, Republican incumbent Herman T. Schneebeli spent $16,938 in overcoming a determined challenge by Robert F. Smith, who spent $23,085.

South Dakota's two Republican primaries both had high expenditures. The 1st District had five candidates, and was won by Dexter H. Gunderson, who spent $13,356. Jerry Simmons spent $8,809 and Frank Gibbs $4,361 in losing efforts. In the 2nd District, Fred D. Brady spent $11,837 in a successful campaign over James Abdnor, who spent $7,166. Neither Republican candidate won his general election contest.

Finally, two primary races in Texas had spending of more than $10,000 by candidates. In the 5th District, Rep. Earle Cabell (D) spent $10,078 in defeating challenger Mike McCool, who spent $5,253. And in the 7th District Republican primary, Bill Archer spent $29,955 in winning the nomination over Ross Baker, who spent $17,831, and Dudley Sharp Jr., who spent $21,055.

Broadcast Costs Per Vote. When measured on a cost-per-vote basis, the most expensive general election campaign for statewide office was conducted by Gov. Winthrop Rockefeller (R Ark.). His losing campaign for re-election cost $1.56 for each vote he received. The winner, Dale Bumpers (D), spent 31 cents per vote.

The smallest expenditure by a winning gubernatorial candidate was the 5 cents per vote of J.J. Exon (D Neb.) who defeated incumbent Norbert T. Tiemann (R). Tiemann spent 9 cents per vote.

Sen. Howard W. Cannon (D Nev.) spent 80 cents per vote in his successful re-election bid—the highest amount expended by a winner in a statewide race. His opponent, William Raggio (R), spent $1.36 per vote.

The smallest amount spent by a winner in a statewide campaign was the .56 cents per vote outlay of Sen. John C. Stennis (D Miss.) who had no Republican opponent. Among winning statewide candidates who were opposed, Sen. Robert C. Byrd (D W. Va.) spent the least, 2 cents per vote. His opponent also spent 2 cents per vote.

The lowest cost per vote for a losing candidate was the 1½-cents expenditure of William Sesler (D Pa.) who opposed Sen. Hugh Scott (R).

Wyoming had the least expensive campaign by a losing gubernatorial candidate. John J. Rooney (D) spent 4 cents per vote, compared to 15 cents for his opponent, Gov. Stanley K. Hathaway (R).

WELL-HEELED CANDIDATES: MIXED RESULTS IN 1970 ELECTIONS

The outstanding political primary upsets of 1970 were made by men of great wealth, presenting their politics to the voters on television and spending their way from obscurity to success in a matter of weeks.

With big-city machines no longer in complete command of working-class votes, and with expenses for major campaigns running into the millions, many organizations were unable or unwilling to defeat rich men who could pay their own bills in November.

The profusion of affluent office-seekers made campaign spending a major political issue in itself and brought bitter resentment from candidates who found it difficult to campaign against men with vast personal fortunes.

Democratic Senate candidates Richard L. Ottinger in New York and Lloyd M. Bentsen Jr. in Texas won primary victories over better-known and heavily favored opponents. Their successes indicated that they had perfected their own form of the new politics, in which cash and manipulation of the media do the work that used to be done by regular party organizations.

One instance in which an old-style political organization found itself up against a candidate of considerable wealth was in New York's 22nd House District. Redistricting placed two incumbents, organization Democrat Jacob H. Gilbert and rich reformer James H. Scheuer, in the same Bronx district, and the two opposed each other in the June primary. Scheuer won.

In Ohio, Howard M. Metzenbaum, through a radio and television advertising blitz, defeated famous former astronaut John Glenn for the Democratic Senate nomination. In Pennsylvania, Democrat Milton J. Shapp—whose style and viewpoint are strikingly similar to those of Metzenbaum—was nominated for Governor. Both men are reform Democrats, fiercely independent of party regulars and willing to dip generously into their personal resources to build campaign funds.

And in New York, Democrat Howard Samuels ran a well-financed campaign similar to those of Metzenbaum and Shapp. But he failed to defeat Arthur J. Goldberg, who had regular party backing, for the gubernatorial nomination.

Ottinger: Plywood

The 1970 season produced one campaign in which wealth and candidate spending turned out to be the single decisive issue. This was New York's Democratic primary, which saw Ottinger build a Senate nomination out of the plywood his family began manufacturing in 1919.

Ottinger's late father, Lawrence, founded the U.S. Plywood Corporation in 1919. The firm later merged with the Champion Paper Company and by 1968 had become the nation's 70th largest corporation, with sales that year of over $1-billion and a net income of $54,678,000. The

Ottinger family no longer manages the company, and Ottinger himself owns no stock.

Ottinger, 41, was elected Representative from New York's Westchester County in 1964. Unknown to nearly two-thirds of the state's voters when the 1970 Senate campaign began, and facing three opponents with whom he agreed on nearly every major issue, he won a convincing victory with the help of a flood of television advertisements.

Ottinger hired media consultant David Garth and allowed him to spend a reported $1-million producing and airing six spot commercials. The theme of the ads was "Ottinger delivers," and they featured the candidate detailing his record on the Vietnam war, environmental pollution and legislative subjects. The commercials closed with an announcer saying, "It's easy to promise—it's a lot tougher to deliver. Ottinger delivers. Make Ottinger Senator Ottinger." Garth timed the commercials so that at least one appeared in prime time every night on every New York City station during the last three weeks of the campaign.

In all, Ottinger's Senate campaign cost $1.8-million, according to reports filed in New York the following month. More than $1.7-million was money borrowed from his mother, Mrs. Lawrence Ottinger of Manhattan. Ottinger said he intends to pay back his mother for her contributions, and soon he had returned some $31,000. In addition, Ottinger reported spending $86,000 of his own money.

The Ottinger total represented more than six times as much money as was spent by his three primary opponents, former Kennedy aide Theodore Sorensen, former New York City Councilman Paul O'Dwyer and U.S. Rep. Richard D. McCarthy. Sorensen and O'Dwyer each reported spending $103,000; McCarthy, $30,000. When the votes were counted, O'Dwyer was Ottinger's closest rival, with 33.1 percent of the vote to Ottinger's 39.1 percent. Sorensen, who had the endorsement of party regulars, finished a poor third, and McCarthy was a distant last.

For McCarthy, the lack of available funds led to a series of eccentric campaign stunts designed to produce free media publicity. McCarthy, a former public relations man, jumped into the Hudson River in diving equipment to dramatize his opposition to water pollution and flew over Central Park in a balloon to show his concern for clean air. New York City officials prevented him from entering a manhole to check on underground sanitation conditions. "If I had Ottinger's money," said McCarthy, "I wouldn't have to do these things."

Ottinger's commercials generated considerable resentment among all three of his opponents. Both McCarthy and O'Dwyer accused Ottinger of violating a New York primary law that provides that no candidate may spend more than the equivalent of 10 cents for every registered voter in his party. This would have been about $350,000 for the Democrats. The law is easily evaded, however, by borrowing or by establishing numerous campaign committees and allowing each of them to contribute no more than $350,000.

"I wonder how those 18-year-olds, if they are going to vote, will regard his flouting of the law," said O'Dwyer of Ottinger.

McCarthy charged that "what it boils down to is this: Can you buy a seat in the U.S. Senate?"

Ottinger defended his spending by saying that he was not attempting to buy a seat but was simply bringing his already established views before the voters. "You can't buy an election," he said. "You can't win if you don't stand for something." He said his free-spending campaign differed little from those conducted by Mayor John V. Lindsay of New York City in 1965 and 1969 and by John F. Kennedy for President of the United States in 1960. "I don't understand why they can't raise money," Ottinger said of his opponents. "Anybody who can't raise money against me just isn't on his toes."

Postscript. Ottinger was less successful in the general election in November, losing narrowly to Conservative Party candidate James L. Buckley in a three-way race that also included incumbent Republican Sen. Charles E. Goodell. With the Nixon Administration disowning Goodell for his increasingly liberal views, and Ottinger making no effort to hide his own liberalism, Buckley was able to appeal to conservative voters in both parties and surprise his divided opposition.

Bentsen: Insurance

Insurance executive Lloyd M. Bentsen Jr. of Houston emerged from 15 years of political obscurity to defeat Texas Sen. Ralph W. Yarborough in a primary and gain a major victory for the conservative wing of the state's Democratic party.

Elected as a U.S. Representative at age 27 in 1948, Bentsen retired from the House in 1955 to devote full time to his business interests. Bentsen was president of Lincoln Consolidated, a holding company that controls the Lincoln Liberty Life Insurance Company as well as several mutual funds and the Ben Franklin Savings Association. According to the *Texas Observer*, Lincoln Liberty Life reported assets in 1969 of more than $75-million and net profits of $444,293.49.

After the primary, Bentsen said he spent about $800,-000 in his campaign against Yarborough. Yarborough reported spending $275,096. Before the election, Yarborough predicted that Bentsen's effort might cost several million dollars. U.S. Rep. George Bush, facing little opposition for the Republican Senate nomination, reported spending $165,989.

Bentsen declined to make a financial disclosure during the campaign. "I assume the reason we want to give financial statements is to show what a man's worth is when he is elected and what his financial losses and gains are when he gets out," he was quoted as saying.

The financial disclosure issue came up again in the fall campaign. Bush made a financial disclosure in 1967 and introduced legislation to make such disclosures mandatory for Members of Congress and for Congressional candidates. According to his last disclosure, in 1969, Bush had net assets of $1,310,933.18. He called on Bentsen to make a similar disclosure.

Bentsen's primary campaign, although it included extensive personal appearances throughout the state, made

heavy use of television and newspaper advertising. A special Sunday supplement entitled "What Makes Bentsen Run?" appeared in many of the state's largest newspapers on April 5, four weeks before the election.

Bentsen criticized Yarborough's liberal views on race, his opposition to the war in Vietnam and his alleged failure to vote on a proposal to allow prayer in public schools. One television commercial featured scenes of rioting at the 1968 Democratic convention and announcements that Yarborough supported Sen. Eugene J. McCarthy (D Minn.) for President and backed an anti-war moratorium in November 1969. Bentsen then appeared on camera, looked toward the demonstrators and said of Yarborough, "Does he support your view?"

Yarborough backers said after the primary that repeated showings of the commercial gave Bentsen statewide recognition within days and helped contribute to Yarborough's defeat. Yarborough, whose supporters concede he is more effective in person than on television, made little use of the media during the campaign.

Postscript. Bentsen went into the fall campaign an underdog against Bush, but won the election following a low-key campaign that involved heavy spending but few substantive differences on the issues. A heavy turnout helped Bentsen by allowing him to take advantage of the state's sizeable Democratic registration edge.

Scheuer: Real Estate

Rep. Jacob H. Gilbert of New York was known as the last member of Congress who owed his election to the Democratic machine forged by the late U.S. Rep. Charles A. Buckley (D N.Y. 1935-65) decades ago. Rep. James H. Scheuer, a reform Democrat, was a wealthy attorney with extensive real estate holdings. Not a native of the Bronx, he moved to the district shortly before his initial election in 1964.

Scheuer won the 1970 primary, 11,567 votes to 8,264. He denied that his wealth was responsible for his victory, saying that he spent about $130,000 on the primary but that Gilbert had access to equal amounts through labor and other organizational sources.

Gilbert told a far different story, saying that his own campaign cost only $30,000 and that he believed Scheuer spent several hundred thousand dollars. Gilbert said labor unions provided him with only $5,000 to $10,000 and that he went into debt to pay for the rest of the effort. "People didn't make the contributions I thought they would make," said Gilbert. "I had to go to the bank to borrow money." Gilbert said his shortage of cash prevented him from producing the campaign literature he needed. But Scheuer charged that the Gilbert campaign made use of 30 sound-trucks paid for by union campaign funds.

Since there were few issue differences between the two men, the primary turned on their personal familiarity and popularity. Unlike other wealthy candidates at statewide levels, Scheuer did not make extensive use of the mass media. He reported spending about $1,500 for commercials on Spanish-language radio stations and $3,000 for newspaper advertisement. Scheuer said he depended primarily on personal campaigning.

According to Gilbert, wealth is an electoral advantage not only during a campaign but throughout the year. He said that Scheuer, although he was an outsider in the Bronx, was able to develop a constituency by contributing

Rich Candidates Spent $1 to $11 A Vote in Primaries

Candidate	Party	State	Primary Contest	Number of Votes Received	Estimated Expenses*	Cost Per Vote	Outcome
James H. Scheuer	D	New York	U.S. House	11,733	$ 130,000	$11.07	Won
Richard L. Ottinger	D	New York	Senate	370,273	$1,800,000	$ 4.86	Won
Norton Simon	R	California	Senate	670,106	$1,900,000	$ 2.83	Lost
Milton J. Shapp	D	Pennsylvania	Governor	519,161	$1,200,000	$ 2.31	Won
Charles Woods	D	Alabama	Governor	148,887	$ 300,000	$ 2.01	Lost
Howard M. Metzenbaum	D	Ohio	Senate	430,469	$ 812,900	$ 1.89	Won
Howard J. Samuels	D	New York	Governor	455,482	$ 675,000	$ 1.48	Lost
Lloyd M. Bentsen Jr.	D	Texas	Senate	814,316	$ 800,000	$ .98	Won

*Based on official expense reports or on estimates by the candidates themselves. Technicalities in state election laws may result in discrepancies between the two sources.

to religious and civic organizations in his district. "If I walk into a synagogue and say, 'I'm Jack Gilbert—here's $25,' that doesn't mean anything. Or if I could give maybe $100, he could give $500....All of a sudden, the guy with wealth seems to be the most righteous guy in the world. Just because a man is rich doesn't mean he's more righteous than anyone else."

Gilbert had received significant contributions from organized labor in the past. A Jack Anderson column of June 8, 1970, reported that the Justice Department was investigating a 1968 contribution of $5,000 by the Seafarers Union. According to the column, Gilbert reported only $500 of the contribution.

Evidence shows that Scheuer spent money profusely in previous campaigns. When he ran for mayor of New York City in 1969, Scheuer reportedly spent about $550,000 on the Democratic primary, although he finished fifth in a five-man primary field. Scheuer's expenditure represented $14.23 for every vote he received. This was about seven times as much money per vote as the second-highest-spending Democrat and equaled more than twice as much per vote as all the other Democratic candidates combined.

Postscript. The general election posed few problems for Scheuer in his heavily Democratic Bronx district. Scheuer received 71.6 percent of the vote to 28.4 percent for his Republican opponent, Robert M. Schneck.

Metzenbaum: Parking Lots

At the outset of the Ohio campaign for the Democratic Senate nomination, the name of John Glenn, a national hero, was a household word. The name of Howard M. Metzenbaum was virtually unknown. A poll taken in November 1969 showed that only 10 percent of Ohio's voters knew who Metzenbaum was. All but 5 percent knew who Glenn was.

But the 50-year-old Metzenbaum closed the gap with a radio and television advertising blitz, 65 percent of which he paid for himself. The television time alone was estimated to cost more than $500,000.

To handle his television campaign, Metzenbaum hired Charles Guggenheim of Washington, D.C., one of the nation's leading producers of TV documentaries. Guggenheim produced a variety of ads ranging from 20-

second spots to 5-minute speeches. The commercials ran during prime time in Ohio's largest cities.

By concentrating his commercials in Ohio's largest metropolitan areas, Metzenbaum got the most for his money. He lost 72 of the state's 85 counties, but he did so well in the most populous ones that he defeated Glenn by about 14,000 votes.

Glenn, despite his recognition, had trouble raising money for an extensive campaign. He concentrated on the traditional formula of rallies and public appearances, traveling throughout the state but failing to reach the mass audiences that Metzenbaum reached with his commercials.

Metzenbaum told Congressional Quarterly he resented charges that he bought the election. "I don't agree with the concept that only rich men get elected," he said. "I ran Steve Young's Senate campaign for $45,000 in 1964 and beat the strongest vote-getter in the state." Metzenbaum managed the 1964 re-election campaign of Sen. Stephen M. Young, who won a narrow victory over Rep. Robert Taft Jr. Young retired in 1970 at age 80, and it was his seat that Metzenbaum sought. Taft was again the Republican nominee.

Metzenbaum admitted that a poor man starting from his low level of recognition could not have defeated Glenn. But he attributed this primarily to Glenn's refusal to debate him on television. "If you can get the other fellow to debate you, you can always run a low-cost campaign," he said.

Despite his past obscurity, Metzenbaum was not a political novice. A lawyer, he served seven years in the Ohio Legislature in the 1940s, then retired to make a fortune as the developer of a string of airport parking lots. Later he returned to private law practice and bought a group of community newspapers in the Cleveland area. Meanwhile, he remained active in traditional liberal causes—the National Hunger and Malnutrition Council, the Legal Aid Society and the Citizens' Crusade Against Poverty. When Sen. Young announced his retirement in December 1969, Metzenbaum jumped into the race.

Postscript. Metzenbaum ran a close race against Taft in November, but lost by a total of 70,420 votes statewide. Metzenbaum had the benefit of a Republican scandal that brought down virtually the entire GOP statewide ticket, but he was unable to overcome the magic of the Taft family reputation in Ohio and the low Cleveland turnout that resulted from bickering among the city Democratic politicians.

Shapp: Television

Pennsylvania's Milton J. Shapp fit the Metzenbaum mold in several ways. A liberal, Jewish, self-made millionaire, he bucked Democratic regulars starting with his first campaign for Governor in 1966. Shapp won the Democratic nomination that year but lost in November to Republican Raymond P. Shafer. In 1970 he won the nomination again and faced Republican Lt. Gov. Raymond J. Broderick.

In both primaries, Shapp's opponent was State Auditor Robert P. Casey. Both times, Shapp cast himself as the independent liberal crusading against the party bosses.

Shapp admitted after the 1970 primary that it took about $1-million to defeat Casey. Nearly one-third of this money, Shapp said, was spent for television time in the last two weeks of the campaign.

In 1966, Shapp reported spending $1.4-million in the primary and $2.4-million in the general election.

Shapp said nearly half the money spent in the primary came from his personal fortune. But he hoped for $2-million from outside sources in the general election, and added that he expected private individuals to help even though they were aware of his wealth. Shapp said he believed this is important. "If you go out and get contributions, you get more people involved in the campaign," he said. "So fund-raising has to be an important part of any campaign, no matter who the candidate is."

Shapp defended his spending by claiming that his opponents spent even more to defeat him. "The way things are now," he said, "nothing's improper. It's a hard fact of life."

In the primary, Shapp and Casey spent considerable time arguing over who was the more extravagant spender. Shapp began attempts to counter the negative aspects of this issue by claiming Broderick would outspend him in the fall. He claimed the Republicans spent at least $8.5-million to defeat him in 1966 and that they were willing to spend up to $15-million in 1970. Republicans denied it.

Unlike Metzenbaum, Shapp said he saw real problems with existing methods of campaign financing.

Shapp said he would prefer legislation guaranteeing free media time for candidates who cannot afford to buy it at market prices. "Each TV or radio station should be required to allow so much time for each candidate—a fixed amount each month," he said.

Shapp himself was a television executive. He worked his way through college during the depression, then became sales manager for an electronics firm. In 1948, he set up the first successful cable television company in the United States, which he called the Jerrold Corporation after his middle name. When it was founded, Jerrold was worth $500 and had two employees. In 1966, when Shapp sold out his holdings for $10-million, the company employed 2,100 persons.

Postscript. In 1970, better known than he had been in 1966, Shapp won the general election and went on to become the first Democratic Governor in 12 years. In addition to his greater familiarity, Shapp was helped by voter resentment over tax increases in the previous Republican administration. Broderick, as lieutenant governor in that administration, was unable to avoid the association.

Samuels: Plastics

Howard Samuels, 51, was narrowly defeated by former Supreme Court Justice Arthur J. Goldberg in the Democratic primary for Governor of New York June 23, 1970.

Samuels is an engineer who founded the Kordite plastic packaging corporation and turned it into a $100-million-a-year business. He served as U.S. Under Secretary of Commerce and head of the Small Business Administration during the Johnson years. In 1966, he was the Democratic nominee for lieutenant governor of New York.

During the 1970 primary campaign, Samuels charged that Goldberg "is manipulated by the same handful of old-line Democratic leaders who have maneuvered the party into repeated defeat." Most of Samuels' accusations were made in advertisements in newspapers and on television and in televised Samuels-Goldberg debates.

"He's running on his name," protested Samuels. "I'm depending on the need for exposure." Samuels said early in the campaign that he expected to spend up to $1-million before primary day, but reports filed after the primary placed his expenditures at $650,000.

Samuels argued that it would take at least $2-million, and possibly $5-million, to defeat Republican Gov. Nelson A. Rockefeller in the fall. He said Goldberg would run out of cash but that he himself would be able to raise whatever was required if he were the nominee.

Even though Samuels was willing to sink large amounts of his own money into the campaign, he was a bitter critic of the system he believed makes this necessary. According to Samuels, existing campaign financing methods ensure that only rich men can remain independent of party bosses. "They can't own us," he said of the Democratic regulars he linked unfavorably to the Goldberg campaign. Samuels called the existing system "disastrous," referring to the "nefarious influence of money." He said he would limit the amount any candidate could spend, limit the amount of contributions any candidate could receive, authorize low-cost candidate appearances on public television and set up strict accounting procedures after elections are over.

Samuels insisted that he participated in multi-candidate spending sprees only because there is no other way for reformers to be elected. "Unless we deal with campaign financing, we'll never get the best people into politics," he said.

Postscript. Twice unsuccessful in campaigns at the statewide level in New York, Samuels found an appointed political home in the Republican-turned-Democratic administration of Mayor John V. Lindsay in New York City. He was placed in charge of the newly legalized off-track betting system run by the city.

The publicity and the controversy associated with his new job made Samuels a frequently mentioned prospect for future statewide political campaigns

1968 PRESIDENTIAL CAMPAIGN: WEALTHIEST FAVOR GOP 13-1

Forty-six of the richest people in America contributed a total of at least $1,494,502 to political campaigns during the 1968 Presidential election year.

These wealthy donors, each estimated to have a fortune of $150 million or more in 1968, gave Republicans the larger share of their money, favoring them over Democrats by almost a 13-to-1 margin.

Republican candidates received $1,377,313 to $106,-488 for the Democrats. The average contribution was $32,489. *(Top 10 contributors, p. 40)*

The data on campaign contributions came from a study of the 66 Americans estimated by *Fortune* in 1968 to be the "richest of the rich." The information was compiled from Federal, and, where available, state records by Citizens' Research Foundation of Princeton, N.J.

Also studied were the donations of members of the Business Council, a national group of business executives which is organized to advise Government agencies.

Business Council members gave at least $367,213 to finance campaigns in 1968. Contributions to the Republicans totaled $280,913 compared to $83,000 for the Democrats.

Because of loopholes in the Federal Corrupt Practices Act of 1925, these figures must be considered the minimum contribution for each individual. *(Discussion of 1925 act in chapter on campaign spending laws p. 15)*

The Act does not apply to state elections, primary campaigns or campaign committees operating within one state.

Contributions of the Very Rich

Of the 66 Americans who possessed fortunes in excess of $150 million in 1968, 46—or about 70 percent—are on record as having contributed to political campaigns in that Presidential election year.

Forty super-rich donors gave the Republicans a total of $1,377,313 with individual contributions averaging $34,433. Twelve of the elite group gave the Democrats $106,488 with contributions averaging $8,874.

Contributions to miscellaneous committees and candidates not affiliated with the two major parties amounted to $10,701.

The four contributors making the largest total donations all gave exclusively to Republican candidates.

New York Governor Nelson A. Rockefeller and his wife made the largest contributions in 1968. After reported contributions of $356,000 to his own campaign for the Republican Presidential nomination, Rockefeller supplied an additional $127,500 to various Republican committees.

Insurance executive W. Clement Stone of Chicago, a strong backer of the Presidential bid of Richard M. Nixon in 1968, gave $200,000 to Republican campaign committees.

The third-highest gift total also went to Republicans. The late Richard King Mellon of Pittsburgh, a director of General Motors Corporation, and his wife gave $65,000 to Republican candidates.

John Hay Whitney of New York, publisher of the defunct *New York Herald Tribune* and ambassador to Great Britain (1956-61), and his wife donated $57,500 to the Republicans.

Gifts by very wealthy donors to Democrats were small compared to those received by Republicans.

Xerography inventor Chester Carlson of Rochester, N.Y., gave the Democrats their largest contribution of $30,700. Carlson also contributed $1,000 to the Republicans.

Placing second among contributors to Democrats was William Clay Ford of Detroit, a Ford Motor Company vice president, who donated $20,000. His wife gave $1,000 to Republican committees.

Jacob Blaustein of Baltimore, a director of Standard Oil Company (Indiana), and his wife provided $17,000 to the Democrats and $1,000 to the Republicans.

In addition to Carlson, Ford and Blaustein, five other individuals or couples on the list of 66 multimillionaires split their contributions between Republican and Democratic committees.

David Rockefeller of New York, chairman of the Chase Manhattan Bank, and his wife gave $20,500 to the Republicans and $5,000 to the Democrats.

Others who split their contributions were investment banker Charles Allen Jr. of New York ($1,500 R; $3,000 D), industrialist Charles W. Engelhard Jr. of Newark ($250 R;

(Continued on p. 34)

1968 Campaign Contributions of Wealthiest Americans [1]

	1968	
	Republican	Democratic
$1 Billion to $1.5 Billion [2]		
J. Paul Getty		
Getty Oil Co.		
Howard Hughes		
Hughes Aircraft, Hughes Tool,		
real estate		
$500 Million to $1 Billion		
H. L. Hunt	4,000	
Independent oil operator		
Dr. Edwin Land		
Polaroid		
Daniel K. Ludwig		
Shipping		
Ailsa Mellon Bruce [3]	30,000	
Paul Mellon	47,000	
Richard King Mellon [4]	$65,000	
$300 Million to $500 Million		
N. Bunker Hunt		
Independent oil operator		
John D. MacArthur		
Bankers Life & Casualty		
William L. McKnight	44,000	
Minnesota Mining & Manu-		
facturing		
Charles S. Mott		
General Motors		
R. E. (Bob) Smith		
Independent oil, real estate		
$200 Million to $300 Million		
Howard F. Ahmanson		
Home Savings & Loan Asso-		
ciation		
Charles Allen Jr.	1,500	3,000
Investment banking		
Mrs. W. Van Alan Clark Sr.	6,000	
Avon products		
John T. Dorrance Jr.	20,101	
Campbell Soup		
Mrs. Alfred I. DuPont		
Charles W. Engelhard Jr.	250	5,750
Mining and metal		
fabricating		
Sherman M. Fairchild		
Fairchild Camera, IBM		
Leon Hess		5,500
Hess Oil & Chemical		
William R. Hewlett	500	
Hewlett-Packard		
David Packard	11,000	
Hewlett-Packard		
Amory Houghton	19,500	
Corning Glass Works		
Joseph P. Kennedy		
Eli Lilly		
Eli Lilly & Company		
Forrest E. Mars	4,000	
Mars candy		
Samuel I. Newhouse		
Newspapers		
Majorie Merriweather Post	600	2,500
General Foods		
Mrs. Jean Mauze (Abby Rocke-	8,000	
feller)		
David Rockefeller	20,500	5,000
John D. Rockefeller III	17,500	
Laurance Rockefeller	23,500	
Nelson Rockefeller [5]	483,500	
Winthrop Rockefeller	6,500	
Cordelia Scaife May	52,000	
Mellon family		
Richard Mellon Scaife	55,462	
DeWitt Wallace	35,900	
Reader's Digest		
Mrs. Charles Payson	28,000	
(Joan Whitney)		
John Hay Whitney	57,500	
$150 Million to $200 Million		
James S. Abercrombie		1,000
Independent oil; Cameron		
Iron Works		
William Benton		12,538
Encyclopaedia Britannica		
Jacob Blaustein	1,000	17,000
Standard Oil of Indiana		
Chester Carlson	1,000	30,700
Inventor of xerography		
Edward J. Daly		
World Airways		
Clarence J. Dillon		
Investment banking		
Doris Duke		
Lammot DuPont Copeland	14,000	
Henry B. DuPont	3,000	
Benson Ford	41,000	
Ford Motor Company		
Mrs. W. Buhl Ford II	4,500	
Ford Motor Company		
William C. Ford	1,000	20,000
Ford Motor Company		
Helen Clay Frick	19,500	
William T. Grant	4,000	
W. T. Grant stores		
Bob Hope	16,000	
Arthur A. Houghton Jr.	12,000	2,500
Corning Glass Works		
J. Seward Johnson		
Johnson & Johnson		
Peter Kiewit	9,000	
Construction		
Allen P. Kirby		
Woolworth, Alleghany Cor-		
poration		
J. S. McDonnell Jr.		
McDonnell Douglas aircraft		
Mrs. Lester J. Norris	7,000	
(Dellora F. Angell)		
E. Glaiborne Robins	2,500	
A. H. Robins drugs		
W. Clement Stone	200,000	
Insurance		
Mrs. Arthur Hays Sulzberger		
The New York Times		
S. Mark Taper		500
First Charter Financial Cor-		
poration		
Robert W. Woodruff		500
Coca-Cola		
Subtotal:	$1,377,313	$106,488
TOTAL:	$1,494,502	

---

1 *Contributions of spouses are included with those of individual listed.*
2 *Estimates of net worth by* Fortune *were made in 1968 and relate to the financial position of the individuals in that year.*
3 *Now deceased.*

4 *Now deceased.*
5 *Includes $356,000 contribution by Nelson A. Rockefeller to his own campaign for the Republican Presidential nomination in 1968.*

$5,750 D), Arthur A. Houghton Jr. of New York, a director of Corning Glass Company ($12,000 R; $2,500 D) and General Food heiress Marjorie Merriweather Post of Washington, D.C., ($600 R; $2,500 D).

Neither of the country's two billionaires, Howard Hughes and J. Paul Getty, was recorded as having contributed to political campaigns in 1968.

Hughes maintains a screen around most of his activities and lives as a recluse in Las Vegas, Nev. Although his oil holdings are in the United States, Getty now lives in England.

Among America's families of great wealth, the Mellon name stands highest in the rankings of Republican contributors. In addition to the $65,000 gift by Mr. and Mrs. Richard King Mellon, others include Mr. and Mrs. Richard Mellon Scaife of Pittsburgh ($55,462), Mrs. Cordelia Scaife May of Pittsburgh ($52,000), Paul Mellon of Pittsburgh ($47,000) and the late Ailsa Mellon Bruce of New York ($30,000).

Close behind as Republican party patrons are the five Rockefeller brothers. The contributions of Gov. Nelson Rockefeller to his own Presidential primary campaign are not counted here.

These donors are: banker David Rockefeller of New York ($20,500), businessman John D. Rockefeller III of New York ($17,500), businessman Laurance Rockefeller of New York ($23,500), New York Governor Nelson Rockefeller ($127,000) and Arkansas Governor Winthrop Rockefeller of Little Rock ($6,500).

David Packard of Palo Alto, Calif., now Deputy Secretary of Defense, and his wife contributed $11,000 to Republican causes; his partner in the electronic firm Hewlett-Packard, William R. Hewlett of Palo Alto, gave $500 to the Republicans, according to the survey.

National Honor America Day cochairman, comedian Bob Hope, and his wife provided $16,000 for the Republicans. In 1964, Mrs. Hope gave $10,000 to the successful campaign of Sen. George Murphy (R Calif.)

Business Council Donors

Business executives who were members of the Business Council in 1968 gave Republicans more than $3 for every $1 to the Democrats.

This is in sharp contrast to the situation in 1964 when council members provided the Johnson campaign 50 percent more than was received by the Goldwater forces.

The 1968 Republican total of $280,913 was a record high for contributions by Business Council members to Republicans in the last four Presidential election years. Democrats received a total of $83,000.

The following totals were contributed by the indicated number of Business Council members to Republican (R) and Democratic (D) campaign committees since 1956 in Presidential election years: 1968, (R) $280,913 (67), (D) $83,000 (5); 1964, (R) $87,100 (36), (D) $135,450 (33); 1960, (R) $241,060 (73), (D) $35,140 (7); 1956, (R) $268,499 (68), (D) $4,000 (4).

The Business Council is a private, nonprofit group of businessmen which meets to act as an advisory body to Government. Membership is by invitation, and, while a variety of industries and geographic areas are represented, each member must be either a president, chairman or chief executive officer of his company.

Contributing much smaller amounts on the average than the very rich, members of the Business Council (considered here with their wives) made average contributions of $5,322. The average for the 46 richest Americans who contributed was $32,489.

John Hay Whitney, who along with Packard and Corning Glass honorary chairman Amory Houghton also appears on the list of richest Americans, was the Business Council's leading individual donor with his $57,500 to Republicans.

The second largest donor was Henry Ford II of Dearborn, chairman of the board of Ford Motor Company. He donated $30,000 to the Democrats and $7,250 to the Republicans.

Ford shifted in 1964 from his previous stance as a solid Republican supporter and in that year gave Democratic committees $40,000 and Republican ones $4,100.

Industrialist Edgar F. Kaiser donated the third highest amount in 1968, $25,000, exclusively to Democratic fund-raising groups.

At the top of the list of Republican financial supporters after Whitney were Charles B. Thornton, chairman of Litton Industries, ($19,500); Amory Houghton ($19,500); clothing manufacturer Barry T. Leithead, president of Cluett, Peabody & Company, ($17,200); and James A. Linen III, president of Time Inc., ($12,500).

Third, behind Ford and Kaiser, among large contributors to the Democrats was Thomas J. Watson Jr., International Business Machines board chairman, who split his campaign gifts in favor of the Democrats $21,000 to $7,875.

The members of the Business Council who split their contributions, Ford, Watson and Allied Chemical chairman John T. Connor ($500 R; $1,000 D), all did so to the advantage of the Democrats.

Frederick R. Kappel, former chairman of the board of American Telephone and Telegraph Corporation, and an appointee of President Lyndon Johnson to head both the Postal Organization and Executive, Legislative and Judicial Salaries commissions, contributed $6,000 to Republican committees.

Banker C. Douglas Dillon, Secretary of the Treasury under Democratic Presidents Kennedy and Johnson, gave just to Republicans ($9,000) in 1968 after having switched to the Democrats for the first time in 1964 with a donation of $42,000.

Thirty members of the Business Council gave at least $3,000 to political campaigns in 1968.

The names of these officials follow in alphabetical order. After each name and affiliation is the amount of the 1968 donation and the party, Republican (R) or Democrat (D), receiving the money.

The amounts below represent only those contributions listed on official state or Federal reports.

S. D. Bechtel (and Mrs. Bechtel), senior director, Bechtel Corporation: $3,000 (R).

S. D. Bechtel Jr., president, Bechtel Corporation: $4,500 (R).

Howard L. Clark, chairman, American Express Company: $4,000 (R).

Paul L. Davies, senior partner, Lehman Brothers: $8,000 (R).

C. Douglas Dillon: $9,000 (R).

Henry Ford II, chairman, Ford Motor Company: $7,250 (R); $30,000 (D).

R. V. Hansberger (and Mrs. Hansberger), president, Boise Cascade Corporation: $4,988 (R).

Amory Houghton (and Mrs. Houghton), honorary chairman, Corning Glass Works: $19,500 (R).

Gilbert W. Humphrey (and Mrs. Humphrey), chairman, M. A. Hanna Company: $3,000 (R).

Edgar F. Kaiser (and Mrs. Kaiser), chairman, Kaiser Industries Corporation: $25,000 (D).

F. R. Kappel, former chairman, American Telephone and Telegraph Company: $6,000 (R).

George E. Keck, president, United Air Lines: $3,000 (R).

John R. Kimberly (and Mrs. Kimberly), chairman, Kimberly-Clark: $3,500 (R).

Barry T. Leithead, chairman, Cluett, Peabody & Company: $17,200 (R).

James A. Linen III (and Mrs. Linen), president, Time Inc.: $12,500 (R).

S. M. McAshen Jr. (and Mrs. McAshen), chairman, Anderson, Clayton & Company: $6,000 (D).

Neil McElroy, chairman, Procter & Gamble: $3,000 (R).

J. Irwin Miller (and Mrs. Miller), chairman, Cummins Engine Company: $4,000 (R).

Frank R. Milliken, president, Kennecott Copper Corporation: $4,000 (R).

Roger Milliken, president, Deering Milliken Inc.: $1,000 (R); $2,500 (Misc.).

Charles F. Myers Jr., chairman, Burlington Industries: $3,500 (R).

David Packard (and Mrs. Packard), chairman, Hewlett-Packard Company: $11,000 (R).

T. F. Patton (and Mrs. Patton), chairman, Republic Steel Corporation: $3,000 (R).

M. J. Rathbone, retired chairman, Standard Oil of New Jersey: $3,000 (R).

Charles B. Thornton, chairman, Litton Industries: $19,500 (R).

Juan T. Trippe, honorary chairman, Pan American World Airways: $5,000 (R).

Thomas J. Watson Jr., chairman, International Business Machines Corporation: $7,875 (R); $21,000 (D).

John Hay Whitney (and Mrs. Whitney), chairman, Whitney Communications Corporation: $57,500 (R).

Henry S. Wingate, chairman, International Nickel Company: $3,000 (R).

Top Corporate Contributors

Campaign contributions on record for 1,013 officers and directors of the 25 largest industrial corporations listed in the *Fortune Directory* in 1968, favored the Republicans nearly 6 to 1.

Twenty-three percent of all officials of these companies gave donations in 1968 totaling at least $921,239.

Republicans received $782,839 from 219 contributors contrasted to $132,150 from 26 contributors for the Democrats. Miscellaneous committees not affiliated with the major parties received $6,250 from six donors.

The companies with the largest total contributions from executives, and the amounts given to Republicans (R) and Democrats (D), were: Ford Motor Company, (R) $87,100, (D) $53,000; International Business Machines Corporation, (R) $104,250, (D) $32,000; General Motors Corporation, (R) $114,675, (D) $1,000.

Corporations are prohibited from making donations to Presidential, Vice Presidential or Congressional candidates

---

Impact of Campaign Contributions

Many legislators, writers, and civic groups have deplored the erosion of political integrity likely to result from large campaign contributions. Among the more pungent statements on this subject are the following:

"Individuals and organizations providing substantial gifts at critical moments can threaten to place a candidate in moral hock."—President's Commission on Campaign Costs (1962).

"The accelerating cost of campaigning is the single most important factor in corrupting and degrading our politicians."—James M. Perry, political columnist, in *The National Observer*, April 13, 1970.

Acceptance of funds from "labor organizations or other private interests...means that a candidate is placed in the position of being in the pocket of such contributors, or assumed to be by the contributor and by the public."—Sen. John Sherman Cooper (R Ky.), Senate speech, Nov. 23, 1970.

---

by the Federal Corrupt Practices Act. But it is legal for corporate executives to contribute as individuals.

Of the 25 leading industrial corporations, thirteen also appear on listings of the top 25 contractors in fiscal 1970 for the Department of Defense (DOD), Atomic Energy Commission (AEC) and National Aeronautics and Space Administration (NASA). *(Analysis of contributions of top defense contractors, p. 36)*

Executives of Gulf Oil Corporation led the donors from companies which were not on the top contractor lists, with $73,800 to Republicans and nothing to Democrats.

Conclusions

The return of the large contributor to the Republican camp in 1968 is perhaps the most important fact shown by the data. These funds complemented those from a wide base of donors who were first mobilized during the Goldwater campaign and stuck with the Republicans to contribute $6,600,000 in 1968.

For Business Council members, the very rich, as well as the top officials of the country's 25 leading industrial corporations, the percentage of individuals in each group who contributed to political campaigns is high when compared to estimates of the proportion of the general population who contribute.

A national survey in the last two months of 1968 by the Survey Research Center at the University of Michigan reported that only 8.3 percent of a sample of 1,346 adults said that they had contributed to a political party in the recent election.

Significantly, of the 23 percent of this sample who said they were asked to contribute during the campaigns, 38 percent indicated they had. This figure is higher than the 23 percent who contributed among officers and directors of the top industrial firms, all of whom were likely to have been asked.

Contributions from each group were greater in 1968 than in either 1960 or 1964, with the very rich leading the other categories in both percentage of their number who contributed and the average amount given.

CONTRACTORS' OFFICERS FAVOR GOP 6-1 IN CONTRIBUTIONS

Officials of companies ranking among the top 25 defense, space and nuclear contractors in fiscal 1968 contributed at least $1,235,402 to political campaigns during the 1968 Presidential election year.

Officers and directors of these companies favored the Republicans over the Democrats by almost 6 to 1 in their donations, according to data gathered by the Citizens' Research Foundation of Princeton, N.J.

Republicans received $1,054,852 compared to $180,-550 for the Democrats. The figures are based on a tabulation of contributions from 294 officials. *(Table p. 38)*

The Federal Corrupt Practices Act of 1925 forbids corporations from making political contributions. Officers or directors of corporations may make contributions as individuals.

The survey, one of the most comprehensive ever made of political contributions by corporate executives, covered the top 25 contractors in fiscal 1968 for the Department of Defense (DOD), Atomic Energy Commission (AEC) and National Aeronautics and Space Administration (NASA). *(Box p. 37)*

Because several companies appear on two or all three lists of the 25 top contractors, and two companies are subsidiaries of larger corporations, fewer than 75 separate contractors were included in the survey.

The study was based on 56 companies. Available records showed 49 companies had officials who made political donations. The average contribution was $4,202. No donations were reported for officials of seven companies.

The reported total of $1,235,402 in contributions is a minimum figure. Many executives included in the study may have made other large contributions that did not have to be reported because of loopholes in the Federal Corrupt Practices Act. *(p. 15)*

The Citizens' Research Foundation did not include all state reports on campaign contributions in its survey, and some information was not readily accessible for inspection. *(For sources of data, see box p. 32)*

Furthermore, the study covered only the top 25 DOD, AEC and NASA contractors and therefore represents only a portion of total political donations by officials of all contractors in these fields. Hundreds of other companies received sizeable DOD, AEC and NASA contracts in 1968.

Defense Contractor Donations

Twenty-four of the 25 top DOD contractors had officers or directors who made political contributions in 1968. Hughes Aircraft, number 24 on the list, was the lone exception.

Of the 856 officials serving in administrative positions or on boards of these 25 defense contractors, 178, or about 21 percent, showed up as contributors in available records.

Republicans got more than six dollars for every one received by the Democrats. The military contractor executives donated $671,252 to Republican party coffers and $110,000 to the Democrats. Another $5,501 went to miscellaneous committees without formal party ties.

Litton Industries, which ranked 14th on the DOD contractor list in 1968, led the givers with a total of $156,000. Eleven of Litton's 29 officers and directors made donations. The Republican party got $151,000, Democrats got nothing, and miscellaneous committees received $5,000.

Litton also supplied the most generous donors, Mr. and Mrs. Henry Salvatori, who contributed a total of $90,000 to the Republicans and $5,000 to miscellaneous committees. Salvatori, a Litton director, is a wealthy California oilman who supported Sen. Barry Goldwater (R Ariz.) for the Presidency in 1964.

Nineteen of the Ford Motor Company's 47 leading officials donated a total of $140,100 to political candidates in 1968. Republicans got $87,100 and Democrats received $53,000.

Henry Ford II, chairman of the board, gave the Democrats $30,000 and Republicans $7,250. On the other hand, Benson Ford, vice president of the company, gave all his contributions totaling $41,000 to the Republicans.

The Ford Motor Company ranked 19th among DOD contractors in fiscal 1968. A Ford subsidiary, Philco-Ford was 16th on the list of NASA contractors in the same year. *(Box p. 37)*

NASA Contractor Contributions

Twenty-four of the 25 leading NASA contractors in fiscal 1968 had officials who contributed to 1968 political campaigns, according to the records. The exception was Brown Engineering which ranked 23rd on the list.

There were 856 officers and directors for these 25 companies of whom 165, or 19 percent, gave money to candidates in the Presidential election year.

But considerable duplication occurred between the top NASA contractors and companies on the DOD and AEC lists. Fourteen of the NASA contractors also ranked among the top 25 DOD contractors and two were on the AEC list.

If all 24 NASA companies with campaign contributors are counted, the Republicans received $502,102 compared to $129,000 for the Democrats.

Officials of the eight contractors appearing only on the NASA list donated a total of $300,750 with the Republicans getting $201,750 and the Democrats $99,000.

Of the eight companies appearing only on the NASA list, International Business Machines Corporation (IBM) registered the highest total in contributions—$136,250 from 12 of the company's 44 officers and directors.

Defense, AEC and NASA Contractors for 1968 and 1970

The following lists show the top 25 Defense Department, AEC and NASA contractors as they ranked in fiscal 1968. Numbers in parentheses indicate the company's rank in fiscal 1970. Companies appearing in these lists but not in the chart on p. 38 did not have officers or directors who reported 1968 campaign contributions.

Defense	AEC	NASA
1. General Dynamics (2)	1. Union Carbide (1)	1. North American Rockwell (1)
2. Lockheed Aircraft (1)	2. Sandia Corp. (2)#	2. Grumman Aircraft (2)
3. General Electric (3)	3. General Electric (6)	3. Boeing (4)
4. United Aircraft (6)	4. duPont (3)	4. McDonnell-Douglas (3)
5. McDonnell-Douglas (5)	5. Reynolds Electrical (5)	5. General Electric (6)
6. American Telephone and Telegraph (4)	6. Westinghouse Electric (7)	6. IBM (5)
7. Boeing (12)	7. Bendix (4)	7. Bendix (7)
8. Ling-Temco-Vought (11)	8. Holmes and Narver (12)	8. Aerojet-General (9)
9. North American Rockwell (7)	9. Douglas United Nuclear (10)	9. RCA (11)
10. General Motors (17)	10. Dow Chemical (8)	10. Chrysler (22)
11. Grumman Aircraft (8)	11. Goodyear Atomic (14)	11. General Dynamics (14)
12. Avco (20)	12. Idaho Nuclear (9)	12. TRW (10)
13. Textron (13)	13. Aerojet-General (18)	13. General Motors (20)
14. Litton Industries (9)	14. Atlantic-Richfield (13)	14. Ling-Temco-Vought (21)
15. Raytheon (18)	15. E. G. and G. (11)	15. Lockheed Aircraft (13)
16. Sperry-Rand (15)	16. Gulf General Atomic (23)	16. Philco-Ford (19)
17. Martin Marietta (26)	17. Monsanto (15)	17. Sperry-Rand (12)
18. Kaiser Industries	18. Kerr-McGee (22)	18. Martin Marietta (8)
19. Ford Motor (19)	19. National Lead (21)	19. TWA (15)
20. Honeywell (16)	20. Mason and Hanger (16)	20. Federal Electric (18)
21. Olin Mathieson (28)	21. North American Rockwell (17)	21. Catalytic-Dow (39)
22. Northrop (33)	22. Homestake-Sapin (24)†	22. United Aircraft (17)
23. Ryan Aeronautical (29)*	23. United Nuclear (26)	23. Brown Engineering (29)
24. Hughes Aircraft (10)	24. Pan American (26)	24. Honeywell (26)
25. Standard Oil (N.J.) (30)	25. Phillips Petroleum	25. Control Data (38)

*1970 ranking is for Teledyne Inc., which now owns Ryan Aeronautical. If still listed separately Ryan would have ranked 54th in fiscal 1969.

#Subsidiary of Western Electric, the manufacturing unit of A T & T.
†.Now known as United Nuclear-Homestake Partners.

SOURCES: Department of Defense, NASA, AEC.

Republicans got $104,250 from IBM officials and the Democrats received $32,000.

Arthur K. Watson, vice chairman of the IBM board of directors, made the largest donation—$54,875 to the Republicans. Thomas J. Watson, chairman of the board, gave the Democrats $21,000 and the Republicans $7,875.

Officials of Trans World Airlines Inc. (TWA), also among the group of eight NASA contractors not on the other lists, donated $47,700 to the candidates. Eight of 65 TWA executives contributed a total of $45,200 to the Republican party and $2,500 to the Democrats.

AEC Contractor Contributions

Twenty of the 25 top AEC contractors for fiscal 1968 showed officials contributing to political races in 1968.

The survey showed no contributors among the executives of five companies on the AEC list: Reynolds Electric Co. (5), Holmes & Narver Inc. (9), Goodyear Atomic Corp. (11), E. G. & G. (15) and Mason & Hanger-Silas Mason Co. (20).

Two of the AEC contractors also appeared on the DOD list. Of the 700 officials with the 25 leading AEC contractors, 106 or 15 percent, made contributions according to available records.

If all 20 AEC companies with contributors are counted, the company officials donated a total of $308,701 in 1968. The Republicans got $272,700, the Democrats $30,050 and miscellaneous committees $5,951.

Executives of the 18 AEC companies not duplicated on the DOD list contributed a total of $257,100 with the Republicans getting $224,600 and the Democrats $27,050 and miscellaneous committees $5,450.

The Atlantic Richfield Company recorded the largest amount of contributions, $66,000, among those 18 AEC contractors not also on the DOD list.

Twelve of 33 Atlantic Richfield executives donated money to political campaigns in 1968. The Republicans received $65,000 and the Democrats got only $1,000.

(Continued on p. 39)

Contributions by Officials of Federal Contractors

COMPANY	Number Contributing	Republicans	Democrats	NET VALUE Prime Military Contract Awards (in millions of dollars) Fiscal Years 1968	1969	1970	TOTAL COSTS AEC Prime Industrial Contractors (in millions of dollars) Fiscal Years 1968	1969	1970	NET VALUE NASA Direct Contract Awards [1] (in millions of dollars) Fiscal Years 1968	1969	1970
Aerojet-General Corp.	2	$ 8,000	$15,000				$ 34.8	$ 25.9 $	26.3	$ 67.1	$ 64.9	$ 71.6
American Telephone and Telegraph Co.	9	16,500	1,000	$ 775.9	$ 914.6	$ 931.2	197.9[2]	214.3[2]	220.3[2]	5.5[3]	5.8[3]	6.5[3]
Atlantic Richfield Co.	12	65,000	1,000		54.3	46.3	32.2	31.6	36.6			
Avco Corp.	6	3,000	13,000	583.6	456.1	269.7				5.3	3.9	1.3
Bendix Corp.	2	2,000		223.6	184.4	167.7	73.8	85.0	92.2	123.8	127.6	109.8
Boeing Co.	4	5,000		762.1	653.6	474.7				296.7	228.7	158.6
Catalytic-Dow [4]	1		2,000							18.8	19.4	6.1
Chrysler Corp.	20	30,550	5,500	146.6	121.8	92.0				62.6	42.5	16.7
Control Data Corp.	3	4,000	1,000	56.8	56.9	80.6				15.5	7.2	6.7
Douglas United Nuclear Inc.	1	1,000					52.8	44.8	42.9			
Dow Chemical Co.	3	3,000	3,550				40.2	42.8	58.2			
E. I. duPont de Nemours and Co.	11	42,800		170.6	212.0	161.7	90.2	99.1	116.6			
Federal Electric Corp.	2	1,500	500							22.0	27.0	26.3
Ford Motor Co.	19	87,100	53,000	381.3	396.3	345.9				32.0[5]	22.4[5]	24.0[5]
General Dynamics Corp.	9	17,265	1,000	2,239.3	1,243.1	1,183.2				54.4	34.0	38.0
General Electric Co.	17	27,600	1,000	1,488.7	1,620.8	1,000.5	103.0	95.1	87.4	190.7	150.1	131.7
General Motors Corp.	29	114,675	1,000	629.6	584.4	385.7				46.8	30.9	20.4
Grumman Aircraft Engineering Corp.	4	6,500		629.2	417.1	660.8				394.1	369.2	284.4
Gulf General Atomic Inc.	3	2,800					29.6	14.6	8.2			
Honeywell Inc.	4	6,000	3,000	351.7	405.6	397.9				15.7	8.1	11.5
Idaho Nuclear Corp.	1	2,000					36.5	48.4	48.1			
International Business Machines Corp.	12	104,250	32,000	223.7	256.6	256.1				147.7	112.5	133.4
Kaiser Industries Corp.	3	8,000	25,000	386.3	142.4							
Kerr-McGee Oil Industries Inc. [6]	3	2,500	1,000				24.2	20.9	9.1			
Ling-Temco-Vought Inc.	4	7,500	1,500	758.3	914.1	479.3				42.7[7]	20.4[7]	17.9
Litton Industries Inc. [8]	11	151,000		465.7	317.1	543.1						1.8
Lockheed Aircraft Corp.	5	38,880	1,000	1,870.2	2,040.2	1,847.7				40.5	39.8	41.0
Martin-Marietta Corp.	5	3,500	4,500	393.5	264.3	250.9	9.0			26.8	56.0	108.0
McDonnell-Douglas Corp.	5	26,432		1,100.8	1,069.7	882.7				209.0	207.5	236.3
Monsanto Co.	4	4,500	2,500				27.4	30.4	33.2			
National Lead Co.	2	6,000					23.8	20.6	17.5			
North American Rockwell Corp. [9]	8	20,500	2,000	668.6	674.2	707.1	21.1	23.2	26.4	838.7	680.9	531.5
Northrop Corp.	2	23,500		310.3	178.9	184.2				15.4	12.4	9.4
Olin Mathieson Chemical Corp.	7	58,300	3,000	329.4	354.4	247.7						
Pan American World Airways Inc.	11	34,500		205.7	167.4	143.1	16.4	10.3	5.4			1.3
Phillips Petroleum Co.	1		500				13.5					
Radio Corporation of America	6	7,000	5,500	255.0	299.0	262.8				63.2	51.6	54.5
Raytheon Co.	3	6,000		451.1	546.8	379.6						3.1
Ryan Aeronautical Co.	2	10,000		293.2	121.2[10]	98.4[10]						
Sperry Rand Corp.	6	7,000		447.2	467.9	398.9				31.8	34.1	48.1
Standard Oil Co. of New Jersey	6	12,000		274.3	291.1	229.2						
Textron Inc.	5	6,000		500.7	428.3	430.9				2.1		4.2
Trans World Airlines Inc.	8	45,200	2,500							25.3	35.4	36.0
TRW Inc.	1	1,000		127.5	170.4	179.1			5.0	52.4	50.0	58.3
Union Carbide Corp.	6	8,000	1,000				284.0	317.4	319.1	15.3	8.9	5.5
United Aircraft Corp.	6	9,500		1,321.0	997.4	873.8				18.1	26.2	27.1
United Nuclear Corp.	1	2,500					16.8	15.9	6.7			
United Nuclear-Homestake Partners	3	1,000	1,000				17.2[11]	14.9	7.5			
Westinghouse Electric Corp. [12]	14	38,500	1,500	251.0	429.6	417.7	73.8	75.9	83.5	7.4	6.9	7.2
TOTALS	312	$1,089,352	$186,050	$19,072.5	$17,452.0	$15,010.2	$1,198.2	$1,230.8	$1,250.2	$2,887.4	$2,484.3	$2,238.2
LESS DUPLICATIONS [13]	18	34,500	5,500									
ADJUSTED TOTALS	294	$1,054,852	$180,550									

(Footnotes p. 39)

(Continued from p. 37)

The top giver from Atlantic Richfield was Robert O. Anderson, chairman and chief executive officer of the company, who sent the Republicans $44,000 and the Democrats nothing.

E. I. duPont de Nemours & Company showed the second highest total for contributions among this group of 18 AEC contractors. Eleven of 35 chief duPont executives contributed $44,300—$42,800 to Republicans, none to the Democrats and $1,500 to miscellaneous groups.

General Conclusions of Survey

One obvious deduction to be made from the study is that eight consecutive years in power (1961-1968) did little to sway major Federal contractors to the Democratic party cause in 1968.

From among the 49 top DOD, NASA and AEC contractors, officials of only seven companies donated more money to the Democrats than they did to the Republicans.

In each case these Democratic party financial triumphs were small. Kaiser Industries officials gave the Democrats the largest margin of contributions—$25,000 compared to $8,000 for the Republicans.

The six other companies with officials who gave more to the Democrats than to the Republicans were: Aerojet-General Corporation, Avco Corporation, Catalytic-Dow, Dow Chemical Company, Martin-Marietta Corporation and Phillips Petroleum Company. *(Chart, p. 38)*

Donations Increase. Contributions from corporate executives to both major parties in 1968 were almost always larger than in either 1960 or 1964.

The top two individual contributors provided dramatic examples of increasing donations. Mr. and Mrs. Salvatori were listed as contributing $95,000 in 1968 and $6,000 in 1964. The late Richard King Mellon, a director of General Motors, gave $65,000 in 1968 compared to $18,000 in 1964. *(Forty-three top contributors listed below)*

Directors usually gave more money to political campaigns than the officers of companies, according to the data. These directors, many of them wealthy men serving on the boards of several companies, are frequently bankers, lawyers or Wall Street investors.

(Footnotes for chart p. 38)

1 *Data for individual companies include awards on research and development contracts of $1,000 and over and on all other contracts of $25,000 and over.*
2 *Amounts listed are for Sandia Corp., a subsidiary of Western Electric Co., which is the manufacturing unit of American Telephone and Telegraph Co.*
3 *Combined amounts for separate contracts let to American Telephone and Telegraph Co. and Western Electric Co.*
4 *Joint venture of Catalytic Construction Co. and Dow Chemical Co.*
5 *Amounts listed are Philco-Ford Corp., a subsidiary of Ford Motor Co.*
6 *One officer of Kerr-McGee Oil Industries Inc. also made $700 in miscellaneous contributions.*
7 *Combined amounts for separate contracts let to LTV Aerospace Corp. and LTV Electro Systems.*
8 *One director of Litton Industries Inc. also made $5,000 in miscellaneous contributions.*
9 *One officer of North American Rockwell Corp. also made $501 in miscellaneous contributions.*
10 *Ryan Aeronautical Co. is now a subsidiary of Teledyne Inc. Amount listed does not reflect any Teledyne contracts except those let to Ryan Aeronautical Co.*
11 *Amounts are for Homestake-Sapin Partners, since merged into United Nuclear-Homestake partners.*
12 *One director of Westinghouse Electric Corp. also made $3,250 in miscellaneous contributions.*
13 *Eighteen individuals were listed as officers or directors of more than one of the above companies. The totals next to each company include the duplicate amounts.*

Top 43 Individual Contributors

Forty-three officers or directors of companies among the top 25 DOD, NASA and AEC contractors in fiscal 1968 gave at least $5,500 to political campaigns in 1968.

The names of these officials follow in alphabetical order. After each name is the amount of the 1968 donation and the party, Republican (R) or Democrat (D), receiving the money. Donations, if any, in 1964 and 1960 also are listed.

The amounts below represent only those contributions listed on official state or Federal reports.

Robert O. Anderson, chairman and chief executive officer, Atlantic Richfield: 1968, $44,000 (R); 1960, $500 (R).

Roy L. Ash, president, Litton Industries: 1968, $8,500 (R).

Walker G. Buckner, director, IBM: 1968, $9,000 (D); 1964, $6,000 (D).

John S. Bugas, vice president, Ford Motor Co.: 1968, $20,000 (R); 1964, $3,000 (R).

William A. M. Burden, director, Lockheed Aircraft Co.: 1968, $14,500 (R); 1964, $1,000 (R); 1960, $3,500 (R).

Walter S. Carpenter Jr., honorary chairman, duPont: 1968, $7,000 (R); 1964, $6,500 (R); $500 miscellaneous; 1960, $12,000 (R).

Lammot DuPont Copeland, president, duPont: 1968, $14,000 (R); 1964, $9,000 (R); 1960, $13,000 (R).

Paul L. Davies, director, IBM: 1968, $8,000 (R); 1964, $1,000 (R); 1960, $1,000 (R).

George P. Edmunds, director, duPont: 1968, $5,500 (R); 1964, $500 (R); 1960, $1,000 (R).

Edward F. Fisher, director, General Motors: 1968, $8,000 (R).

John C. Folger, director, IBM: 1968, $9,000 (R); 1964, $4,000 (R); 1960, $16,100 (R).

Benson Ford, vice president, Ford Motor Co.: 1968, $41,000 (R); 1960, $3,000 (R).

Henry Ford II, chairman, Ford Motor Co.: 1968, $7,250 (R), $30,000 (D); 1964, $3,600 (R), $39,500 (D); 1960, $6,000 (R).

William Clay Ford, vice president, Ford Motor Co.: 1968, $1,000 (R), $20,000 (D); 1960, $6,000 (R).

Amory Houghton Jr., director, IBM: 1968, $19,500 (R); 1960, $900 (R).

David S. Ingalls, director, Pan American World Airways: 1968, $12,000 (R); 1964, $1,500 (R); 1960, $2,000 (R).

Charles S. Jones, director, Atlantic Richfield: 1968, $9,000 (R); 1964, $1,000 (R).

Earle M. Jorgenson, director, Northrop Corp.: 1968, $22,500 (R).

Edgar F. Kaiser, president, Kaiser Industries: 1968, $25,000 (D); 1964, $6,000 (D).

Frederick R. Kappel, chairman of executive committee, A T & T; director, Standard Oil of New Jersey: 1968, $6,000 (R); 1964, $1,000 (R); 1960, $3,000 (R).

Willard W. Keith, director, Lockheed Aircraft Co.: 1968, $19,880 (R); 1964, $4,500 (R); 1960, $1,000 (R).

Dan A. Kimball, chairman of executive committee, Aerojet-General: 1968, $15,000 (D); 1964, $2,000 (D).

Barry T. Leithead, director, TWA: 1968, $17,200 (R); 1964, $500 (R); 1960, $1,000 (R).

Edward H. Litchfield, director, AVCO Corp.: 1968, $10,000 (D).

Glen McDaniel, senior vice president, Litton Industries: 1968, $11,500 (R).

Jackson R. McGowen, corporate vice president, McDonnell Douglas Corp.: 1968, $18,700 (R).

Richard King Mellon, director, General Motors: 1968, $65,000 (R); 1964, $18,000 (R); 1960, $20,000 (R).

Andre Meyer, director, RCA: 1968, $1,000 (R); $5,500 (D); 1964, $35,500 (D).

Thomas S. Nichols, chairman of executive committee, Olin Mathieson Chemical Corp.: 1968, $4,000 (R); $3,000 (D); 1964, $4,000 (D); 1960, $7,000 (R).

Spencer T. Olin, director, Olin Mathieson Chemical Corp.: 1968, $12,500 (R); 1964, $11,900 (R); 1960, $24,500 (R).

John M. Olin, honorary chairman, Olin Mathieson Chemical Corp.: 1968, $31,500 (R); 1964, $31,000 (R); 1960, $12,000 (R).

M. G. O'Neil, chairman, Aerojet General: 1968, $8,000 (R).

David Packard, director, Ford Motor Co.: 1968, $11,000 (R).

Thomas L. Perkins, director, General Motors: 1968, $9,000 (R).

Willard F. Rockwell Jr., chairman, North American Rockwell: 1968, $7,000 (R).

Henry Salvatori (and Mrs. Salvatori), director, Litton Industries: 1968, $90,000 (R), $5,000 miscellaneous; 1964, $6,000 (R); 1960 $1,000 (R).

John M. Schiff, director, Westinghouse Electric: 1968, $24,500 (R); 1964, $10,000 (R); 1960, $11,500 (R).

Hugh A. Sharp Jr., director, duPont: 1968, $6,500 (R); 1960, $4,000 (R).

C. Arnholt Smith, director, Ryan Aeronautical Co.: 1968, $8,000 (R); 1960, $1,000 (R).

Vernon Stouffer, director, Litton Industries: 1968, $27,000 (R); 1964, $900 miscellaneous.

Charles B. Thornton, director, TWA: 1968, $19,500 (R); 1964, $3,000 (D); 1960, $1,000 (R).

Arthur K. Watson, vice chairman, IBM: 1968, $54,875 (R); 1964, $13,000 (D); 1960, $7,500 (D).

Thomas J. Watson, chairman, IBM: 1968, $7,875 (R), $21,000 (D); 1964, $37,000 (D); 1960, $10,500 (D).

Top Corporate Contributors

Following are the 10 companies among top defense, space and nuclear contractors, whose officers and directors were reported to have contributed the largest amounts to election campaigns in 1968.

The totals are divided within the parentheses between donations to Republicans (R) and Democrats (D).

1. Litton Industries Inc., $151,000 ($151,000 R)
2. Ford Motor Company, $140,000 ($87,100 R; $53,000 D)
3. International Business Machines Corp., $136,250 ($104,250 R; $32,000 D)
4. General Motors Corporation $115,675 ($114,675 R; $1,000 D)
5. Atlantic Richfield Company, $66,000 ($65,000 R; $1,000 D)
6. Olin Mathieson Chemical Corporation, $61,300 ($58,300 R; $3,000 D)
7. Trans World Airlines Incorporated, $47,700 ($45,200 R; $2,500 D)
8. E. I. duPont de Nemours & Company, $42,800 ($42,800 R)
9. Westinghouse Electric Corporation, $40,000 ($38,500 R; $1,500 D)
10. Lockheed Aircraft Corp., $39,880 ($38,880 R; $1,000 D)

Political Contributions in 1968: The 10 Highest Contributors †

Contributor	Background	Amounts given to	
		Republicans	Democrats
W. Clement Stone	Chicago insurance multimillionaire	$148,916*	
Jack J. Dreyfus Jr.	Former board chairman of investment fund	76,000	$ 63,000
Max M. Fisher	Detroit oil executive and industrialist	105,000	
Rella Factor	Wife of John (Jake the Barber) Factor, who served six years in jail for mail fraud.		100,000
Henry Salvatore	Los Angeles oil executive	95,000	
Margery F. Russell	Daughter of Oregon department store magnate	**	
Mary Lasker	Widow of advertising executive Albert D. Lasker		69,400
J. Howard Pew	Board chairman of Sun Oil Co.	63,834	
Elmer H. Bobst	Executive of Warner-Lambert Pharmaceuticals	63,000	
Richard K. Mellon	Pittsburgh banker	62,000	

*Stone told reporters in January 1971 that he had also given more than $500,000 earmarked for the Nixon-Agnew campaign and that his political contributions to Nixon supporters in 1970 totaled almost $1 million.

†See p. 32-35. Richest Contributors.

**Contributions of $94,613 were made to promote the campaign of ultraconservative Walter S. Blake for election as Oregon's superintendent of schools. Blake was defeated.

SOURCES: Herbert E. Alexander and Caroline D. Jones (eds.), *Political Contributors of $500 or More in 1968* (Citizens' Research Foundation, 1971).

CONGRESS 1945-1970: MANY PROPOSALS, FEW RESULTS

Congress from 1945-1970 considered a number of proposals aimed at tightening regulations over election spending and freeing candidates from over-dependence upon large contributors and special interest groups.

Only in 1966 and 1970 did bills regulating campaign financing clear Congress. In 1966 Congress cleared a bill, signed by President Johnson, which set up a public fund to finance presidential campaigns; in 1967, however, Congress rendered the 1966 act inoperative. In 1970 Congress cleared a bill limiting political broadcasting, but President Nixon vetoed the bill and the Senate failed to override the veto.

Following is a year-by-year review of Congressional action.

1948—In its final report on a study of the 1948 Congressional elections, the House Campaign Expenditures Committee recommended a "substantial raise" in existing limits on campaign expenditures, pointing to the increased costs of goods and services, as well as the large population increase since passage of the Corrupt Practices Act of 1925.

1951—The House Special Committee to Investigate Campaign Expenditures, in a report on the 1950 House elections, Jan. 3 said it favored repeal of a number of provisions of the Federal Corrupt Practices Act of 1925 and the Hatch Act (1939). The Committee said it was "patently impossible for a candidate to conduct a Congressional or Senatorial campaign" within the existing limitations of expenditures, and that the "unrealistic" $3 million annual limitation on the national political committees was "an invitation to criminal violation." The Committee also recommended that primaries be included under political financing regulations, political committees be precluded from receiving and spending funds on behalf of a candidate without his written authorization and that the prohibition against participation in elections by federal employees be eliminated or liberalized.

1953—In a Jan. 24 report, the 82nd Congress Elections Subcommittee of the Senate Rules Committee proposed that the limit on spending for national political campaign committees be increased from $3 million to $10 million a year. The Subcommittee also recommended that the limit for spending by Senatorial candidates be increased from $25,000 to $50,000 or an absolute limit of $250,000, based upon a sliding scale of up to 10 cents for each vote case in the last primary or general election for the office in the candidate's state. On June 10, Sens. Carl Hayden (D Ariz.), Thomas C. Hennings Jr. (D Mo.) and Robert C. Hendrickson (R N.J.) introduced a bill (S 2081) containing these provisions, plus a ceiling of $25,000 (instead of the existing $5,000) on spending by candidates for the House. No action was taken on the bill.

1955—The Senate Rules and Administration Committee June 22 reported a bill (S 636), which had been introduced by Hennings (D Mo.), to include campaign costs in primary elections under the federal regulation limiting expenditures; require all committees active in campaigns for federal office to file financial reports (instead of only those active in more than one state); and increase the spending limit for Senatorial candidates in both primary and general elections to $50,000 and for House candidates to $12,500. The bill also would have raised the existing $3 million limit on spending by national committees, according to a formula based on the number of votes in recent elections, to approximately $12 million. The bill received no floor action.

1956—A Select Senate Committee, in an April 7 report, recommended that Congress re-evaluate the Federal Corrupt Practices Act. Specifically, the report suggested that Congress consider the advisability of amending the election laws to require that every candidate for federal office designate a fiscal agent officially authorized to solicit and accept campaign contributions and required to make this information a matter of public record. The Committee also recommended that every person, political committee or organization making more than $5,000 in campaign contributions in any one year be required to file a detailed accounting with the Secretary of State of each state.

1957—A bill (S 2150) increasing the maximum spending limits for political campaigns was reported Aug. 2 by the Senate Rules and Administration Committee but received no further action. As reported, S 2150 would have increased the limit for national committees to a figure equal to 20 cents for each person who voted in the last presidential election; for Senate and Representative-at-Large candidates to $50,000 or more, depending upon the number of voters in the preceding general election; and for other House candidates to $12,500 or more based on the number of voters.

1960—A bill (S 2436) increasing the limits on campaign spending but tightening provisions for disclosure was passed by the Senate but not acted on by the House. S 2436 was reported July 23, 1959, by the Senate Rules and Administration Committee and passed Jan. 25, 1960, by a 59-22 (D 38-15; R 21-7) roll-call vote. As passed by the Senate, the bill increased the spending limit for Senate and Representative-at-Large candidates to $50,-000 or a level established by the number of voters in the previous election; for other House candidates to $12,500, or a sliding maximum based upon the number of voters in the preceding election; and for nominees for President and Vice President at an amount equal to 20 cents times the number of votes cast in any of the three preceding elections, which would have set the ceiling at approximately $12 million and $6 million, respectively, in 1960. The House took no action.

1961—A truncated version of the "clean elections" bill passed by the Senate in 1960 was approved by the Senate Sept. 15, 1961, by voice vote but was not acted upon by the House. As passed, the bill (S 2426) raised the annual limit on campaign spending by political committees to an estimated $14 million, under a sliding scale formula; increased the spending limits for Senate and Representative-at-Large candidates to $50,000, and for other House candidates to $12,500.

Also in 1961, Sen. Maurine B. Neuberger (D Ore.) and four co-sponsors introduced a bill (S 1555) to establish a federal election finance fund which would share up to half of a candidate's radio-television expenses. No action was taken on the measure.

1962—The President's Commission on Campaign Costs April 18 issued a report recommending a series of proposals to encourage greater citizen participation in financing presidential campaigns. The Commission had been named Oct. 4, 1961, by President Kennedy. Chairman was Alexander Heard, dean of the University of North Carolina Graduate School. Among the Commission's recommendations were that:

• Individuals be given a credit against their federal income tax of 50 percent of political contributions, up to a maximum of $10 per year or, as an alternative, a deduction from taxable income for contributions up to $1,000 a year.

• The current $3 million annual limit on expenditures of interstate political committees and the $5,000 limit on contributions by individuals to those committees be repealed, leaving no limit.

• All candidates for President and Vice President and committees spending at least $2,500 a year be required to report expenditures made in both primary and general election campaigns.

• A Registry of Election Finance be established to help enforce political financing regulations.

• The Government pay the "reasonable and necessary costs" of a President-elect's facilities and staff during the "transition" period between election and inauguration.

President Kennedy May 29 submitted five draft bills to Congress encompassing proposals identical or similar to those made by the Commission. The only bill reported (HR 12479) was one to finance transition costs. This bill was reported by the House Government Operations Committee Sept. 19, but the measure died when Rep. Gerald R. Ford (R Mich.) Oct. 1 objected to consideration of the measure under the Consent Calendar, stating that the $750,000 authorization figure for each fiscal year concerned was too high.

1963—President Kennedy April 30 sent to Congress two draft bills to stiffen reporting requirements for campaign finances and to give tax benefits to campaign contributors in order to encourage support of political candidates and committees. Both proposals had been recommended by the President's Commission on Campaign Costs in 1962, but neither was acted upon.

1964—A provision to allow taxpayers to claim a deduction for campaign contributions of up to $50 for individuals and $100 for married couples was added to the Administration's omnibus tax bill (HR 8363—PL 88-272) by the Senate Finance Committee but was dropped in the Senate-House conference.

1966: Campaign Fund Subsidy

Reform of U.S. political campaign finances advanced on a number of fronts in 1966. For the first time in U.S. history, Congress approved a form of federal subsidy for the costs of Presidential campaigning. President Johnson sent Congress a comprehensive campaign finance reform law that covered all presidential and congressional campaigns, both in the primary and general election stage. Congress also clamped down on corporate tax deductions for advertisements in political journals.

Significant developments of 1966:

• President Johnson's draft of a campaign spending reform bill, forwarded to Congress May 26, envisaged sweeping reforms in the field. Not only were primary campaigns, both for President and for Congress, brought under the reporting requirements, but also a provision was added requiring all Members of Congress to report annually all gifts and income from personal services of more than $100 which they received from sources other than Government salary and securities income. Taxpayers were to be allowed to deduct from taxable income up to $100 for contributions to any candidate or political committee—local, state or federal—in each calendar year.

The Senate Rules and Administration Committee refused to hold hearings on the Presidential recommendations, reporting out instead a much weaker reform bill sponsored by Sen. Howard W. Cannon (D Nev.). But in the House Administration Committee, several days of hearings were held and a subcommittee drafted a bill closing loopholes in the presidential measure and strengthening it in several respects. No House action was taken.

• At the urging of Senate Finance Committee Chairman Russell B. Long (D La.), the Senate added to the Foreign Investors Tax Act, and both houses of Congress approved, a measure establishing a Presidential Election Campaign Fund, to be financed by voluntary $1 tax form checkoffs by the country's taxpayers. The measure was expected to channel $30 million or more into the Presidential campaign chests of each major party in presidential election years. Though the legislation was criticized on a number of counts, President Johnson signed it into law and it was expected to act as a catalyst for further congressional action in financing federal campaigns. Congress, however, in 1967 made the bill inoperative. *(Below)*

• In the wake of widespread adverse publicity about political journals published by the major political parties with tax-deductible corporate ads at rates of up to $15,000 a page, Sen. John J. Williams (R Del.) persuaded the Senate Finance Committee to attach an amendment to the Administration's excise tax bill totally prohibiting tax deductions for the cost of advertisements in political advertising journals. No move was made to strike the amendment as it went through the House and Senate, and it became law with the President's signature March 15. The amendment deprived national political committees of a growing source of indirect income and cut off a traditional source of funds for state and local political committees, thus adding to pressures for other laws to help the parties with their financing problems.

1967—Congress made inoperative Sen. Long's 1966 measure establishing a Presidential Election Campaign Fund, but the fight over the action (HR 6950) tied up the Senate for more than five weeks.

The Senate passed a bill (S 1880) that extended the reporting requirements of the Corrupt Practices Act to spending in all primaries and conventions for President, Senator or Representative. The bill, the broadest campaign finance reform measure ever to clear a chamber of

Congress, also required reports from intrastate political committees, which were exempted by existing law, and removed the existing ceilings on spending by political committees and Congressional candidates.

A subcommittee of the House Administration Committee reported an even more comprehensive bill (HR 11233), sponsored by Reps. Robert T. Ashmore (D S.C.) and Charles E. Goodell (R N.Y.), but the bill remained stalled in the full committee. A coalition of Northern Democrats, who feared restrictions on spending by organized labor, and of Southern Democrats, who opposed the bill's reporting requirements for primaries, blocked full committee approval.

Sen. Long's Finance Committee in November reported a bill (HR 4890) which embodied S 1880 plus a comprehensive plan for federal subsidies to Presidential and Senate campaigns. However, no further action was taken on the measure.

1968—Congress again failed to act on campaign financing and reporting reform. Congress, however, did pass a bill (HR 17325) to permit tax deductions for corporate advertising in Presidential nominating convention programs.

Action in Congress, 1969-70

Both sessions of the 91st Congress (1969-70) showed signs of readiness to take action to regulate campaign spending. However, only one bill (S 3637), which concerned allocation of broadcasting time, was passed by both houses and it was vetoed.

S 2876, 91st Congress, was a bill to provide television time at reduced rates to candidates for the Senate and the House. The bill would have allowed candidates to purchase a limited amount of spot advertising time at 30 percent of commercial rates, and a limited amount of program time at 20 percent of commercial rates. Philip A. Hart (D Mich.) and James B. Pearson (R Kan.) introduced the bill, with 34 additional sponsors. A similar bill, having 34 sponsors, was introduced in the House. The Senate Commerce Subcommittee on Communications in October 1969 conducted hearings on S 2876 but submitted no report to the full committee. There were no hearings on the corresponding bill in the House.

The Senate Committee on Rules and Administration reported July 15 the Election Reform Bill of 1970 (S 734), which would allow a tax credit for political contributions, repeal the $3 million limit on spending by a political committee and require the Secretary of the Senate and the Clerk of the House to publicize reports filed by candidates and political committees. No further action was taken.

NIXON VETO

The one campaign-financing bill passed by Senate and House in 1970 was limited to political broadcasts. President Nixon vetoed the bill, largely on the ground that it was not more comprehensive. More than half of the Senators voted to override the veto, but their votes were short of the required two-thirds majority.

Passage of the Bill. S 3637 would have limited spending on political broadcasts by candidates for election to the two houses of Congress, the Presidency and the governorship of a state. The limits for Senate and House candidates in the primaries would have been $10,000 or three and one-half cents per vote cast in the previous general election, whichever was greater, and, in the general election, $20,000 or seven cents per vote cast in the previous general election, whichever was greater. The bill also would have made possible television debates between the major parties' candidates for President by repealing the equal-time requirements of the Communications Act of 1934.

The Senate passed S 3637 on April 14, 1970, by a vote of 58-27. The House on Aug. 11 passed the bill with amendments which, among other things, applied the bill's restrictions to primary as well as general elections. Conferees accepted the House version after changing the effective date of the measure from Jan. 1, 1971, to 30 days after enactment. Neither House nor Senate Republican conferees signed the conference report. The House adopted the report, by a vote of 247-112, on Sept. 16. By this time, it was too late for the measure's restrictions to be applied in the 1970 campaign. Final Congressional action came when the Senate on Sept. 23 adopted the report by a vote of 60-19.

Unexpected Veto. President Nixon vetoed S 3637 on Oct. 12, 1970, the last day on which he could sign or veto the bill. If he had kept it longer, it would have become law without his signature. Since the President had not made known his opposition, Members of both houses were under the impression that he would sign the bill.

S 3637, the President said in his veto message, represented "a good aim gone amiss." He called it a measure which "plugs only one hole in a sieve," and said he was vetoing it because it:

• "Discriminates against the broadcast media" by imposing spending limits on only one means of communication and leaving unrestricted campaign advertising in print media.

• "Might tend to increase rather than decrease the total amount that candidates spend in their campaigns." Wealthy candidates "would simply shift their advertising out of radio and television into other media."

• "Unfairly endangers freedom of discussion." By restricting the amount of time a candidate could obtain on television and radio, it "would severely limit the ability of many candidates to get their message to the greatest number of the electorate."

• "Gives an unfair advantage to the famous" over "the worthy but little-known" and to "the incumbent officeholder over the office-seeker."

Veto Sustained. On Nov. 20, before the Senate voted again on the vetoed bill, the President wrote to Senate Minority Leader Hugh Scott (R Pa.) endorsing Scott's announced plan to propose a comprehensive election reform bill early in 1971. The President's letter said: "Reform is needed in this area, but this issue need not and should not be dealt with in a hurried and contentious fight over a veto. There will be no major elections between now and the time that Congress can consider this legislation in the next session."

The Senate on Nov. 23 sustained the President's veto by a four-vote margin. The vote was 58 for overriding (62 needed) and 34 against. Failure of the Senate to override made a House vote unnecessary.

CONGRESSIONAL ACTION: REFORM BILL NEAR ENACTMENT

Members of the House and Senate, with more than a casual interest and expertise in the field of campaign financing, acted in 1971 on election reform plans designed to end the spiraling costs of running for public office.

The Federal Election Campaign Act of 1971 (S 382) was passed by the Senate Aug. 5 and the House Nov. 30. The legislation placed limits on the amounts candidates for Congress and the Presidency could spend for television and other communications media, and included comprehensive requirements for reporting and disclosure of political contributions and expenditures.

Legislators were under considerable pressure to meet an early deadline on political finance reform if it were to apply to the 1972 presidential and congressional elections. Even as the proposals were introduced, potential candidates from major parties were collecting and spending sizeable amounts to fund campaign organizations in preparation for the 1972 campaigns.

The House-Senate conference committee filed a report on S 382 Dec. 14, and the Senate adopted the report the same day. However, final action by the House was postponed until after Congress returned from the holiday recess Jan. 18. The law would become effective 60 days after the President signed it.

Mr. Nixon issued a statement Dec. 11 through his congressional liaison Clark MacGregor that he would sign the bill when it was cleared by Congress.

The reform thrust was spurred by constant pressure from various groups, including National Committee for an Effective Congress, Common Cause, labor organizations and some media representatives.

Attempts at reform began in the early days of the 92nd Congress, when numerous election change measures were introduced in the House and Senate. The Senate bills were referred simultaneously to three Senate committees—Commerce (with jurisdiction over broadcasting), Rules (with jurisdiction over election matters), and Finance (with jurisdiction over tax proposals).

Of the many campaign finance reform plans introduced, the one which came closest to being a Nixon Administration bill was S 956, cosponsored by Senate Minority Leader Hugh Scott (R Pa.) and Sen. Charles McC. Mathias (R Md.).

Although Scott stressed March 3 that his bill had not been written by the Nixon Administration, he said "The President is aware of the contents of our bill, and 85 to 90 percent of it has his approval. If S 956 were passed as introduced, the President would sign it."

Mr. Nixon was committed to some form of major campaign overhaul. In his veto message Oct. 12, 1970, he said "I am as opposed to big spending in campaigns as I am to big spending in government," and he praised the "highly laudable and widely supported goals of controlling political campaign expenditures."

Lack of Partisanship. Proponents of campaign reform, cognizant of the partisan considerations that could have

---

Key Provisions of S 382

As cleared by the Senate-House conference committee Dec. 14, the Federal Election Campaign Act of 1971 (S 382) contained the following key provisions:

- Retained the "equal time" requirement of the Communications Act of 1934.
- Limited to 10 cents per voter the amount that could be spent by candidates for Congress and the Presidency for advertising on television, radio, newspapers, magazines, billboards and automatic telephone equipment. Up to 60 percent of the over-all media limitation could be spent for broadcasting purposes.
- Required broadcasters to sell candidates advertising at the lowest unit rate in effect for the time and space used. The requirement would be in effect during the last 45 days preceding a primary election and the last 60 days preceding a general election.
- Provided for an escalation in the media spending limit based on annual increases in the Consumer Price Index.
- Strengthened the requirements for reporting to the public how much a candidate spent on his campaign and his sources of contributions and other income.
- Specified that all candidates and political committees report names and addresses of all persons who made contributions or loans in excess of $100, and of all persons to whom expenditures in excess of $100 were made.
- Authorized as the supervisory officers for collection of campaign reports the Secretary of the Senate for Senate candidates, the House Clerk for House candidates and the Comptroller General for presidential candidates. Copies of reports would be filed with the secretaries of state in those states where the election was held.
- Defined more strictly the roles unions and corporations could play in political campaigns.
- Limited the amount a candidate or his family could contribute to his own campaign to $50,000 for President or Vice President, $35,000 for Senator and $25,000 for Representative.
- Repealed the Corrupt Practices Act of 1925.

---

threatened revision of campaign laws, worked to avoid writing a law that could benefit any political party or candidate. Republicans, aware of the relatively healthy financial state of their party in 1971, were eager to protect their coffers, while Democrats did not want to jeopardize their contributions from organized labor.

(Continued on p. 46)

Conflicting Pressures On 1971 Spending Bill

Although not officially a lobby group, the National Committee for an Effective Congress (NCEC) served as the umbrella organization for groups attempting to create a strong campaign finance law in 1971. NCEC, a nonpartisan group formed in 1947, raised $236,231 for congressional campaigns in 1968.

"NCEC designated campaign finance reform as a major legislative goal about 2½ years ago," said Susan King, representing the Washington office of the group. "When we saw that media budgets for campaigns were doubling and tripling with every election, we decided to concentrate on reducing the broadcast costs."

Congress agreed, but broadcasters and the Nixon Administration didn't. The result was a veto of the 1970 bill, because, Mr. Nixon said, the bill "discriminates against the broadcast media."

NCEC initiated a 1971 reform attempt by working with Senate Republican Leader Hugh Scott (Pa.) on a bill (S 956) that removed all limitations on campaign spending but placed restrictions on the amounts that could be contributed by individuals. In testimony March 3, 1971, before the Senate Commerce Communications Subcommittee, Scott said, "If S 956 were passed as introduced, the President would sign it."

Administration Intervention

But then a confusing set of signals emanated from the Nixon Administration. The first came in mid-March when *The Wall Street Journal* told of a visit by Eugene S. Cowen, special assistant to the President, to Rep. John B. Anderson (R Ill.), sponsor of House legislation to put money limits on campaign expenses.

Cowen was reported to have told Anderson to throw out specific limits on campaign spending and endorse the Scott plan. Anderson, however, did not revise his own bill.

No spokesman for the Administration appeared during Senate hearings on campaign finance. But on March 22, in a television interview, President Nixon set forth another Administration approach.

"We do favor a limitation on expenses. There is no question about that. The point is how can we have one which will do two things: One, it must be comprehensive, and the other is it must not give an advantage to incumbents over challengers," Mr. Nixon said.

The following day, Senate Republicans blocked a markup session by the Commerce Committee on a campaign finance bill. Committee Republicans then demanded that hearings be reopened because, as Sen. Marlow W. Cook (R Ky.) said, "There are a number of uncertainties as to the full effects of this legislation."

Regarding the Administration's seeming vacillation on campaign financing, NCEC director Russell D. Hemenway charged March 31: "The Administration has found itself caught in the noose of its own rhetoric, and will be forced to publicly support reform while seeking behind the scenes to render any prospective legislation either toothless, or so riddled with controversial provisions as to defy congressional passage."

Broadcasters

The electronic media—radio and television—opposed the 1970 attempt to place limits on broadcast media spending by candidates. In 1971, they repeated that any limits on broadcasters should apply to all media, including newspapers, billboards and magazines. The bill reported by the Senate Commerce Committee April 23 complied with those stipulations.

The National Association of Broadcasters (NAB), representing 3,363 AM and FM radio stations, 537 television stations and all national radio and television networks, made its position clear March 5. "To require broadcasters to charge political candidates a lesser rate than charged other comparable purchasers of time would constitute an enforced subsidy for political broadcasting—a subsidy required of no other industry," said Vincent T. Wasilewski, president of the NAB.

Labor, Common Cause

Major labor organizations have not cited campaign finance revision as a prime legislative target in the 92nd Congress, although most have supported the concept of reform.

Howard McGuigan, registered lobbyist for the AFL-CIO, said his organization was "waiting to see what is sent to the floor. In the meantime, we're making our views known to the committee members."

At the AFL-CIO's Executive Council meeting in Miami in February, the group adopted a resolution calling for laws that would "give major party candidates equitable opportunities to reach the voters while at the same time minimizing dependence on wealthy individual contributors."

Evasion of legal restrictions on campaign financing was the motive for an action taken in 1971 by Common Cause, a new lobbying group that claimed 53,000 dues-paying members.

Common Cause on Jan. 11, 1971, filed with the U.S. District Court for the District of Columbia a "class action" complaint as authorized by the Federal Rules of Civil Procedure, alleging noncompliance with the Federal Corrupt Practices Act of 1925, with harmful results to members of the organization and others, and requesting "declaratory and injunctive relief."

Other groups which have endorsed tightened political finance laws include the Americans for Democratic Action, the United Auto Workers, International Association of Machinists, the American Association of Political Consultants and Twentieth Century Fund.

Final Provisions

As adopted Dec. 14 by a Senate-House conference committee, S 382 contained the following major provisions:

Title I—Campaign Communications

• Limited the total amount that could be spent by federal candidates for advertising time in communications media to 10 cents per eligible voter, or $50,000, whichever was greater. The limitation would apply to all candidates for President and Vice President, Senator, and Representative, and would be determined annually for the geographical area of each election by the Bureau of the Census.

• Included in the term "communications media" radio and television broadcasting stations, newspapers, magazines, billboards, and automatic telephone equipment. Of the total spending limit, up to 60 percent could be used for broadcast advertising time.

• Prohibited radio and television stations from charging political candidates more than the lowest unit cost for the same advertising time available to commercial advertisers. Lowest unit rate charges would apply only during the 45 days preceding a primary election and the 60 days preceding a general election.

• Required non-broadcast media to charge candidates no more than the comparable amounts charged to commercial advertisers for the same class and amount of advertising space. The requirement would apply only during the 45 days preceding the date of a primary election and 60 days before the date of a general election.

• Specified that candidates for presidential nomination, during the period prior to the nominating convention, could spend no more in primary or non-primary states than the amount allowed under the 10-cent-per-voter communications spending limitation.

• Provided that broadcast and non-broadcast spending limitations be increased in proportion to annual increases in the Consumer Price Index over the base year 1970.

• Provided that amounts spent by an agent of a candidate on behalf of his candidacy would be charged against the over-all expenditure allocation. Fees paid to the agent for services performed also would be charged against the over-all limitation.

• Stipulated that no broadcast station could make any charge for political advertising time on a station unless written consent to contract for such time had been given by the candidate, and unless the candidate certified that such charge would not exceed his spending limit.

Title II—Criminal Code Amendments

• Defined "election" to mean any general, special, primary or runoff election, nominating convention or caucus, delegate selection primary, presidential preference primary or constitutional convention.

• Broadened the definitions of "contribution" and "expenditure" as they pertain to political campaigns, but exempted a loan of money by a national or state bank made in accordance with applicable banking laws.

• Prohibited promises of employment or other political rewards or benefits by any candidate in exchange for political support, and prohibited contracts between candidates and any federal department or agency.

• Placed a ceiling on contributions by any candidates or his immediate family to his own campaign of $50,000 for President or Vice President, $35,000 for Senator, and $25,000 for Representative.

• Provided that the terms "contribution" and "expenditure" did not include communications, non-partisan registration and get-out-the-vote campaigns by a corporation aimed at its stockholders or by a labor organization aimed at its members.

• Provided that the terms "contribution" and "expenditure" did not include the establishment, administration and solicitation of voluntary contributions to a separate segregated fund to be utilized for political purposes by a corporation or labor organization.

Title III—Disclosure of Federal Campaign Funds

• Required all political committees that anticipated receipts in excess of $1,000 during the calendar year to file a statement of organization with the appropriate federal supervisory officer, and to include such information as the names of all principal officers, the scope of the committee, the names of all candidates the committee supported and other information as required by law.

• Required all political committees to have a chairman and a treasurer and prohibited any expenditure by the committee without the authorization of the chairman or treasurer.

• Stipulated that the appropriate federal supervisory officer to oversee election campaign practices, reporting and disclosure was the Clerk of the House for House candidates, the Secretary of the Senate for Senate candidates and the Comptroller General for presidential candidates.

• Required each political committee to report any individual expenditure of more than $100 and any expenditures of more than $100 in the aggregate during the calendar year.

• Required disclosure of all contributions to any committee or candidate in excess of $100, including a detailed report with the name and address of the contributor and the date the contribution was made.

• Required that any committee that accepted contributions or made expenditures on behalf of any candidate without the authorization of such candidate to include a notice on the front page of all literature published by the committee stating that the committee was not authorized by the candidate and that the candidate was not responsible for the activities of the committee.

• Required the supervisory officers to prepare an annual report for each committee registered with the commission and make such reports available for sale to the public.

• Required candidates and committees to file reports of contributions and expenditures on the 10th day of March, June and September every year, on the 15th and fifth days preceding the date on which an election was held and on the 31st day of January. Any contribution of $5,000 or more was to be reported within 48 hours after its receipt.

• Required reporting of the names, addresses and occupations of any lender and endorser of any loan in excess of $100 as well as the date and amount of such loans.

• Required reporting of the total proceeds from the sale of tickets to all fund-raising events, mass collections made at such events and sales of political campaign materials.

● Required any person who made any contribution in excess of $100, other than through a political committee or candidate, to report such contribution to the commission.

● Required a full and complete financial statement of the costs of holding a presidential nominating convention within 60 days after the end of the convention.

● Prohibited any contribution to a candidate or committee by one person in the name of another person.

● Authorized the office of the Comptroller General to serve as a national clearinghouse for information on the administration of election practices.

● Required political parties in states where presidential nominating conventions were held to file detailed reports on the financing of the convention with the office of the Comptroller General.

● Required that copies of reports filed by a candidate with the appropriate supervisory officer also be filed with the secretaries of state for the state in which the election was held.

Title IV—General Provisions

● Repealed the Federal Corrupt Practices Act of 1925 (2 U.S. Code 241-256).

● Required the Civil Aeronautics Board, the Federal Communications Commission and the Interstate Commerce Commission to promulgate regulations with respect to the extension of credit without collateral by any person, business or industry regulated by the federal government to any person on behalf of any candidate for federal office.

● Prohibited funds appropriated for the Office of Economic Opportunity from being used for any political activity.

Senate Committee Action

The Senate Commerce Committee May 6 reported with amendments S 382 (S Rept 92-96), the Federal Elections Campaign Act of 1971, placing limits on political campaign expenditures and contributions.

Title I of the bill limited campaign spending by candidates for federal office to 5 cents per eligible voter for broadcast media and 5 cents per voter for non-broadcast media in both primary and general elections.

The committee said the limitation would allow an estimated $13,956,300 for all media spending by a presidential candidate in the 1972 general election.

The 10-cent-per-voter limit would allow total media spending in 1972 Senate campaigns of $756,300 per candidate in Illinois, $394,700 in Massachusetts and $758,900 in Texas. Varying amounts were listed by the committee for other states, based on voting age population estimates of the Census Bureau.

Although the measure was reported by an 18-0 roll-call committee vote, 10 separate amendments to the bill offered by Republicans were defeated by record roll-call votes. Republicans gave dissenting views in the committee report.

Committee Views. In reporting the bill, the committee concluded "the legislation represents a major effort at reform in an area vital to our democratic society. The necessity for campaign reform is now beyond question and transcends special or partisan interests."

Minority Views. In a dissenting statement, five Republican committee members said the bill contained weaknesses which "stem not from its innovations, but rather from its adherence to some of the undesirable provisions of existing law."

In summary, the Republicans said the bill's defects were that it did not exempt all candidates for federal office from the equal time provisions; that it provided unrealistically low spending and contribution limits, and that it failed to provide for an independent Federal Elections Commission.

SENATE RULES COMMITTEE

The Senate Rules and Administration Committee June 21 reported a bill (S 382—S Rept 92-229), the Federal Election Campaign Act of 1971, placing limits on spending for political campaigns and requiring full disclosure of such spending.

The same bill had been reported May 6 by the Commerce Committee, and was referred to the Rules and Administration Committee for consideration of provisions within its jurisdiction.

Individual Views. Democratic and Republican members of the committee, although voting to report S 382, split in their opinions on the bill. Senators Prouty, Scott and John Sherman Cooper (R Ky.) said the bill "represents effective, meaningful and workable election campaign reform legislation which is long overdue."

Sen. James B. Allen (D Ala.) said the bill "did not go far enough" in limiting campaign expenditures. "I feel that an over-all limit should be placed on the total amount of campaign contributions and expenditures that a candidate may receive or spend."

Allen listed expenditures on which the bill placed no limits as "mass mailings, telephone lines, postage, stationery, automobiles, trucks, telegrams, campaign headquarters, campaign workers, airplane rentals, buses, trains, campaign newspapers, movie theater film advertisements, campaign staffs, public relations firms, production expenses for broadcasts, public opinion polls, paid campaigners and poll watchers, novelties, bumper stickers and sample ballots."

Sen. Howard W. Cannon (D Nev.), objecting to certain amendments added by the committee, said the provisions "go too far and will either create new outlets for excessive expenditures or impose inordinate reporting burdens upon political committees and certain businesses." Such amendments, he said, were "politically inspired."

Senate Floor Action

The Senate Aug. 5, by an 88-2 roll-call vote, passed a bill (S 382), the Federal Election Campaign Act of 1971.

The bill was debated in the Senate over a four-day period. The two Senators voting against S 382 were Arizona Republicans Barry Goldwater and Paul J. Fannin.

Majority Leader Mike Mansfield (D Mont.), noting the overwhelming support for the bill, said after the vote: "It is difficult to conceive of how this legislative measure could favor one party or the other."

The National Committee for an Effective Congress, chief pressure group supporting reform of campaign financing, called S 382 "the first real campaign controls in American political history" and labeled passage "a stunning reform victory."

As passed by the Senate, S 382 was more comprehensive than the bill vetoed in 1970 by President Nixon that only placed limits on radio and television spending.

Amendments introduced by Republican Senators and adopted by the Senate during the debate Aug. 2-5 were expected to make the bill acceptable to President Nixon. The Administration favored repeal of the equal time clause for all candidates for federal office and did not want any limitation placed on the amount private individuals could contribute to any campaign. Both Administration requirements were included in the Senate-approved bill.

DEBATE

Debate on S 382 began Aug. 2. Pastore said: "We have striven to give to the people of the country and also to candidates for federal office, whoever they may be—whether incumbents or opponents of incumbents—a guideline which is reasonable in measuring the costs and arriving at a ceiling" in order to bring about a sensible program of election reform.

Howard W. Cannon (D Nev.), chairman of the Senate Rules and Administration Elections Subcommittee, said the provisions on reporting and disclosure of campaign finances were to replace the Federal Corrupt Practices Act of 1925, which he termed old, obsolete and of no use at all today.

Republican floor manager of the bill Winston L. Prouty (R Vt.) said the "existing law is but a farce and the public knows it. The whole purpose of this legislation is to restore public confidence in the election process. We cannot afford to procrastinate."

Campaign Commission. Debate Aug. 3 began with consideration of an amendment by James B. Pearson (R Kan.) to establish an independent federal regulatory agency to oversee election costs and campaign practices. "I do not think we ought to turn it over to an agency which is bound by long association to be highly responsive to Congress, as is the General Accounting Office. I think we need a truly, genuinely independent commission."

Cannon, who spoke against the amendment because "it would set up another bureaucracy" and "would not be completely removed from politics," eventually supported the change. The amendment was adopted by an 89-2 roll-call vote.

Minority Leader Hugh Scott (R Pa.) introduced an amendment to prohibit extension of credit to candidates by federally regulated industries. "Because of their inability to protect themselves adequately, the airlines, telephone and telegraph companies have been placed in a position of unlawfully, unavoidably, and unintentionally—and I might add illegally—subsidizing political campaign expenses," Scott said.

The amendment was approved by voice vote after being modified to allow federal regulatory agencies to establish regulations regarding the extension of credit.

Senate Spending Limits

Under S 382 as passed by Senate, bill would allow use of up to 60 percent of allowable funds (based on 10 cents per eligible voter in each state) for either broadcast or non-broadcast media advertising. Table below reflects spending ceilings permitted for 1972 Senate elections if candidate chooses to spend maximum on broadcast advertising.

State	Broadcast 60 Percent	Non-Broadcast 40 Percent	Media Limit
Ala.	$137,460	$ 91,640	$229,100
Alaska	36,000	24,000	60,000*
Ariz.	73,620	49,080	122,700
Ark.	79,080	52,720	131,800
Calif.	854,220	569,480	1,423,700
Colo.	91,920	61,280	153,200
Conn.	127,020	84,680	211,700
Del.	36,000	24,000	60,000*
Fla.	305,280	203,520	508,800
Ga.	186,660	124,440	311,100
Hawaii	36,000	24,000	60,000*
Idaho	36,000	24,000	60,000*
Ill.	453,780	302,520	756,300
Ind.	209,220	139,480	348,700
Iowa	113,220	75,480	188,700
Kan.	92,340	61,560	153,900
Ky.	130,620	87,080	217,700
La.	141,360	94,240	235,600
Maine	39,720	26,480	66,200
Md.	162,900	108,600	271,500
Mass.	236,820	157,880	394,700
Mich.	352,500	235,000	587,500
Minn.	151,380	100,920	252,300
Miss.	84,720	56,480	141,200
Mo.	193,320	128,880	322,200
Mont.	36,000	24,000	60,000*
Neb.	60,120	40,080	100,200
Nev.	36,000	24,000	60,000*
N.H.	36,000	24,000	60,000*
N.J.	301,080	200,720	501,800
N.M.	37,980	25,320	63,300
N.Y.	762,840	508,560	1,271,400
N.C.	209,580	139,720	349,300
N.D.	36,000	24,000	60,000*
Ohio	429,900	286,600	716,500
Okla.	107,460	71,640	179,100
Ore.	88,380	58,920	147,300
Pa.	488,160	325,440	813,600
R.I.	40,260	26,840	67,100
S.C.	102,900	68,600	171,500
S.D.	36,000	24,000	60,000*
Tenn.	162,600	108,400	271,000
Texas	455,340	303,560	758,900
Utah	40,440	26,960	67,400
Vt.	36,000	24,000	60,000*
Va.	193,920	129,280	323,200
Wash.	142,860	95,240	238,100
W.Va.	70,500	47,000	117,500
Wis.	176,880	117,920	294,800
Wyo.	36,000	24,000	60,000*

Minimum figure under Senate bill.

SOURCE: Bureau of the Census Estimates of the Total Resident Population of Voting Age, November 1972.

Equal Time. An amendment then was introduced by Prouty to repeal the equal broadcast time clause for all candidates for federal office and to give candidates "maximum flexibility" in choice of television and radio program format. Pastore, who warned that the amendment "would place a campaign more or less at the whim of an affluent licensee," said he approved the change "because I think over-all the industry has reached the stage of maturity in which it can be trusted."

Cannon said: "We are putting a tremendous weapon in the hands of the broadcaster, whether television or radio. He could select the people to whom he wants to give time and he would not have to give equal time to all candidates." The amendment was passed by a 71-21 roll-call vote.

Coverage. Charles McC. Mathias Jr. (R Md.) offered an amendment to bring under the requirements of the bill all candidates—announced or unannounced—who were allowing money to be collected for a political campaign. "When we are talking about a man who has publicly announced his candidacy for office or who allows other people to puff up his candidacy with his knowledge and without any denial on his part, we are talking about a man who ought to be covered," Mathias said. "I think the loophole is too big."

A motion to table the amendment was accepted by a 51-40 vote which divided closely on party lines. Among Democratic Senators who voted to table were potential 1972 presidential candidates Fred R. Harris (Okla.), Hubert H. Humphrey (Minn.), Henry M. Jackson (Wash.), Edward M. Kennedy (Mass.), George McGovern (S.D.) and Edmund S. Muskie (Maine.)

Limit Increase Proposal. Another controversial amendment, introduced by Prouty, would have doubled from 5 cents to 10 cents per voter the amount candidates could spend for either broadcast or non-broadcast advertising. Under the amendment, candidates could transfer funds, after the 5-cent-per-vote limit was reached in one medium, to the other.

Prouty said the 5-cent-per-voter limit for radio and television spending—and a similar limit for print media—was "incumbent insurance." He said it would aggravate a situation in which "more than 93 percent of the Congressmen and Senators who have run for re-election since 1940 have been successful."

Howard H. Baker Jr. (D Tenn.) supported the change: "The lack of interchangeability of campaign allowances is a distinct step backward. We do not need to regiment and institutionalize the process of campaigning," he said.

Pastore, adamantly opposed to the amendment, said he would compromise only on a partial interchangeability allowance. Prouty modified his amendment to allow a 20-percent transfer from one spending limit to another. The effect of the amendment, which passed by voice vote, was to allow a candidate to spend up to 6 cents per voter for either broadcast or non-broadcast media advertising. *(Box, p. 48)*

Rich Man's Amendment. Another hotly contested debate occurred Aug. 4 over an amendment by Mathias and Lawton Chiles (D Fla.) to place a limit of $5,000 on the amount an individual could contribute to any one candidate or campaign committee. The proposal also limited the amount a wealthy candidate could contribute to his own campaign.

Scott, who early in 1971 favored a limit on individual contributions, said the Mathias-Chiles amendment was "another rich man's amendment," that would not be constitutional, would be opposed strongly in the House and would be "unworkable and unenforceable."

Norris Cotton (R N.H.), who moved to table the amendment, said: "The people can determine if a man is trying to buy a seat. But there is nothing we can put on that will not give a rich man an advantage." Sen. Peter H. Dominick (R Colo.) said: "I do not see any reason why, just because somebody's family may have some money, they are prohibited from contributing. This is an exercise of free speech, of political participation." The Cotton motion was then rejected by a 33-58 vote.

The amendment eventually was agreed to after the $5,000 individual contribution limit was deleted. As approved, the amendment placed limits on the amounts candidates could contribute to their own campaigns.

Another attempt to force a vote on the $5,000 individual contribution limit was made by Mathias and Chiles. Chiles said the amendment would prevent a wealthy contributor from "buying a stable of favors and considerations from beholding Senators and Representatives."

Veto Threat. Scott added: "If this amendment goes into the bill, we are not going to get any bill, because the bill will be vetoed, and I would support the veto."

Baker said the amendment was a "morass of uncertainty" that could cause "disastrous trouble" if enacted without thorough investigation. Pastore, who did not commit himself on the amendment, said "this is a very, very controversial area. I do not want to do anything to jeopardize the bill." The amendment was rejected by voice vote.

Spot Advertisements. Vance Hartke (D Ind.) and Adlai E. Stevenson III (D Ill.) sponsored an amendment to prohibit television stations from selling advertising time to candidates in periods of less than one minute duration, thus reducing the use of "spot" advertising in campaigns.

Hartke said spot ads were "diabolical," promoted "superficial imagery" and were used "to cloud the issues and belie the truth." Hartke cited estimates that candidates for major offices spend 95 percent of their broadcast funds on spot ads. The amendment was tabled by a 74-17 roll-call vote.

Labor Fund. Dominick put forth an amendment to prohibit dues or assessments collected by any organization from its members to be used in support of any political candidacy. Robert P. Griffin (R Mich.), in support of the change, said: "I do not see how any Senator can maintain he is for campaign spending reform if he is against this amendment."

Mike Gravel (D Alaska) called the amendment "sheer anti-labor legislation" and an "effort to gut the ability of organized labor to participate in the democratic process." Gravel said the amendment made "second class citizens out of people who belong to labor unions" and suggested that similar controls be placed on corporation executives who made political contributions. The amendment was tabled by a 56-38 roll-call vote.

Voter Registration Drives. An amendment by Robert W. Packwood (R Ore.) to require disclosure of $500 or more where used to sponsor get-out-the-vote drives or voter education projects was tabled by a 60-28 roll-call vote.

Advertising Costs. Carl T. Curtis (R Neb.) sponsored an amendment to eliminate provisions requiring broadcasters and newspapers to provide the lowest unit advertising rate to political candidates. "It is not morally right that we should impose price fixing for our benefit." The amendment was defeated by a 31-55 vote which closely divided on party lines.

Possible Loophole. Edward M. Kennedy (D Mass.), in a brief exchange with Pastore at the close of debate on S 382, asserted there was a possible loophole in the bill. Kennedy said that an escalator clause to raise the limits on media spending based on increases in cost of living would produce "generous" limits by 1972. Pastore conceded that the limit would be pushed up by the cost-of-living provision.

The escalator clause was inserted in the bill by Marlow W. Cook (R Ky.) during committee consideration. It allowed the limits to be increased and rounded to the next highest cent based on the annual increase in the Consumer Price Index.

Senate Provisions

As passed by the Senate, S 382 contained the following major provisions:

Title I—Amendments to Communications Act of 1934; Limitations on Campaign Expenditures

• Repealed the equal time provision of the Communications Act of 1934 for all major candidates for President, Vice President, Senator, Representative, Delegate and Resident Commissioner.

• Required broadcast station licensees who granted air time to candidates to permit such candidates maximum flexibility in choosing program format.

• Prohibited radio and television stations from charging political candidates more than the lowest unit cost for the same advertising time available to commercial advertisers. The lowest unit cost would be determined by using the published advertising rates for commercial buyers and charging the lowest amount listed for the same quantity and time period (such as prime time). Lowest unit rates would apply only during the 45 days preceding the date of a primary election and 60 days before the date of a general or special election. The limitation on the time period for using the lower rates was stipulated in an effort to shorten campaigns.

• Required non-broadcast media—newspapers, magazines and other periodical publications and billboards—to charge candidates no more than the lowest unit cost for the same class and amount of advertising space charged to commercial advertisers. The requirement would apply only during the 45 days preceding the date of a primary election and 60 days before the date of a general or special election.

• Limited the expenditures made by a candidate during any primary, runoff, special or general election to a combined total of 5 cents per eligible voter for non-broadcast media advertising and 5 cents per eligible voter for broadcast media advertising, or a combined total of $60,000, whichever figure was larger. The number of eligible voters would be determined in advance by the Bureau of the Census.

• Allowed a candidate to transfer up to 20 percent of either the broadcast or non-broadcast spending limit from one category to the other.

• Specified that amounts spent for campaign advertising on behalf of a candidate would be deemed to have been spent by such candidate and that no person could make any charge for the use of broadcast or non-broadcast facilities unless the candidate, or an individual specifically authorized by such candidate in writing to do so, certified that the payment would not violate the spending limitation.

• During presidential primary elections, the spending limit would be determined by the entire resident population of voting age in the state in which the primary was being held.

• Limitations on media spending would be increased according to the percentage rise in the cost of living as computed through the Consumer Price Index by the Bureau of Labor Statistics, Department of Labor. Differences in percentage increases from the previous calendar year would be rounded to the next highest cent.

Title II—Criminal Code Amendments

• Defined "election" to mean any general, special, primary or runoff election, nominating convention or caucus, delegate selection primary, presidential preference primary or constitutional convention.

• Broadened the definitions of "contribution" and "expenditure" as they pertain to political campaigns.

• Prohibited promises of employment or other political rewards or benefits by any candidate in exchange for political support, and prohibited contracts between candidates and any federal department or agency.

• Placed a ceiling on contributions by any candidate or his immediate family to his own campaign of $50,000 for President or Vice President; $35,000 for Senator, and $25,000 for Representative, Delegate or Resident Commissioner.

Title III—Disclosure of Federal Campaign Funds

• Established a Federal Elections Commission, composed of six members appointed by the President on a bipartisan basis for staggered 12-year terms, to oversee election campaign practices and monitor disclosures of contributions and expenditures.

• Required all political committees to have a chairman and a treasurer and prohibited any expenditure by the committee without the authorization of the chairman or treasurer.

• Required all political committees that anticipated receipts in excess of $1,000 during the calendar year to file a statement of organization with the Federal Elections Commission, including such information as the names of all principal officers, the scope of the committee, the names of all candidates the committee supported and other information as required by the commission.

• Required each political committee to report to the commission any individual expenditure of more than $100 and any expenditures of more than $100 in the aggregate during the calendar year.

• Required disclosure of all contributions to any committee or candidate in excess of $10, including a detailed report with the name and address of the contributor and the date the contribution was made.

• Required that any committee that accepted contributions or made expenditures on behalf of any candidate without the authorization of such candidate to include a notice on the front page of all literature published by the committee stating that the committee was not authorized by the candidate and that the candidate was not responsible for the activities of the committee.

• Required the Federal Elections Commission to prepare an annual report for each committee registered with the commission and make such reports available for sale to the public.

• Required candidates and committees to file reports of contributions and expenditures on the 10th day of March, June and September every year, on the 15th and fifth days preceding the date on which an election was held and on the 31st day of January. Any contribution of $5,000 or more was to be reported within 48 hours after its receipt.

• Required reporting of the names, addresses and occupations of any lender and endorser of any loan in excess of $100 as well as the date and amount of such loans.

• Required reporting of the total proceeds from the sale of tickets to all fund-raising events, mass collections made at such events and sales of political campaign materials.

• Required any person who made any contribution in excess of $100, other than through a political committee or candidate, to report such contribution to the commission.

• Required a full and complete financial statement of the costs of holding a presidential nominating convention within 60 days after the end of the convention.

• Required that any financial statement of contributions or expenditures filed with the commission also be filed with the clerk of the United States district court for the judicial district in which was located the principal office of the candidate or political committee.

• Prohibited any contribution to a candidate or committee by one person in the name of another person.

• Repealed the Federal Corrupt Practices Act of 1925 (2 United States Code 241-256).

Title IV—Extensions of Credit by Regulated Industries

• Required the Civil Aeronautics Board, the Federal Communications Commission and the Interstate Commerce Commission to promulgate regulations with respect to the extension of credit without collateral by any person, business or industry regulated by the federal government to any person on behalf of any candidate for federal office.

Amendments Rejected. Aug. 3—Charles McC. Mathias Jr. (R Md.)—Broaden definition of legally qualified candidate to include any person who, although not an announced candidate, has knowledge that contributions and expenditures are being made for the purpose of bringing about his nomination or election to office. A motion to table the amendment was made by John O. Pastore (D R.I.) and agreed to by the Senate. Roll-call vote, 51-40.

Robert W. Packwood (R Ore.)— Require that any loan of $10,000 or more during a calendar year to a candidate be reported within five days to the Federal Elections Commission. Motion to table amendment made by Howard W. Cannon (D Nev.) and agreed to by the Senate. Roll call, 48-43.

Aug. 4—Mathias—Limit to $5,000 the amount which an individual may contribute to any one political candidate, and limit to $5,000 the amount which any individual can contribute to a political committee for a political candidate. Voice vote.

Vance Hartke (D Ind.)—Prohibit any television station from selling or otherwise making available broadcast time in segments of less than one minute duration for use by or on behalf of a candidate for federal office. Motion to table made by John O. Pastore (D R.I.) and agreed to by the Senate. Roll call, 74-17.

Peter H. Dominick (R Colo.)—Prohibit use of dues, assessments or other money collected by any labor organization from its members to be used for the benefit of any candidate for federal office. Motion to table amendment made by Pastore and agreed to by the Senate. Roll call, 56-38.

Aug. 5—Packwood—Require reports of campaign contributions to be completed two days ahead of the filing deadline, instead of the five days required under the bill. Motion to table amendment made by Pastore and agreed to by the Senate. Roll call, 73-10.

Packwood—Require disclosure of the names of individuals who act as guarantors or surety of extension of credit for any debt incurred by a political committee in behalf of a candidate. Motion to table amendment made by Cannon and agreed to by the Senate. Roll call, 53-30.

Packwood—Require disclosure of any transfer of $500 or more in funds for the purpose of sponsoring get-out-the-vote drives or voter-education projects by any organization. Motion to table amendment made by Pastore and agreed to by the Senate. Roll call, 60-28.

Packwood—Prohibit extension of additional credit to political committees by industries or businesses regulated by the Interstate Commerce Commission, the Federal Communications Commission and the Civil Aeronautics Board if previous such debts of political committees have not been paid within two years. Motion to table amendment made by Pastore and agreed to by the Senate. Roll call, 46-42.

James B. Allen (D Ala.)—Allow an additional 10 cents per eligible voter or $60,000, whichever is greater, for campaign expenses other than broadcast and non-broadcast advertising. Roll call, 31-60.

Carl T. Curtis (R Neb.)—Delete provisions requiring broadcast and non-broadcast media to charge the "lowest unit rate" for advertising to political candidates. Roll call, 31-55.

House Committee Action

Two House committees Oct. 13 reported separate bills designed to curb political campaign spending and provide for full disclosure of election financing.

Jurisdiction over the subject of campaign practices was divided between the House Administration and Interstate and Foreign Commerce Committees, but the two bills reported (HR 8628 and HR 11060) were merged during floor consideration.

Although similar in intent, the bills differed in their approaches. HR 8628 placed limits on various media expenses in federal elections and repeals the equal time requirements for presidential and vice presidential candidates. HR 11060 places over-all spending ceilings on federal election campaigns and requires detailed disclosure of all contributions and expenditures.

Bipartisan support for revision of existing campaign spending laws was made clear when House Speaker Carl Albert (D Okla.) and Minority Leader Gerald R. Ford (R Mich.) declared they would push for House passage of a campaign spending bill.

COMMERCE COMMITTEE

The Interstate and Foreign Commerce Committee Oct. 13, by a 23-20 record vote, reported HR 8628, repealing the equal time requirement of the Communications Act of 1934 for presidential and vice presidential candidates and placing spending limits on broadcast and newspaper advertising.

The vote to order the bill reported came Oct. 6, when Torbert H. Macdonald (D Mass.), chairman of the communications subcommittee, offered a substitute bill to the committee version. The Macdonald subsitute contained a key provision limiting broadcast expenses to 5 cents per voter in federal elections.

Committee Views. Urging passage of the bill, the committee said, "The media covered by the legislation are today the most important and effective means of campaigning for federal elective office. If the federal elective process is not to be dominated by special monied interests there must be reasonable and effective limitations on the cost of these media to candidates and on expenditures by candidates for such media."

The committee said the broadcast limitation was "the heart of the legislation. Without it there are no reasonable limitations on expenditures for broadcast time." It was noted, however, that any candidate could, if he wanted, be able to spend all or any part of the total 10-cent-per-voter media limitation on newspaper and magazine advertising.

In defending repeal of the equal time clause for presidential and vice presidential but not other federal candidates, the committee said that without "the spotlight of national attention" on House and Senate candidates, there would be no safeguard against abuse by local licensees.

Dissenting Views. In separate views filed by William L. Springer (R Ill.) and 10 other Republicans, HR 8628 was termed a "sweetheart bill designed to assure as far as legislation can do the continuation of incumbent Congressmen in office, and as such it should be substantially changed or rejected."

ADMINISTRATION COMMITTEE

The House Administration Committee Oct. 13, by a 20-4 roll-call vote, reported HR 11060, the Federal Election Reform Act of 1971.

The four votes against reporting the bill were cast by Republicans Samuel L. Devine (Ohio), James Harvey (Mich.), John Ware (Pa.) and Bill Frenzel (Minn.).

Before reporting the measure, Republican members attempted to substitute the Senate-passed bill (S 382) for the committee version—an effort that failed by a 15-8 vote.

Committee Views. The committee defended its provisions which set an over-all campaign spending limitation by labeling as "unfair" a legal ceiling on media spending. "To insist that no more than a certain percentage may be spent in a particular manner is to operate unfairly as to those candidates who cannot utilize a predesignated type of campaign spending effectively. It is also manifestly unfair to the constituencies which those candidates seek to represent since it deprives the voters of communications from their candidates and from receiving information which as voters they are entitled to receive."

Other Views. Three Democrats on the committee filed separate views on the report. The three, Jonathan B. Bingham (N.Y.), Lucien N. Nedzi (Mich.) and Augustus F. Hawkins (Calif.), criticized provisions that made congressional employees the supervisory officers of campaign disclosures. The members also said the dates that reports should be filed were not sufficient to allow the public to know of "ongoing activities" of political committees.

Another view on the bill was given by Devine and seven other Republicans. They attacked the spending limits in the bill as "arbitrary and unrealistic" and said they would constitute an "incumbent's bill" if enacted. "Placing a limitation on total campaign spending amounts to a classic case of legislating in the dark," the members said.

In additional views, Frenzel said "the sweeping over-all restriction may invite violations of the law because such violations may be extremely difficult to document or prove."

Frenzel also termed "a serious loophole" the provision that allowed for only two reporting dates.

House Floor Action

The House Nov. 30, by a 372-23 roll-call vote, passed the Federal Election Campaign Act of 1971 (HR 11060), to regulate political campaign spending by candidates for Congress and the Presidency.

The bill was substantially the same as S 382, a bill passed Aug. 5 in the Senate by an 88-2 vote. After passage, the House requested a conference with the Senate to resolve differences between the two versions.

Although campaign reform encountered opposition during floor debate to some provisions of the bill, House members exhibited bipartisanship during much of the debate.

Pressure groups such as the National Committee for an Effective Congress and Common Cause hailed the House passage and expressed optimism that President Nixon would sign the bill.

Mr. Nixon Dec. 1 was reported by Clarence J. Brown (R Ohio) as "very pleased with the House-passed bill."

Combined Bills. As passed by the House, the bill was a combination of the reporting and disclosure provisions of the Senate-passed bill, introduced in a House companion bill by Clarence J. Brown (R Ohio) and Bill Frenzel (R Minn.), and the media spending limitations provisions introduced by Torbert H. Macdonald (D Mass.), chairman of the Communications and Power Subcommittee of the Interstate and Foreign Commerce Committee. Most of the reporting and disclosure provisions of the original House bill (HR 11060) introduced by House Administration Committee Chairman Hays were eliminated by the substitution of the Senate version.

Morris K. Udall (D Ariz.) and John B. Anderson (R Ill.), who headed a bipartisan movement in the House to reform campaign financing practices, praised the House action. "We have a crackerjack bill here," Udall said. "It will stop millionaries from buying Senate seats and the Presidency. It brings this television monster under control."

Anderson concluded the more than two days of debate with: "We have accomplished the almost miraculous task of melding together two House committee bills and a Senate bill and have come up with a very acceptable piece of legislation."

Debate Nov. 18

Fewer than 40 members of the House were present during general debate on the campaign spending issue Nov. 18. Major points of contention were repeal of the equal broadcast time provision for all candidates, the question of partisanship on setting over-all campaign expenditure limits and the charge that the bills would provide "incumbent protection insurance."

Macdonald said the legislation was "a public interest bill" that would eliminate "the spectre of money running politics." He supported repeal of the equal time clause for presidential and vice presidential candidates but not for Senate or House candidates. He told House members: "If we repeal equal time for House candidates, a local broadcaster can give free time to your opponent, and then refuse to sell time to you."

Rep. John B. Anderson (R Ill.) said repeal of equal time only for presidential candidates was "an obvious partisan political swipe at President Nixon."

Representatives William L. Springer (R Ill.) and Samuel L. Devine (R Ohio) said the legislation was "rife with politics" and there were "serious constitutional doubts" about the validity of placing spending limits on candidates. Springer said the bills should be recommitted because they would "assure the re-election of every member of this House until he retires or dies."

Rep. Morris K. Udall (D Ariz.), supporting the Senate-passed bill, noted that 90 percent of House incumbents won re-election in 1968 and 96.7 percent in 1970. He asked: "How much more showing for the incumbent can we have than we have now?"

Rep. James Harvey (R Mich.) said the House should adopt the Senate bill because "the President has said he would live with it and would not veto it, the House minority leadership supports it and the Senate has already passed it."

Nov. 29

Equal Time. The divisive issue of allowing candidates for the same political office equal air time on local and network broadcasts threatened during early consideration of the bill to delay final action.

The first of three amendments on the subject was offered by Lionel Van Deerlin (D Calif.). He recommended repeal of Section 315(a) of the Communications Act of 1934 (the equal time provision) for presidential, vice presidential and Senate candidates and sought a study of the effects of repeal for House candidates.

James Harvey (R Mich.), opposing the amendment, told House members: "The sole question when you repeal Section 315...is whether or not you believe that the broadcasters across America have achieved that degree of maturity so that you can trust them."

Hays responded: "I do not trust them at all. I do not think you can trust them to be discreet about whom they give time to and whom they do not. I do not think you can trust them to be fair about how and to whom they give time and from whom they withhold it. I do not think there is a remote possibility that they would not be prejudiced and do exactly as they please."

Morris K. Udall (D Ariz.) said campaigns for the House were "special situations" that presented "435 special problems" of equal time considerations. "There are members on both sides of the aisle in this House who are under the thumb of just one broadcaster in particular situations," Udall said. "I do not trust (the broadcasters) either, but I support this amendment because it is a middle-ground position that puts us on the right track."

Calling the amendment "inconsistent and inequitable," Minority Leader Gerald R. Ford (R Mich.) said it made the House look "ridiculous." He added: "I think you might call it a House of Representatives self-interest or self-protection amendment."

In a particularly strong attack on network television, Chet Holifield (D Calif.) said he had "no confidence in the integrity" of the networks and said candidates should have the protection of equal time because of broadcasters who "victimize the American people."

The Van Deerlin amendment was defeated by a 23-83 standing vote.

A second attempt to change the equal time clause was made by Louis Frey Jr. (R Fla.), who offered an amendment to repeal Section 315(a) for all candidates—for President, the Senate and the House. Frey said the amendment would promote public interest in elections by giving major candidates the opportunity to debate on radio and television.

Macdonald called the Frey amendment "terribly dangerous" and said that if it passed "the broadcasters of this country are going to run our political life." The amendment was defeated by a 95-277 recorded teller vote.

An amendment by Harvey to retain Section 315(a) as written in the Communications Act subsequently won approval by voice vote after several hours of debate on the issue.

Speaking in support of the Harvey amendment, Udall warned that the entire reform bill could be jeopardized by modifying the equal time clause. "If we hang on to this very divisive issue, it may be that we will lose the whole bill in the thought that we somehow can force an incumbent President to debate. We cannot," Udall said. "I believe the thing to do is to take the issue out of debate entirely. It does not amount to a hill of beans."

Lowest Unit Cost. An amendment by J.J. Pickle (D Texas) was approved by a 219-150 recorded teller vote permitting broadcasters and newspapers to charge political candidates the same rate charged to commercial advertisers.

Supporting the amendment, James Abourezk (D S.D.) said: "Asking broadcasters or newspapermen to sell advertising to political candidates at artificially low rates is nothing more than asking them to subsidize political campaigns."

Nov. 30

Union Dues Restrictions. A successful attempt to tighten regulations on use of political funds by labor unions and corporations was made by Orval Hansen (R Idaho). He introduced an amendment to prohibit use of such money for active electioneering directed at the general public. Under the Hansen amendment, approved by a 233-147 recorded teller vote, unions could promote get-out-the-vote drives and voter registration activities only among union members, and corporations could sponsor such activities only among their stockholders.

Hansen said his amendment sought to clear up "undesirable confusion" of Section 610 of Title 18 of the U.S. Code pertaining to political activities by unions and corporations. He said deficiencies of the law had "led to numerous charges that the law is defective or that it is not being observed."

Hansen added that his amendment would maintain the interpretation of existing law which "strikes a balance between organizational rights and the rights of those who wish to retain their shareholding interest or membership status but who disagree with the majority's political views."

Udall said the amendment would make it "very clear that labor unions and corporations are no longer going to be able to play unfair games, that there is a limited role for them in the political process."

Philip M. Crane (R Ill.) urged defeat of the amendment, saying it was not stringent enough in its restrictions on organized labor. Crane had earlier offered an amendment to HR 11060 that was opposed by the AFL-CIO.

Crane maintained that the chief issue was whether union dues were received voluntarily or through compulsion, *i.e.*, as a condition for employment. "We are talking about compulsion, and I think it is unjust, unfair and inequitable to take money involuntarily from union members and to use that money to promote ideals that are contrary to their own."

John M. Ashbrook (R Ohio) supported Crane, saying that "partisan politicking is strongly resented by those wage earners who are compelled by collective bargaining agreements to pay for unwanted union representation."

Reporting-Disclosure. A prime target of campaign finance reformers was removal from the Clerk of the House and the Secretary of the Senate the responsibility for collecting and compiling reports of campaign contributions and expenditures. A provision in the bill to place these duties with an independent Federal Elections Commission was killed by an amendment introduced by Hays.

The Hays amendment retained the existing system whereby House candidates report to the House Clerk and Senate candidates report to the Secretary of the Senate. Presidential candidates, however, were required to report to the Comptroller General in the General Accounting Office.

Hays objected to the independent commission because of its cost—which Hays estimated at $10 million to $20 million—and because it would transfer to the executive branch part of the control over congressional elections which, he contended, would be a violation of the separation of powers.

Harley O. Staggers (D W.Va.), citing Article 1, Section 5 of the Constitution, said each house should be sole judge of the elections, returns and qualifications of its own members. "I do not see how we can give away authority to any other body or any other group to judge what qualifications for office shall be and how we run our campaigns."

Frenzel objected strongly to the Hays amendment: "This is tantamount to putting the fox in charge of the chicken coop. The employees of the House and Senate are inappropriate people to be judging how this law is going to operate. I think they will not be credible in the eyes of the public."

Jonathan B. Bingham (D N.Y.): "Surely the Congress can delegate its responsibilities in this regard. It would be better to have a uniform procedure that would give the whole job of supervision to one office."

Distribution of Reports. A provision requiring copies of each candidate's campaign report to be filed in the federal district court nearest his hometown was deleted through an amendment introduced by freshman Rep. George E. Danielson (D Calif.).

Danielson maintained that "an absolute, complete separation of powers" was necessary for campaign practices and added that many congressional districts did not have federal courthouses in them.

John B. Anderson (R Ill.), chairman of the House Republican Conference, opposed the amendment: "It is important to the public's right to know that campaign statements be on file in the federal district court in the constituency where a man is running."

Hays, who supported the amendment to "keep the courts out of the Congress," said he would promise to support a more acceptable system in the conference committee. "I give my word that I will help write a plan into the final bill that will guarantee distribution of campaign reports to every congressional district—but not through the federal courts," he said.

Election Administration. An effort to improve the efficiency of election procedures was approved by the House by acceptance of an amendment by William J. Keating (R Ohio) to give the Comptroller General's office authority to serve as a national clearinghouse for information on the administration of elections.

Under the amendment, the Comptroller General would collect data and conduct research on the duties and makeup of local election boards, voter registration and voting and counting methods. The Comptroller General could distribute information to local agencies when requested, but he could not advise local election boards on the conduct of elections.

"When the government fails to function efficiently on election day, a tremendous credibility gap occurs between the government and the people. Campaign reform is meaningless if we are unable to properly execute the election itself," Keating said.

Computer, Telephone Systems. Bingham introduced an amendment, subsequently approved, to control campaign expenditures through use of telephone "banks", by which potential voters could be called at home during a campaign, and computer systems used to send mass mailings of campaign literature to homes of voters.

Hays endorsed the amendment, saying it "plugs up the biggest loophole of all—computerized mail can be the most expensive thing and can put a candidate of modest means out of business."

Stewart B. McKinney (R Conn.), another freshman member, supported the amendment: "For those who live in large urban areas and cannot afford the TV market and cannot afford newspaper ads, the boilerroom and computerized mail operations have become one of the most vicious unreported campaign tactics going."

Frenzel said the amendment "imperiled the bill because these expenditures are really not auditable. In addition, this amendment extends the advantages of the incumbent over the challenger. Incumbents have staff, we have telephone privileges, we have access to the media and we have a vast arsenal of weapons with which to campaign in a legitimate way."

$50,000 Campaign Ceiling. Bertram L. Podell (D N.Y.) attempted to place an over-all limit of $50,000 on total campaign expenditures for House candidates. The amendment was defeated after a heated floor discussion.

Podell called the proposal "a poor man's amendment" and said "there comes a point when more than enough money is spent on elections for public office."

Harvey contended that the amendment discriminated against candidates in districts with particularly large populations and negated the specific communications limits set up in Title I of the bill.

Udall, admitting that the Title I provisions were an "imperfect" answer to comprehensive expenditure limitation, said the Podell amendment was improper because "there are certain kinds of expenditures that cannot be effectively monitored or controlled, and you breed hypocrisy and evasion when you try to do so." Anderson (Ill.) added that "to impose that kind of ceiling on the challenger is to truly make this a pro-incumbent bill."

John H. Dent (D Pa.) observed that the $50,000 limit was more than the yearly salary of a member of Congress and said: "Do not put up barriers of gold against the honest but not rich candidate."

Brown (Ohio) opposed the amendment: "We must have some confidence in the ability of the people to make a judgment on when their vote and their support is being purchased with the challenger's money and when incumbents are trying to purchase voter support with the voting taxpayer's own money." Frenzel added that a $50,000 limit would not protect an incumbent from a celebrity challenger, such as a movie star or sports figure.

Individual Contributions. An amendment was offered by Bingham to prohibit any individual running for federal office or any member of his immediate family from contributing to his campaign more than $5,000 if he were running for Senator or Representative and $35,000 if he were running for President. The amendment, opposed by the Nixon Administration, was defeated by a 38-12 standing vote.

Harvey stated that the amendment was unconstitutional and that it was "violently opposed by the

White House." He added that the amendment "discriminates against a person who chooses to exercise his political activity by making a contribution." The bill would be "scuttled," Harvey said, if the amendment were adopted.

Udall, who reminded that "the President is looking for an excuse to veto the bill," told Democratic members: "We had better decide right now whether we want a bill or an issue for the 1972 campaigns. The surest way to get the bill killed is to load it down with all kinds of peripheral, emotional and divisive elements that are not really essential to campaign finance reform."

Rep. Frenzel spoke against the Bingham amendment: "The provision to establish limitations on personal contributions is probably unconstitutional; it is probably unfair, and it is obviously discriminatory since it is many times more restrictive on presidential candidates than on other candidates."

"I do not know which President it happens to be aimed at, but it looks like it is aimed at the incumbent," Frenzel said.

Bob Eckhardt (D Texas) spoke in favor of the amendment and contended there were no constitutional questions involved. "We regulate the right of various organizations to contribute at all, and therefore we cut off the right of expression in some areas with respect to a campaign, but we cut off no one's right to express his own views on his own time, and on issues which he desires to express himself."

House Provisions

As passed by the House, HR 11060 contained the following major provisions:

Titles I and II—Limitations on Campaign Communications Expenditures

● Restricted the amounts candidates for federal offices could spend on radio, television, cable television, newspapers, magazines, billboards, automated telephone systems and computerized postal mailings in any primary, runoff, special or general election.

● Limited the amount a candidate could spend on communications media in each election to 10 cents times the voting-age population of the geographical unit covered by the election, or $50,000, whichever was greater.

● Provided that if a newspaper or magazine sold or made available free space to a candidate, all other candidates for the same office would be entitled to buy equivalent space on the same charge basis.

● Provided that no candidate could spend more than 60 percent of his media expenditure limit on broadcast advertising.

● Provided that broadcast facilities and newspapers and magazines could not charge political candidates more than the actual charges made for comparable commercial advertising purposes.

● Prohibited transferring to a general election campaign funds which had not been used by a candidate in the primary campaign.

● Required the Bureau of the Census to provide a biennial estimate of the voting age population in each state and congressional district.

● Included escalator provisions to reflect future increases in the cost of media advertising charges.

Title III—Criminal Code Amendments

- Defined election to mean any general, special, primary or runoff election, nominating convention or caucus, delegate selection primary, presidential preference primary or constitutional convention.
- Broadened the definitions of "contribution" and "expenditure" as they pertained to political campaigns.
- Prohibited promises of employment or other political rewards or benefits by any candidate in exchange for political support, and prohibited contracts between candidates and any federal department or agency.
- Placed a ceiling on contributions by any candidate or his immediate family to his own campaign of $50,000 for President or Vice President; $35,000 for Senator, and $25,000 for Representative, Delegate or Resident Commissioner.

Title IV—Disclosure of Federal Campaign Funds

- Required all political committees that anticipated receipts in excess of $1,000 during the calendar year to file a statement of organization with the appropriate federal supervisory officer, and to include such information as the names of all principal officers, the scope of the committee, the names of all candidates the committee supported and other information as required by law.
- Required all political committees to have a chairman and a treasurer and prohibited any expenditure by the committee without the authorization of the chairman or treasurer.
- Stipulated that the appropriate federal supervisory officer to oversee election campaign practices, reporting and disclosure was the Clerk of the House for House candidates, the Secretary of the Senate for Senate candidates and the Comptroller General for presidential candidates.
- Required each political committee to report any individual expenditure of more than $100 and any expenditures of more than $100 in the aggregate during the calendar year.
- Required disclosure of all contributions to any committee or candidate in excess of $100, including a detailed report with the name and address of the contributor and the date the contribution was made.
- Required that any committee that accepted contributions or made expenditures on behalf of any candidate without the authorization of such candidate to include a notice on the front page of all literature published by the committee stating that the committee was not authorized by the candidate and that the candidate was not responsible for the activities of the committee.
- Required the supervisory officers to prepare an annual report for each political committee and make such reports available for sale to the public.
- Required candidates and committees to file reports of contributions and expenditures on the 10th day of March, June and September every year, on the 15th and fifth days preceding the date on which an election was held and on the 31st day of January. Any contribution of $5,000 or more was to be reported within 48 hours after its receipt.
- Required reporting of the names, addresses and occupations of any lender and endorser of any loan in excess of $100 as well as the date and amount of such loans.
- Required reporting of the total proceeds from the sale of tickets to all fund-raising events, mass collections made at such events and sales of campaign materials.
- Required any person who made any contribution in excess of $100, other than through a political committee or candidate, to report such contribution.
- Required a full and complete financial statement of the costs of holding a presidential nominating convention within 60 days after the end of the convention.
- Prohibited any contribution to a candidate or committee by one person in the name of another person.
- Repealed the Federal Corrupt Practices Act of 1925 (2 United States Code 241-256).
- Defined more explicitly the role which unions and corporations could take in political campaigns, get-out-the-vote drives and voter registration activities.
- Exempted from the definition of "contribution" a loan of money by a national or state bank made in accordance with the applicable banking laws and regulations.
- Authorized the office of the Comptroller General to serve as a national clearinghouse for information on the administration of election practices.

Title V—Extensions of Credit by Regulated Industries; Use of OEO Funds for Political Activity

- Required the Civil Aeronautics Board, the Federal Communications Commission and the Interstate Commerce Commission to promulgate regulations with respect to the extension of credit without collateral by any person, business or industry regulated by the federal government to any person on behalf of any candidate for federal office.
- Prohibited funds appropriated for the Office of Economic Opportunity from being used for any political activity.

Amendments Rejected. Nov. 29—Lionel Van Deerlin (D Calif.)—Amendment to adopted Macdonald amendment *(above)*—Repeal the "equal time" provision for candidates for President, Vice President and the Senate but not for the House of Representatives. Standing vote, 23-83.

William L. Springer (R Ill.)—Amendment to adopted Macdonald amendment *(above)*—Remove the provisions establishing regulations for charges made by broadcasters and newspapers for political advertising and eliminate provisions requiring newspapers to give equal access to advertising space for political candidates for the same office. Recorded teller vote, 145-219.

Louis Frey Jr. (R Fla.)—Amendment to adopted Macdonald amendment *(above)*—Repeal the "equal time" provision for all candidates for federal elective office. Recorded teller, 95-277.

Nov. 30—Bertram L. Podell (D N.Y.)—Amendment to adopted Harvey amendment *(above)*—Place a ceiling of $50,000 as the over-all amount that a candidate for the House of Representatives could spend for all campaign expenditures in each primary, runoff and general election. Voice.

Jonathan B. Bingham (D N.Y.)—Amendment to adopted Harvey amendment *(above)*—Prohibit any individual running for political office or any member of his immediate family from contributing to his campaign more than $5,000 for the office of Senator or Representative and $35,000 for the office of President. Standing, 38-122.

TAX CHECKOFF: FAILURE OF PROPOSAL FOR 1972 CAMPAIGN

After bitter partisan debate with important implications for the Democratic Party's challenge to President Nixon's expected 1972 re-election bid, Congress Dec. 8 cleared the Administration's new economic policy tax bill with a Senate rider (non-germane amendment) creating a federal fund to finance presidential election campaigns.

A similar plan cleared Congress in 1966, but was rendered inoperative in 1967. *(p. 42-43)*

As approved by Congress, however, the campaign funding plan could become effective only in time for the 1976 election. House-Senate conferees, faced with the President's threat to veto the bill (HR 10947) reducing taxes to stimulate the economy, delayed the effective date of the campaign financing provision until after 1972 in a conference report filed Dec. 4 (H Rept 92-708).

At the insistence of House conferees, the conference committee also revised the Senate-passed plan to require that Congress annually appropriate to the campaign fund the money designated by federal taxpayers as contributions to presidential campaigns.

Despite his continued opposition to the campaign funding provision, the President signed the bill Dec. 10. Mr. Nixon reportedly planned to leave further challenges to the plan to congressional action or the courts.

House Ways and Means Committee Chairman Wilbur D. Mills (D Ark.), a possible presidential nominee and leader of the House conferees, had been counted on by Democratic Party officials to insist that the conference approve the campaign funding amendment as passed by the Senate.

Mills, however, concluded that a campaign financing plan effective for the 1972 election would provoke a veto killing corporate and individual tax reductions needed for a healthy economy.

"...the Administration has made it perfectly clear that it is opposed to the checkoff procedure and is willing to jettison the entire tax bill if it cannot have its way on this matter," Mills told the House in urging acceptance of the conference report.

Had the plan gone into effect before the 1972 election, about $20.4-million of federal funds would have been made available to each of the major party candidates. About $6.3-million would have been available for Gov. George C. Wallace (D Ala.) if he ran for President as a third-party candidate.

As approved by Congress, the plan gave each taxpayer the option starting in 1973 of designating $1 of his annual federal income tax payment for use by the presidential candidate of the eligible political party of his choice or for a general campaign fund to be divided among eligible presidential candidates.

Democrats, whose party was $9-million in debt, said the voluntary tax check-off was needed to free presidential candidates from obligation to wealthy contributors to their election campaigns.

Republicans, whose party treasury was well stocked, charged that the plan was a device to rescue the Democratic Party from financial difficulty and assure a Wallace candidacy in 1972 that would lessen President Nixon's re-election chances.

The campaign financing plan, proposed as a floor amendment by John O. Pastore (D R.I.), was adopted by the Senate Nov. 22 by a 52-47 roll-call vote divided largely along party lines.

In an effort to win crucial Republican votes in the Senate, Pastore accepted an amendment by Charles McC. Mathias Jr. (R Md.) allowing each taxpayer to designate which party he wanted to donate his $1 to. The Mathias amendment was adopted by a 72-27 roll-call vote.

As introduced, the Pastore amendment would have divided the total amount designated for campaign contributions among eligible major and minor party candidates according to a formula based on the number of Americans 18 years old or over.

After acceptance of the Mathias amendment, Mathias and Clifford P. Case (R N.J.) joined 50 Democrats in voting for adoption of the Pastore amendment.

Four Democrats—James O. Eastland (Miss.), Sam J. Ervin Jr. (N.C.), John L. McClellan (Ark.) and John C. Stennis (Miss.)—joined 42 Republicans and Harry F. Byrd Jr. (Ind Va.) in voting against it.

Before adopting the plan, the Senate by a 82-17 roll call approved a related but less controversial Pastore amendment allowing income tax credits for contributions to candidates for any federal, state or local office.

1971 Senate Debate

Opening debate on the campaign financing plan Nov. 17, Pastore said the proposals present "an opportunity for the ordinary citizen to work his will in an area that all too often has been the special province of the large contributor or the vested interest."

"...there is nothing in the amendment that inhibits President Nixon in any way," Pastore said, "or that affects him in any way unless he chooses to be so affected."

Edward M. Kennedy (D Mass.) termed the Pastore proposals "the best investment the American taxpayer can possibly make to end the most flagrant single abuse in our democracy, the unconscionable power of money."

During the final day of debate Nov. 22 on the campaign financing proposal, Wallace F. Bennett (R Utah) said he questioned "whether the federal Treasury and the U.S. taxpayer should be called upon to bail out the Democratic party from its present financial problems."

Terming the proposal a "hurry-up raid on the Treasury," Roman L. Hruska (R Neb.) asked "why there is such a rush to enact this far-reaching measure, if indeed it is not primarily a benefit for an approaching presidential campaign in desperate need of financing."

The amendment jeopardized enactment of HR 10947 and thus the President's economic program, John G. Tower (R Texas) said. "This so-called reform effort is nothing more than an attempt by a group in Congress to grab taxpayers' money for their own end," he added.

"We Republicans want no part of shifting our campaign burden to the public," Robert Dole (R Kan.), the Republican national chairman, said.

Dole said the American people would judge the Pastore proposal "for what it is—a blatant partisan attempt to fund the Democratic opposition to President Nixon in 1972 and to ensure the success of that effort by paying the American Independence party to take away from the President as many electoral votes as possible."

Mathias Amendment. Mathias said his modification of the Pastore proposal—to permit taxpayers to choose which candidate would receive their tax check-off contributions—"will be a voluntary designation, in contrast to the original scheme, which contemplated an involuntary subscription by every participating taxpayer to friend and foe alike."

Other Changes. In addition to the Mathias amendment, the Senate approved the following modifications to the Pastore amendment:

• Nov. 18—An amendment by James B. Allen (D Ala.) allowing a presidential candidate who received more than 5 percent of the vote in the previous presidential election while running as the candidate of a combination of parties to be eligible for public campaign funds (the effect of the amendment was to assure Gov. Wallace a share of public funds for the 1972 election if he ran as a third-party candidate). Roll-call vote, 63-27.

• Nov. 19—An amendment by James L. Buckley (Cons-R N.Y.) increasing to $50 from $25 the credit for campaign contributions available to a married couple filing a joint return and increasing to $100 from $50 the deduction permitted for campaign contributions by a married couple filing a joint return. Roll call, 82-0.

• Nov. 22—An amendment by Peter H. Dominick (R Colo.) prohibiting tax credits or deductions for contributions to candidates running for nomination by a political convention or caucus (allowing contributions for candidates in primary elections). Voice vote.

• Nov. 22—An amendment by Howard H. Baker Jr. (R Tenn.) allowing judicial review of any decision by the Comptroller General affecting distribution of public campaign funds. Voice.

• Nov. 22—An amendment by Jack Miller (R Iowa) restricting campaign spending by individuals as well as by committees not authorized by a candidate to $1,000. Voice.

Campaign Fund Provisions

As approved by House-Senate conferees, HR 10947 included the following campaign financing provisions:

• Allowed a tax credit of $12.50 ($25 for a married couple) or a deduction against income of $50 ($100 for a married couple) for political contributions to candidates for local, state or federal office.

• Allowed taxpayers to designate on their federal income tax returns $1 of their tax payment as a contribution to the presidential and vice presidential candidates of the political party of their choice, beginning with the 1972 taxable year.

• As an alternative, allowed taxpayers to contribute to a general fund for all eligible presidential and vice presidential candidates by authorizing $1 of their annual income tax payment to be placed in such a fund.

• Required annual appropriation by Congress of payments into the presidential campaign fund not to exceed amounts checked off on tax returns.

• Directed the Secretary of the Treasury to maintain a general account for presidential campaign contributions and separate accounts for candidates of eligible parties.

• Provided that if any account for a specific party fell short of the amount to which its candidates were entitled, funds in the general account would be allocated to each party according to the ratio of contributions in their accounts. No party would receive from the general fund more than the smallest amount needed by a major party to reach the maximum amount of contributions to which it was entitled.

• Authorized to be distributed to the candidates of each major party (one which obtained 25 percent of votes cast in the previous presidential election) an amount equal to 15 cents multiplied by the number of U.S. residents age 18 or over.

• Established a formula for allocating public campaign funds to candidates of minor parties whose candidates received 5 percent or more but less than 25 percent of the previous presidential election vote.

• Authorized payments after the election to reimburse the campaign expenses of a new party whose candidate received enough votes to be eligible or to a minor party whose candidate increased its vote to the qualifying level.

• Prohibited major party candidates who chose public financing of their campaign from accepting private campaign contributions unless their shares of funds contributed through the income tax check-off procedure fell short of the amounts to which they were entitled.

• Prohibited a major party candidate who chose public financing and all campaign committees authorized by the candidate from spending more than the amount to which the candidate was entitled under the contributions formula.

• Prohibited any campaign committee not authorized by a candidate from spending more than $1,000 to promote his candidacy.

• Required candidates receiving public financing to submit weekly statements of campaign expenses to the Comptroller General.

• Provided penalties of $5,000 or one year in prison, or both, for candidates or campaign committees which spent more on a campaign than the amounts they received from the campaign fund or who accepted private contributions when sufficient public funds were available.

• Provided penalties of $10,000 or five years in prison, or both, for candidates or campaign committees who used public campaign funds for unauthorized expenses, gave or accepted kickbacks or illegal payments involving public campaign funds or who knowingly furnished false information to the Comptroller General.

• Created a Presidential Election Campaign Advisory Board made up of the Senate majority and minority leaders, the Speaker and minority leader of the House, two members representing each major party and three public members.

• Set an effective date of Jan. 1, 1973.

RECORD $42.4-MILLION IN 1970 ELECTION SPENDING

Political spending during the 1970 mid-term elections climbed to a non-presidential year record of $42,386,639, according to reports filed at the national level.

This represented an increase of $16,991,121—or 67 percent—over the $25,395,518 reported in 1966, the last non-presidential election year.

The cost of national-level politics of $42.4-million in 1970 fell only $5.4-million short of the $48.1-million figure reported for both presidential and congressional elections in 1964. The record for a presidential year was $70-million in 1968. *(Chart p. 60)*

The 1970 figures included a record of $14,368,035 in reported spending by congressional candidates—a boost of 51.6 percent over the previous high of $9,479,889 reported in 1964.

National-level political committees reported spending $28,018,604 during 1970—an increase of almost 48 percent over the previous mid-term election high of $18,979,234 in 1966.

The 1970 figures were taken from reports to the Clerk of the House and the Secretary of the Senate. The totals, compiled by the Citizens' Research Foundation of Princeton, N.J., represented only a small fraction of actual political spending.

Many congressional candidates did not report funds handled by their campaign committees. Furthermore, expenditures in primary elections and by committees operating within a single state need not be reported under federal law.

Although a large percentage of the $42.4-million reported in 1970 went into congressional races, several million dollars was used for staff and operations of the Republican and Democratic national committees. In addition, a small portion of the reported spending went into races for Governor and other state-level offices.

Party Spending

Republican committees outspent Democratic committees in 1970 by a margin of almost 3-1, according to the reports. Seventeen Republican committees spent $12.7-million while 18 Democratic committees spent $4.3-million.

The spending total for Republican committees was the highest ever for a non-presidential campaign year, topping the previous record of $7,863,092 in 1966.

Although more Democratic committees were active in 1970 than in 1966, 19 compared to 8, the total Democratic spending dropped from $4,282,007 to $4,263,722.

Congressional Reports. Democratic candidates for the House and Senate spent more than Republicans in 1970, according to filed reports. Democratic candidates reported spending $6,653,648 compared to $5,968,080 reported by Republican candidates.

Third-party and independent candidates reported spending $1,746,307 on congressional campaigns, an all-time record. The total was ballooned in 1970 by the candidacies of Sen. James L. Buckley (Cons-R N.Y.), who reported spending $1,141,378, and Sen. Harry F. Byrd Jr. (Ind Va.), who reported $383,080 in expenditures.

Other Committee Reports

Organized labor spent its highest sum ever for a mid-term election—$5.2-million. But for the first time since 1958, Republicans spent more than the combined total of both Democrats and organized labor. Republican spending topped the alliance by $3.2-million in 1970.

Those labor committees recording the largest spending were the Committee on Political Education, AFL-CIO, $913,365; the Machinists' Non-Partisan Political League Education Fund, $310,708, and Machinists' Non-Partisan Political League General Fund, $260,992.

Miscellaneous political committees, their names often giving little clue to their actual intent, spent $5.8-million, more than double their 1966 spending. (1966 spending, in turn, was more than double the 1962 total.)

The number of miscellaneous committees more than doubled from 1966 to 1970. Ninety-eight miscellaneous committees in 1970 included 14 ad hoc peace groups, 56 business and professional groups and 28 other groups of all political ideologies.

Peace groups' spending totalled $624,113. The Universities' Anti-War Fund spent the largest amount, $229,468, and the Washington, D.C., Peace Candidates Fund, the least, $990.

Among business and professional groups were four fast-growing dairy associations established in 1968-69 which reported spending $5.1-million in 1970. The largest is the Trust for Agricultural Political Education (TAPE); the second-largest, Trust for Special Political Agricultural Community Education (SPACE). The Agricultural and Dairy Education Political Trust (ADEPT) and the Agricultural Cooperative Trust (ACT) are smaller groups.

Those four donated $302,001 to Senate and House candidates. (Sometimes contributions went to opposing candidates.) Twelve elected Democratic Senators received $44,536 during their campaigns, according to the groups' reports. They are Hubert H. Humphrey (Minn.), $10,300; William Proxmire (Wis.), $7,160; Edmund S. Muskie (Maine), $6,626; Adlai E. Stevenson III (Ill.), $5,000; Lloyd Bentsen (Texas), $4,500; Vance Hartke (Ind.), $2,500; Harrison A. Williams Jr. (N.J.), $2,500; Gale W. McGee (Wyo.), $2,000; Philip A. Hart (Mich.), $1,250; John V. Tunney (Calif.), $1,200; Harry F. Byrd Jr. (Va.), $1,100, and Birch Bayh (Ind.), $500. Byrd was elected as an independent but caucuses with the Democrats.

Three elected Republican Senators received $25,000. They were Senators Hugh Scott (Pa.), $10,000; Ted Stevens (Alaska), $5,000, and Winston L. Prouty (Vt.), $10,000. This year, the dairy groups have reported giving $85,000 to the Republican party.

Campaign Financing - 1954, 1958, 1962, 1966 and 1970

The table below shows reported campaign spending included in reports to the Clerk of the House for the mid-term campaigns since 1954. Numbers on the committee line indicate the number of groups reporting.

Committee Spending Reported Nationally

	1954	1958	1962	1966*	1970*
Republican Committees	27	14	11	21	17
Receipts	$ 5,380,994	$ 4,686,423	$ 4,674,570	$ 7,640,760	$11,754,305
Expenditures	5,509,649	4,657,652	4,637,586	7,863,092	12,702,215
Percentage of Total Spending	53.5%	53.7%	39.4%	41.5%	45.3%
Democratic Committees	13	7	8	8	19
Receipts	2,168,404	1,733,626	3,699,827	4,055,310	3,809,883
Expenditures	2,224,211	1,702,605	3,569,357	4,282,007	4,263,722
Percentage of Total Spending	21.6%	19.6%	30.3%	22.5%	15.2%
Labor Committees	41	32	33	42	54
Receipts	1,882,157	1,854,635	2,112,677	4,262,077	5,290,822
Expenditures	2,057,613	1,828,778	2,305,331	4,289,055	5,235,173
Percentage of Total Spending	20.0%	21.1%	19.6%	22.7%	18.7%
Miscellaneous Committees	15	11	26	44	89
Receipts	517,804	492,710	1,313,959	2,123,868	5,603,790
Expenditures	514,094	486,430	1,271,214	2,545,080	5,817,494
Percentage of Total Spending	5.0%	5.6%	10.8%	13.3%	20.8%
TOTALS					
Receipts	$ 9,949,359	$ 8,767,394	$11,801,033	$18,082,015	$ 26,458,800
Expenditures	$10,305,567	$ 8,675,465	$11,783,488	$18,979,234	$ 28,018,604

Congressional Campaign Spending Reported

	1954	1958	1962	1966	1970
Republicans	$ 1,596,031	$ 1,670,933	$ 3,475,847	$ 2,230,835	$ 5,968,080
Percentage of Spending	52.4%	50.9%	52.5%	34.8%	41.5%
Democrats	1,436,576	1,600,117	2,950,552	4,081,685	6,653,648
Percentage of Spending	47.2%	48.7%	44.9%	63.6%	46.3%
Third Party and Independents	13,333	12,605	172,622	103,764	1,746,307
Percentage of Spending	0.4%	0.4%	2.6%	1.6%	12.2%
Total Congressional Spending	3,045,940	3,283,655	6,620,627	6,416,284	14,368,035
TOTAL REPORTED CAMPAIGN COSTS	$13,351,507	$11,959,120	$18,404,115	$25,395,518	$42,386,639

The 1966 and 1970 expenditure figures are "less transfers"—i.e., lateral fund transfers between national-level committees have been deducted.

SOURCE: Reports filed with the Clerk of the House and Secretary of the Senate.

1970 Democratic and Republican Receipts, Spending

Following are receipt and expenditure totals for Republican and Democratic committees during 1970:

Democrats

	Receipts	Expenditures
Democratic National Committee	$1,575,076	$1,585,815
National Committee Affiliates		
Commission on Party Structure and Delegate Selection	18,568	23,375
1970 Democratic National Gala Committee (D.C.)	164,239	164,231
1970 Democratic National Gala Committee (Fla.)	14,460	4,260
Let It Be Committee	3,618	3,195
National Democratic Policy Council	17,350	62,000
Project '70 Committee	7,980	6,500
Reform Democratic National Committee	21,856	18,541
Victory '72 Committee	5,000	0
Young Democratic Operating Committee	0	3,850
Standing Congressional Campaign Committees		
Democratic Congressional Campaign Committee	441,870	400,763
Democratic National Congressional Committee	16,689	207,529
Democratic Senatorial Campaign Committee	506,923	628,671
Other Committees		
Committee for Ten	86,883	87,674
Congressional Leadership for the Future	65,686	63,734
Committee for National Unity	64,695	15,201
Democratic Study Group 1970 Campaign Fund	182,793	146,986
Independent Citizens for Johnson and Humphrey (N.Y.)	0	0
The 1970 Campaign Fund	874,956	845,397
Totals Reported by Democratic Committees	$4,068,642	$4,267,722
Less Lateral Transfers to Other Committees	258,759	4,000
Total Adjusted Receipts and Expenditures	$3,809,883	$4,263,722

Republicans

	Receipts	Expenditures
Republican National Committee	$ 2,949,597	$2,974,159
National Committee Affiliates		
Republican Campaign Committee	703,805	696,046
Republican National Finance Committee	2,541,886	2,980,308
Republican National Finance Operations Committee	286,228	553,306
Campaign Committees		
Nixon-Agnew Campaign Committee	3,626	17,648
RN Associates	17,000	0
Republican Victory Committee	30,698	21,299
Standing Congressional Campaign Committees		
National Republican Congressional Committee	2,491,500	2,774,520
National Republican Senatorial Committee	1,511,086	968,534
Republican Congressional Boosters Committee	874,774	1,288,238
Republican National Finance Advisory Committee	166,578	190,171
Other Committees		
Committee of Nine	500	5,912
Institute for Republican Studies	4,610	4,959
National Federation of Republican Women (Ann Arbor, Mich.)	70,764	87,378
Republican Candidates Committee	2,550	2,550
Republican Dinner Committee	137,083	89,083
United Republican Finance Committee of San Mateo County	50,270	50,654
Totals Reported by Republican Committees	$11,842,555	$12,702,215
Less Lateral Transfers to Other Committees	88,250	0
Total Adjusted Receipts and Expenditures	$11,754,305	$12,702,215

SOURCE: Citizens' Research Foundation

Among the top five spenders of the other 28 political groups, "new priority" groups were first and fifth. The National Committee for an Effective Congress, an independent citizens' group, reported spending $695,501. The Council for a Livable World spent $214,626.

Between them were the Conservative Victory Fund, with $412,852; the American Conservative Union, with $335,716, and the Christian Nationalist Crusade with $297,865.

Effectiveness of Spending. A substantial increase in Republican spending in 1966 was followed by substantial party gains in the elections in that year. Democratic

spending in 1966 also increased but not by as much as Republican spending. In 1970, the Republicans made even larger spending increases, but experienced smaller gains in the election. Democratic spending was approximately the same in 1966 and 1970.

John T. Calkins, executive director of the National Republican Congressional Campaign Committee, said the 1970 results did not prove spending was ineffective. "Spending is as effective as ever, but it's wasted on 50 percent of the bases in any political campaign," he said. Republican disappointments in 1970, Calkins said, were caused by other factors.

RECEIPTS AND SPENDING BY 1970 SENATE CANDIDATES

Each candidate for the U.S. Senate in 1970 was required by the Federal Corrupt Practices Act of 1925 to file with the Secretary of the Senate both pre-election and post-election reports of his personal campaign receipts and expenditures. Failure to file through negligence made a candidate subject to a possible $1,000 fine or imprisonment for one year or both, according to the Corrupt Practices Act. Willful failure to file was punishable by a $10,000 fine or two years imprisonment or both.

Following is a state-by-state chart showing candidates' total personal receipts and expenditures plus reported figures for committees working in behalf of a single candidate. Committees working for candidates were not required to file unless they were active in more than one state or were a branch of a national group other than a political party. Most candidates had purely local committees working in their behalf and many indicated so in their personal reports. Since such committees operated in only one state, however, they were not required to report federally and only a few did so. The bulk of congressional campaign expenditures were channeled through such committees and thus were never reported nationally.

Candidates reported their personal expenditures in two parts. Expenditures which need not be reported individually were: charges made by a state for an individual's candidacy, such as filing fees; any personal transportation costs or meals; stationery, postage, writing or printing costs (except for use in newspapers or on billboards); distribution of letters or circulars and telephone costs. These expenditures were not limited and a single sum was reported for all. All other expenditures had to be itemized and were limited by law according to the number of voters in the candidate's state (three cents for each voter in the last senatorial election) with the total not to exceed $25,000. Total personal spending in the chart below includes both itemized and nonitemized expenditures, since numerous loopholes in the law make the distinction almost meaningless.

Candidates were not required to report primary election expenses. Accordingly, a candidate who was unopposed in the general election may report no receipts or expenditures.

(For changes or proposed changes in the federal campaign reporting laws, see the chapter on the 1971 congressional action)

Key to Senate

*Candidate indicated existence of a committee working in his behalf, but did not report its receipts or expenditures.

Total spending figures include both limited and unlimited expenditures. All amounts are rounded off to the nearest dollar. For full names of candidates and a report on the official vote they received, see "Politics in America, Edition IV," published by Congressional Quarterly Inc., 1971.

PARTY DESIGNATIONS

Standard designations used in the chart include the following:

(A)	American	(LU)	Liberty Union
(AI)	American Independent	(NC)	National Conservative
(C)	Conservative	(P)	Prohibition
(COM)	Communist	(PC)	People's Constitutional
(CP)	Consumer	(PF)	Peace and Freedom
(CST)	Constitutional	(R)	Republican
(D)	Democratic	(SL)	Socialist Labor
(IG)	Industrial Government	(WA)	Wisconsin Alliance
(IND)	Independent	(SW)	Socialist Workers

	PERSONAL		COMMITTEE	
	Receipts	Spending	Receipts	Spending
ALASKA				
Kay (D)	$ 5,000	$ 5,000		
STEVENS (R)	15,998	21,735		
ARIZONA				
Grossman (D)	none	none	$ 76,124	$ 180,778
FANNIN (R)	1,565	6,698		
CALIFORNIA				
TUNNEY (D)	none	none		
Murphy (R)	none	none	1,727,725	1,631,402
Ripley (AI)	3,856	3,856		
Scheer (PF)	No Report Available			
CONNECTICUT				
Duffey (D)	none	none		
WEICKER (R)	none	none	*	*
Dodd (IND)	none	none		
DELAWARE				
Zimmerman (D)	350	1,875		
ROTH (R)	1,968	4,690	*	*
Gies (A)	529	1,216		

	PERSONAL		COMMITTEE	
	Receipts	Spending	Receipts	Spending
FLORIDA				
CHILES (D)	17,260	16,966		
Cramer (R)	none	none	354,803	333,986
HAWAII				
Heftel (D)	5,990	5,886		
FONG (R)	none	none	*	*
ILLINOIS				
STEVENSON (D)	none	35,120	*	*
Smith (R)	none	none	*	*
Fisher (SL)	No Report Available			
Henderson (SW)	No Report Available			
Pietrusa (IND)	127	127		
INDIANA				
HARTKE (D)	none	none	*	*
Roudebush (R)	none	none	*	*
MAINE				
MUSKIE (D)	none	none	182,893	205,871
Bishop (R)	4,872	10,076	37,744	37,744
MARYLAND				
Tydings (D)	none	9,000		
BEALL (R)	none	none	466,981	457,188
Wilder (AI)	1,641	1,630		
MASSACHUSETTS				
KENNEDY (D)	none	none	608,617	583,394
Spaulding (R)	none	879		
Shaw (P)	No Report Available			
Gilfedder (SL)	No Report Available			

	PERSONAL Receipts	PERSONAL Spending	COMMITTEE Receipts	COMMITTEE Spending
MICHIGAN				
HART (D)	none	829	*	*
Romney (R)	none	none	*	*
Sims (SL)	No Report Available			
Lodico (SW)	No Report Available			
MINNESOTA				
HUMPHREY (D)	none	150		
MacGregor (R)	none	1,626		
Braatz (IG)	none	50		
Strebe (SW)	none	none		
MISSISSIPPI				
STENNIS (D)	none	3,196		
Thompson (IND)	No Report Available			
MISSOURI				
SYMINGTON (D)	none	none	91,209	95,252
Danforth (R)	none	25,274	192,000	208,870
Chapman (A)	No Report Available			
Digirolamo (IND)	No Report Available			
MONTANA				
MANSFIELD (D)	3,275	3,275		
Wallace (R)	none	none		
NEBRASKA				
Morrison (D)	575	1,250	41,650	29,190
HRUSKA (R)	none	750	184,034	180,576
NEVADA				
CANNON (D)	2,880	3,941		
Raggio (R)	4,860	3,897		
De Sellem (IA)	No Report Available			
NEW JERSEY				
WILLIAMS (D)	77,395	59,538	51,700	46,965
Gross (R)	23,860	23,860		
Levin (SL)	No Report Available			
O'Grady (NC)	No Report Available			
Job (IND)	No Report Available			
Mans (IND)	No Report Available			
NEW MEXICO				
MONTOYA (D)	none	none	*	*
Carter (R)	none	none	*	*
Higgs (PC)	15	15		
NEW YORK				
Ottinger (D)	none	65,204		
Goodell (R)	none	163,950	185,442	21,491
BUCKLEY (C)	none	none	1,178,971	1,141,378
Johnson (COM)	No Report Available			
Emmanuel (SL)	No Report Available			
Dawson (SW)	No Report Available			
NORTH DAKOTA				
BURDICK (D)	none	300		
Kleppe, Tom (R)	none	1,150	*	*
Kleppe, Russell (IND)	No Report Available			
OHIO				
Metzenbaum (D)	300	300	*	*
TAFT (R)	none	1,500	*	*
Kay (AI)	2,606	2,906		
O'Neill (SL)	No Report Available			

	PERSONAL Receipts	PERSONAL Spending	COMMITTEE Receipts	COMMITTEE Spending
PENNSYLVANIA				
Sesler (D)	6,006	16,511	*	*
SCOTT (R)	none	1,603		
McFarland (AI)	No Report Available			
Mimms (CP)	No Report Available			
Gaydosh (CST)	21,391	21,662		
Johansen (SL)	No Report Available			
Maisel	No Report Available			
RHODE ISLAND				
PASTORE (D)	none	none	*	*
McLaughlin (R)	4,450	none		
Fenton (PF)	No Report Available			
Fein (SW)	No Report Available			
TENNESSEE				
Gore (D)	23,984	28,717		
BROCK (R)	none	3,483		
Pitard (A)	No Report Available			
East (IND)	No Report Available			
TEXAS				
BENTSEN (D)	none	none	*	*
Bush (R)	none	8,193		
UTAH				
MOSS (D)	9,566	9,547		
Burton (R)	10,966	12,516		
Freeman (AI)	46	704		
VERMONT				
Hoff (D)	6,675	626	203,000	203,000
PROUTY (R)	none	6,693		
Meyer (LU)	679	1,875		
VIRGINIA				
Rawlings (D)	98,514	136,197		
Garland (R)	1,075	6,078	66,968	95,418
BYRD (IND)	none	1,500	385,046	383,080
WASHINGTON				
JACKSON (D)	143,157	138,829		
Elicker (R)	24,315	24,960		
Fisk (B)	No Report Available			
Massey (SW)	No Report Available			
WEST VIRGINIA				
BYRD (D)	300	300	*	*
Dodson (R)	3,254	3,254		
WISCONSIN				
PROXMIRE (D)	1,519	3,149	350,711	369,785
Erickson (R)	none	none		
Hou-seye (A)	406	406		
Wiggert (SL)	No Report Available			
Quinn (SW)	No Report Available			
WYOMING				
Boardman (WA)				
MC GEE (D)	none	none	173,508	169,087
Wold (R)	21,003	12,419		

RECEIPTS AND SPENDING REPORTED BY 1970 HOUSE CANDIDATES

Each candidate for the U.S. House of Representatives in 1970 was required by the Federal Corrupt Practices Act of 1925 to file with the Clerk of the House both pre- and post-election reports of his personal campaign receipts and expenditures. Failure to file through negligence made a candidate subject to a possible $1,000 fine or imprisonment for one year or both, according to the Federal Corrupt Practices Act. Willful failure to file was punishable by a $10,000 fine or two years imprisonment or both.

Following is a district-by-district chart showing candidates' total personal receipts and expenditures plus reported figures for committees working in behalf of a single candidate. Committees working for candidates were not required to file reports with the Clerk of the House unless they were working in more than one state or were a branch of a national group other than a political party. Most candidates had purely local committees working in their behalf and many indicated so in their personal reports. Since such committees operated in only one state, however, they were not required to report federally and only a few did so. The bulk of congressional campaign expenditures was channeled through such committees and thus never reported federally.

Candidates reported their personal expenditures in two parts. Expenditures which need not be reported individually were: charges made by a state for an individual's candidacy, such as filing fees; any personal transportation costs or meals; stationery, postage, writing or printing costs (except for use in newspapers or on billboards); distribution of letters or circulars and telephone costs. These expenditures were not limited and a single sum was reported for all. All other expenditures had to be itemized and were limited by law according to the number of voters in the candidate's district (three cents for each vote cast in the last House election in the candidate's district) with the total not to exceed $5,000. Total personal spending in the chart below includes both itemized and nonitemized expenditures, since numerous loopholes in the law made the distinction almost meaningless.

Candidates were not required to report primary election expenses. Accordingly, a candidate who was unopposed in the general election may have reported no receipts or expenditures.

(For changes or proposed changes in the federal campaign reporting laws during 1971, see the chapter on 1971 congressional action.)

| | PERSONAL | | COMMITTEE | |
	Receipts	Spending	Receipts	Spending
ALABAMA				
1 Tyson (D)	$ 8,074	$ 8,974		
EDWARDS (R)	none	300	*	*
Beasley (NDPA)	1,374	1,729		
2 Winfield (D)	1,405	1,784		
DICKINSON (R)	none	none	*	*
Smith (NDPA)	1,881	3,215		
3 ANDREWS (D)	50	475		
Lee (NDPA)	100	195		
4 NICHOLS (D)	3,440	2,450		
Andrews (R)	1,800	2,400		
Harrel (NDPA)		No Report Available		
5 FLOWERS (D)	3,101	3,101		
Rogers (NDPA)	none	none		
6 Schmarkey (D)	3,740	4,649		
BUCHANAN (R)	none	none	*	*
Moore (C)		No Report Available		
7 BEVILL (D)	none	none		
8 JONES (D)	1,750	2,050		
Hearn (C)	972	1,203		
Harris (Ind.)	61	802		
Stanley (NDPA)	none	none		

| | PERSONAL | | COMMITTEE | |
	Receipts	Spending	Receipts	Spending
ALASKA				
AL BEGICH (D)	none	none	*	*
AL Murkowski (R)	1,900	2,500		
ARIZONA				
1 Pollock (D)	3,194	7,486		
RHODES (R)	none	none	*	*
2 UDALL (D)	805	2,920	3,590	
			(Udall-Foley)	
Herring (R)	none	none	*	*
Thomallo (AI)	345	710		
3 Beaty (D)	1,093	1,093		
STEIGER (R)	none	none	*	*
ARKANSAS				
1 ALEXANDER (D)	none	none		
2 MILLS (D)	none	150		
3 Poe (D)	2,350	10,259		
HAMMERSCHMIDT (R)	none	2,987		
4 PRYOR (D)	4,300	3,404		
CALIFORNIA				
1 Kortum (D)	28,278	28,008		
CLAUSEN (R)	38,729	34,311		
2 JOHNSON (D)	none	none		
Gilbert (R)	1,222	3,529		
Carrigg (AI)	1,417	1,874		
3 MOSS (D)	186	186		
Duffy (R)	none	none	21,628	21,628
Priest (AI)	150	884		
4 LEGGETT (D)	17,420	19,693		
Gyorke (R)	none	425		
5 BURTON (D)	none	none	*	*
Parks (R)	none	425	*	*

Key to House List

Candidate indicated existence of a committee working in his behalf, but did not report its receipts or expenditures. Winning candidates' names are in capital letters.

Total spending figures include both limited and unlimited expenditures. All amounts are rounded off to the nearest dollar.

For full names of candidates and a report on the official vote they received, see *Politics in America, Edition IV*, published by Congressional Quarterly Inc., 1971.

PARTY DESIGNATIONS

Standard designations used in the chart include the following:

(A)	American	(NC)	National Conservative
(AF)	America First	(NDPA)	National Democratic
(C)	Conservative		Party of Alabama
(CO)	Common People's	(PF)	Peace and Freedom
(CST)	Constitutional	(PLS)	Progressive Labor Socialist
(D)	Democratic	(PP)	Public
(DI)	Dodd Independent	(R)	Republican
(FP)	For the People	(SCI)	South Carolina
(Ind.)	Independent		Independent
(INP)	Iowa New Party	(SL)	Socialist Labor
(LRU)	La Raza Unida	(SW)	Socialist Workers
(LU)	Liberty Union	(UT)	Urban Tax Reform

	PERSONAL		COMMITTEE	
	Receipts	Spending	Receipts	Spending
CALIFORNIA				
6 Miller (D)	none	none	62,454	54,083
MAILLIARD (R)	1,176	1,601		
7 DELLUMS (D)	none	none	68,518	71,889
Healy (R)	none	1,000	*	*
Seahill (PF)	none	8		
8 MILLER (D)	11,905	7,227		
Crane (R)	none	500		
9 EDWARDS (D)	16,920	25,022		
Guerra (R)	none	2,430	*	*
Kaiser (AI)	2,935	3,090		
10 McLean (D)	45,805	45,517		
GUBSER (R)	none	814	*	*
Stancliffe (AI)	462	2,310		
11 Gomperts (D)	3,200	3,129		
MC CLOSKEY (R)	none	none	39,296	32,736
12 Riordan (D)	6,380	6,350		
TALCOTT (R)	none	1,309	*	*
Foster (PF)	835	1,020		
13 Hart (D)	none	662	*	*
TEAGUE (R)	none	43,590	*	*
Jordet (AI)	none	1,276		
14 WALDIE (D)	none	none	*	*
Athan (R)	none	3,847		
15 MC FALL (D)	1,654	2,141		
Van Dyken (R)	none	4,797	*	*
Gillings (AI)	260	3,096		
16 SISK (D)	none	none	35,159	31,405
Sanchez (R)	none	216	*	*
Scott (AI)	1,390	2,156		
17 ANDERON (D)	none	none	*	*
Donaldson (R)	none	941	*	*
Copeland (AI)	425	425		
Matthews (PF)		No Report Available		
18 Miller (D)	6,302	8,986		
MATHIAS (R)	none	425	*	*
Hensley (AI)	25	565		
19 HOLIFIELD (D)	13,675	10,370		
Jones (R)	8,424	11,851		
20 Stolzberg (D)	1,328	532		
SMITH (R)	9,650	1,090		
Harper (AI)	55	1,585		
21 HAWKINS (D)	7,647	7,647		
Johnson (R)	none	725	*	*
22 CORMAN (D)	none	425	*	*
Hayden (R)	88,871	79,304	*	*
Johnson (AI)	1	214	Included in Personal	
23 Chapman (D)	4,157	9,161		
CLAWSON (R)	none	none	*	*
24 Evers (D)	19,341	19,514		
ROUSSELOT (R)	none	725	134,565	134,565
Scanlon (AI)	none	720		
Kaplan (PF)	2,231	2,878		
25 Craven (D)	2,168	5,200		
WIGGINS (R)	none	none	*	*
Scanlen (AI)	none	757		
26 REES (D)	9,042	4,968	11,842	9,719
Friedman (R)	1,934	1,882		
Hallinan (AI)	none	1,246		
McCammon (PF)	537	537		
27 Kimmel (D)	6,907	6,906		
GOLDWATER (R)	none	none		
Hind (AI)	1	740		
Richer (PF)	61	550		
28 McLaughlin (D)		No Report Available		
BELL (R)			*	*
Gordon, Derek (AI)	2,753	2,752		
Gordon, Jane (PF)	525	577		

	PERSONAL		COMMITTEE	
	Receipts	Spending	Receipts	Spending
CALIFORNIA				
La Follette (R)	none	none	60,153	53,638
(Defeated in Primary)				
29 DANIELSON (D)	none	none	*	*
Mc Mann (R)	none	1,462	*	*
30 ROYBAL (D)	15,982	16,938	*	*
Cavnar (R)	none	250	*	*
Belouson (AI)	10	2,251		
31 WILSON (D)	15,565	16,337		
Casmir (R)	13,736	9,754	*	*
32 Mallonee (D)	223	3,436		
HOSMER (R)	none	none	*	*
Donohue (PF)	475	475		
33 Wright (D)	7,742	6,189		
PETTIS (R)	none	none		
34 HANNA (D)	92,092	86,603		
Teague (R)	115,532	119,076	*	*
Rayburn (AI)	36	502		
35 Lenhart (D)	492	1,423		
SCHMITZ (R)	14,768	none	*	*
Halpern (PF)	1,225	3,035		
36 Hostetter (D)	40	485		
WILSON (R)	4,300	4,300	*	*
Davis (AI)	100	193		
Koppelman (PF)	550	550		
37 VAN DEERLIN (D)	none	none	*	*
Kuhn (R)	27,027	27,758		
Brice (AI)	1,825	1,921		
Thygeson (PF)	none	none		
38 Tunno (D)	none	none	59,519	68,609
VEYSEY (R)	none	5,877	*	
Pasley (AI)	330	920		
COLORADO				
1 Barnes (D)	6,500	2,722		
MC KEVITT (R)	12,216	12,217	*	*
Carpio (LRU)	179	313		
2 Gebhardt (D)	13,963	26,635	*	*
BROTZMAN (R)	none	1,535	*	*
3 EVANS (D)	1,778	3,771		
Mitchell (R)	none	66	*	*
Cranson (IP)	365	1,670		
Olshaw (IA)	104	779		
Serna (LRU)	28	348		
4 ASPINALL (D)	none	2,212	49,694	48,273
Gossard (R)	—	1,972	*	*
CONNECTICUT				
1 COTTER (D)	5,750	5,750	*	*
Uccello (R)	none	none	*	*
Coll (PP)	13,378	11,380		
2 Pickett (D)	41,648	52,060		
STEELE (R)	none	none	*	*
3 GIAIMO (D)	none	none	39,953	40,840
Dunn (R)	none	1,000		
Antonetti (DI)	841	1,185		
4 Daly (D)	21,528	138,605		
MC KINNEY (R)	none	1,200	*	*
Emard (AI)	1,939	1,939		
5 MONAGAN (D)	none	none	43,238	42,510
Patterson (R)	4,970	5,425		
Avitabile (CO)	2,056	2,005		
6 GRASSO (D)	none	10,895	58,982	58,881
Kilborn (R)	none	280	*	*
DELAWARE				
AL Daniello (D)	1,360	2,760		
AL DU PONT (R)	2,920	2,818	*	*

	PERSONAL		COMMITTEE	
	Receipts	Spending	Receipts	Spending
FLORIDA				
1 SIKES (D)	2,500	1,708		
Shuemake (R)	7,863	8,288		
2 FUQUA (D)	none	none		
3 BENNETT (D)	2,125	2,125		
4 CHAPPELL (D)	49,094	42,872		
Wood (R)	19,325	16,688		
5 Girod (D)	6,450	6,467		
FREY (R)	none	none	*	*
6 GIBBONS (D)	5,455	1,014		
Carter (R)	none	3,000	*	*
7 HALEY (D)	26,237	23,843		
Lovingood (R)	16,762	16,718		
8 Bailey (D)	none	2,700		
YOUNG (R)	none	2,125	*	*
9 ROGERS (D)	50,718	31,029		
Danciu (R)	9,193	11,443		
10 Ward (D)	10,325	10,883		
BURKE (R)	none	2,625	*	*
11 PEPPER (D)	none	none		
12 FASCELL (D)	30,403	23,194		
Zinzell (R)	none	none	*	*
GEORGIA				
1 HAGAN (D)	none	none		
2 MATHIS (D)	none	none		
Ragsdale (R)	none	none		
3 BRINKLEY (D)	none	none		
4 Shumake (D)	2,125	2,125		
BLACKBURN (R)	none	2,125	*	*
5 Young (D)	500	22,400		
THOMPSON (R)	16,806	16,353		
6 FLYNT (D)	1,800	2,125		
7 DAVIS (D)	—	2,125	*	*
Fullerton (R)	12,988	17,572		
8 STUCKEY (D)	1,000	2,150		
9 LANDRUM (D)	14,474	18,792		
Cooper (R)	none	3,853	*	*
10 STEPHENS (D)	none	none		
HAWAII				
1 MATSUNAGA (D)	none	none	74,369	51,435
Cockey (R)	none	none	*	*
2 MINK (D)	none	1,585	41,886	24,898
IDAHO				
1 Brauner (D)	19,982	19,982		
MC CLURE (R)	none	5,359	*	*
2 Wells (D)	5,638	8,558		
HANSEN (R)	none	744	*	*
Anderson (AI)	none	none		
ILLINOIS				
1 METCALFE (D)	3,910	6,782		
Jennings (R)	none	none	*	*
2 MIKVA (D)	4,173	4,341		
Marks (R)	none	2,108	*	*
3 MURPHY (D)	4,500	5,110		
Rowan (R)	4,655	5,851		
4 Morgan (D)	4,905	5,417		
DERWINSKI (R)	4,562	12,361		
5 KLUCZYNSKI (D)	4,200	3,817		
Ochenkowski (R)	1,295	4,650		
6 COLLINS (D)	1,750	1,788		
Zabrosky (R)	none	4,587	*	*
7 ANNUNZIO (D)	1,230	1,230		
Lento (R)	none	2,100		
8 ROSTENKOWSKI (D)	none	1,465		
Kaplinski (R)	220	775		

	PERSONAL		COMMITTEE	
	Receipts	Spending	Receipts	Spending
ILLINOIS				
9 YATES (D)	3,468	8,884		
Wolbank (R)	1,004	3,447		
10 Logan (D)	No Report Available			
COLLIER (R)	6,607	5,969		
11 PUCINSKI (D)	12,500	13,004		
Mason (R)	1,650	1,950		
12 Cone (D)	none	none	7,377	7,128
MC CLORY (R)	none	none	*	*
13 Warman (D)	none	none		
CRANE (R)	none	none	*	*
14 Adelman (D)	2,420	2,507		
ERLENBORN (R)	1,260	none	*	*
15 Todd (D)	378	557		
REID (R)	none	500	*	*
16 Devine (D)	No Report Available			
ANDERSON (R)	200	none	29,339	36,891
17 Hawthorne (D)	1,775	2,575		
ARENDS (R)	9,915	12,950		
18 Fox (D)	1,540	1,866		
MICHEL (R)	7,905	7,920		
19 Shaw (D)	none	none		
RAILSBACK (R)	none	510	*	*
20 Cox (D)	3,380	4,032		
FINDLEY (R)	6,500	6,500		
21 GRAY (D)	4,000	14,339		
Evans (R)	none	4,990	*	*
22 Miller (D)	No Report Available			
SPRINGER (R)	11,825	12,850		
23 SHIPLEY (D)	none	none	26,650	26,650
Schlafly (R)	none	19,575		
24 PRICE (D)	21,661	21,609		
Randolph (R)	1,480	1,955		
INDIANA				
1 MADDEN (D)	5,750	10,117		
Kirtland (R)	none	358	*	*
2 Sprague (D)	none	1,387		
Landgrebe (R)	none	2,500	*	*
3 BRADEMAS (D)	33,455	41	*	*
Newman (R)	none	2,244		
4 ROUSH (D)	814	1,079		
Adair (R)	none	none	*	*
5 Williams (D)	10,824	12,147		
HILLIS (R)	none	738	*	*
6 Straub (D)	16,130	16,091		
BRAY (R)	1,723	2,709	*	*
7 Roach (D)	4,600	4,603		
MYERS (R)	none	500		*
8 Huber (D)	none	1,500	41,190	37,267
ZION (R)	none	455	*	*
9 HAMILTON (D)	none	none	4,700	5,628
	(Two committees)		52,939	52,658
Wathen (R)	none	none	*	*
10 Sharp (D)	none	340	*	*
DENNIS (R)	none	1,000	*	*
11 JACOBS (D)	none	none	38,891	38,657
Burton (R)	none	none	*	*
IOWA				
1 Mezvinsky (D)	1,531	3,550	*	*
SCHWENGEL (R)	none	none		
Foster (AI)	No Report Available			
2 CULVER (D)	2,620	2,740		
Mc Martin (R)	150	787	*	*
3 Taylor (D)	5,614	5,610		
GROSS (R)	5,845	none	*	*
4 Blobaum (D)	889	1,116		
KYL (D)	none	3,300		

	PERSONAL		COMMITTEE	
	Receipts	Spending	Receipts	Spending
IOWA				
5 SMITH (D)	13,078	14,064		
Mahon (R)	none	none	*	*
Grant (AI)	1	131		
Berger (INP)	none	20	1,193	1,193
6 Moore (D)	300	267	*	*
MAYNE (R)	none	none	*	*
7 Galetich (D)	1,200	2,000	*	*
SCHERLE (R)	6,000	4,218	*	*
KANSAS				
1 Jellison (D)	1,235	1,532	*	*
SIBELIUS (R)	none	900	*	*
2 ROY (D)	none	3,824		
Mize (R)	none	2,145	*	*
Kilian (C)	2,443	3,263		
3 DeCoursey (D)	9,213	12,825		
WINN (R)	none	425	*	*
Redding (C)	384	765		
4 Juhnke (D)	500	950		
SHRIVER (R)	4,250	4,114		
Snell (C)	85	783		
5 Saar (D)	2,240	3,685		
SKUBITZ (R)	3,267	6,107		
KENTUCKY				
1 STUBBLEFIELD (D)	none	none		
2 NATCHER (D)	none	none		
3 MAZZOLI (D)	none	none		
Cowger (R)	none	1	*	*
Watson (AI)	none	68		
4 Webster (D)	8,100	17,296		
SNYDER (R)	none	1,635	*	*
5 Willis (D)	162	162		
CARTER (R)	none	1,000	*	*
6 WATTS (D)	200	325		
Gregory (R)	none	1,015	*	*
7 PERKINS (D)	430	1,315	*	*
Myers (R)	569	845		
LOUISIANA				
1 HEBERT (D)	2,045	2,075		
Fontana (Ind.)	1,460	776		
2 BOGGS (D)	none	none		
Lee (R)	none	none		
Smith (Ind.)	2,141	none		
3 CAFFREY (D)	none	none		
Smith (R)	Withdrew from race			
4 WAGGONER (D)	none	none		
5 PASSMAN (D)	none	none		
6 RARICK (D)	none	none		
7 EDWARDS (D)	none	none		
8 LONG (D)	none	none		
MAINE				
1 KYROS (D)	none	none		
Speers (R)	296	296		
2 HATHAWAY (D)	none	none		
Conners (R)	4,355	4,355		
MARYLAND				
1 Aland (D)	4,233	6,005		
MORTON (R)	11,943	11,859	*	*
Laque (AI)	none	194		
2 LONG (D)	46,958	33,509		
Pierpont (R)	none	2,310	*	*
3 GARMATZ (D)	33,124	33,125		
4 SARBANES (D)	none	none	78,881	78,498
Fentress (R)	3,477	3,477		

	PERSONAL		COMMITTEE	
	Receipts	Spending	Receipts	Spending
MARYLAND				
5 Hart (D)	none	none	82,849	80,802
HOGAN (R)	none	100	139,129	139,129
Brittain (AI)	Withdrew			
6 BYRON (D)	none	none	32,192	32,844
Hughes (R)	7,695	9,953		
Carroll (AI)	59	275		
7 MITCHELL (D)	none	none	49,190	48,953
Parker (R)	26,082	27,160		
Freidler (D)			43,895	42,271
(Defeated in primary)	(2 committees)		5,650	5,478
8 Boggs (D)	none	none	107,305	107,383
GUDE (R)	none	none	54,884	44,756
MASSACHUSETTS				
1 CONTE (R)	none	none		
2 BOLAND (D)	1,000	1,000		
3 DRINAN (D)	none	none		
McGlennon (R)	none	468	*	*
4 DONOHUE (D)	none	713	*	*
Miller (R)	17,440	20,216		
5 Williams (D)	2,825	3,577		
MORSE (R)	1,490	2,690	*	*
6 HARRINGTON (D)	none	1,450		
Phillips (R)	5,000	4,929	*	*
7 MACDONALD (D)	23,686	10,605		
Hughes (R)	185	335		
8 O'NEILL (D)	none	none	12,400	12,400
9 HICKS (D)	none	none		
Curtis (R)	none	6,537	*	*
Houton (Ind.)	none	none		
10 Yaffe (D)	none	1,400		
HECKLER (R)	none	none	*	*
Smith (D)			1,960	3,000
(Defeated in primary)				
11 BURKE (D)	2,010	1,993		
12 Studds (D)	2,000	7,380		
HASTINGS (R)	550	4,263	*	*
MICHIGAN				
1 CONYERS (D)	none	none	*	*
Johnson (R)	240	none		
2 Stillwagon (D)	none	500		
ESCH (R)	none	none	*	*
3 Enslen (D)	none	none	5,440	5,440
			17,051	28,484
			7,600	7,600
			5,000	5,000
			20,381	21,301
	(6 committees)		5,150	5,150
BROWN (R)	none	1,100		
4 Mc Cormack (D)	6,407	6,041		
HUTCHINSON (R)	none	2,912	*	*
5 Mc Kee (D)	14,772	15,583	*	*
Ford (R)	none	1,367	10,500	10,500
Girard (SL)	5	5		
Kus (SW)	none	410		
Cihon (D)	6,260	6,484		
CHAMBERLAIN (R)	4,800	5,938		
7 Ruhala (D)	21,681	25,110		
RIEGLE (R)	306	306		
Mattison (AI)	none	511		
8 Davies (D)	200	1,331		
HARVEY (R)	none	none	*	*
9 Rogers (D)	none	25,938	*	*
VANDER JAGT	none	1,850		
Dillinger (AI)	none	none		
10 Parent (D)	5,229	5,230		
CEDERBERG (R)	4,150	3,253		

	PERSONAL		COMMITTEE	
	Receipts	Spending	Receipts	Spending
MICHIGAN				
11 Green (D)	17,353	17,752		
RUPPE (R)	none	580	*	*
12 O'HARA	none	none		
Driscoll (R)	300	350		
Deschaine (AI)	28	853		
13 DIGGS (D)	675	684		
Engle (R)	none	none		
14 NEDZI (D)	938	938		
Owen (R)	none	none		
15 FORD (D)	none	none	*	*
Fackler (R)	1,329	1,326	*	*
16 DINGELL (D)	4,943	2,662		
Rostrun (R)	102	583		
17 GRIFFITHS (D)	none	none	*	*
Klunzinger (R)	No Report Available			
18 Scholle (D)	17,628	18,790		
BROOMFIELD (R)	4,583	4,674		
19 Harris (D)	none	none		
MC DONALD (R)	1,768	1,768		
Mc Gregor (AI)	23	23		
MINNESOTA				
1 Lundeen (D)	119	435		
QUIE (R)	1,523	1,822		
2 Adams (D)	2,896	2,996		
NELSEN (R)	475	575	29,300	29,300
(Approximate totals compiled by Citizens' Research Foundation from lists not totaled by the committee.)				
3 Rice (D)	none	163		
FRENZEL (R)	none	1,252		
4 KARTH (D)	2,404	2,404	38,180	36,858
Less (R)	none	561	*	*
5 FRASER (D)	none	477	98,712	108,218
Enroth (R)	none	346		
Myers (SW)	No Report Available			
6 Montgomery (D)	none	100		
ZWACH (R)	none	100	*	*
Martin (Ind.)	55	2,383		
7 BERGLAND (D)	none	359	*	*
Langen (R)	none	1,624	*	*
8 BLATNIK (D)	885	1,051		
Reed (R)	none	464	*	*
MISSISSIPPI				
1 ABERNETHY (D)	none	none		
2 WHITTEN (D)	none	2,839		
Carter (Ind.)	No Report Available			
3 GRIFFIN (D)	2,166	7,650		
Lee (R)	none	200	*	*
4 MONTGOMERY (D)	none	none		
5 COLMER (D)	none	234	*	*
Creel (Ind.)	none	263		
MISSOURI				
1 CLAY (D)	none	50		
Fischer (AI)	891	1,156		
2 SYMINGTON (D)	none	624		
Hoffman (R)	none	283	*	*
Lacy (AI)	1,332	8,984		
3 SULLIVAN (D)	4,232	4,555		
Troske (R)	1,644	2,749		
4 RANDALL (D)	2,805	6,174		
Olson (R)	2,978	3,114		
5 BOLLING (D)	7,998	6,503	*	*
Vanet (R)	No Report Available			
Kernodle (AI)	396	499		

	PERSONAL		COMMITTEE	
	Receipts	Spending	Receipts	Spending
MISSOURI				
6 HULL (D)	none	1,390		
Sprague (R)	none	500		
Chaney (AI)	648	3,331	Totals inconsistent	on report
7 HALL (R)	4,500	440	*	*
8 ICHORD (D)	3,616	2,349		
Caskanett (R)	none	50	*	*
Byford (Ind.)	none	400		
9 HUNGATE (D)	none	2,406		
Schroeder (R)	2,159	2,031		
Hale (AI)	261	819		
10 BURLISON (D)	50	50	*	*
Rust (R)	none	50	*	*
MONTANA				
1 Olsen (D)	none	870		
SHOUP (R)	none	2,307	*	*
2 MELCHER (D)	1,095	1,095		
Rehberg (R)	none	3,125	*	*
NEBRASKA				
1 Burrows (D)	none	none	7,148	8,240
THONE (R)	none	1,269		
Callan (Ind.)	3,493	3,493		
2 Hlavacek (D)	none	none	15,425	16,364
MC COLLISTER (R)	none	none	75,418	75,339
	2 Committees		9,626	10,418
3 Searcy (D)	5,787	7,311		
MARTIN (R)	2,780	1,898		
NEVADA				
AL BARING (D)	1,200	5,000	*	*
Charles (R)	85	178		
NEW HAMPSHIRE				
1 Merrow (D)	3,849	2,632		
WYMAN (R)	none	611	*	*
2 Daniell (D)	8,164	8,163		
CLEVELAND (R)	none	none	*	*
NEW JERSEY				
1 Mansi (D)	1,575	1,526		
HUNT (R)	none	none		
Doganiero (SL)	none	none		
2 Hughes (D)	9,368	9,368		
SANDMAN (R)	4,650	4,650		
3 HOWARD (D)	7,718	7,921		
Dowd (R)	2,231	2,231		
Hill (NC)	2,477	5,493		
4 THOMPSON (D)	2,331	1,262		
Costigan (R)	3,500	3,498		
Frank (SL)	none	none		
5 Eisele (D)	6,229	6,219		
FRELINGHUYSEN (R)	2,100	7,097		
Wright (NC)	155	196		
6 Yates (D)	20,268	27,312		
FORSYTHE (R)	3,125	3,125		
Doganiero (SL)	none	none		
Mahalchik (AF)	none	none		
7 Lesemann (D)	25,779	25,417		
WIDNALL (R)	9,830	16,480		
8 ROE (D)	1,810	1,800		
Fontanella (R)	670	670		
9 HELSTOSKI (D)	4,620	4,932		
Hoebel (R)	4,692	4,601		
Cundari (NC)	none	184		
10 RODINO (D)	18,703	17,410		
Jones (R)	none	none		

	PERSONAL Receipts	PERSONAL Spending	COMMITTEE Receipts	COMMITTEE Spending
NEW JERSEY				
11 MINISH (D)	15,430	12,960		
Shue (R)	4,685	6,672		
12 Lundy (D)	16,746	13,326		
DWYER (R)	none	none	10,443	6,685
13 GALLAGHER (D)	4,000	4,000		
Comesanas (R)	4,740	4,770		
Miller (UT)	550	925		
14 DANIELS (D)	9,400	7,504		
DeGennaro (R)	none	1,240	*	*
Dellay (FP)	546	546		
Whaley (NC)	none	none		
15 PATTEN (D)	7,220	7,713		
Garibaldi (R)	none	none	*	*
NEW MEXICO				
1 Chavez (D)	none	none	17,116	18,490
LUJAN (R)	none	none	99,654	96,069
2 RUNNELS (D)	425	3,922	*	*
Foreman (R)	none	2,000	*	*
NEW YORK				
1 PIKE (D-L)	none	none		
Smith (R-C)	none	3,763		
2 Sherman (D-L)	none	none	6,130	14,631
GROVER (R-C)	none	none	*	*
3 WOLFF (D-L)	none	none		
Rice (R)	none	1,647	*	*
Camardi (C)	100	303		
4 Burstein (D-L)	none	5,000	66,970	69,609
WYDLER (R)	none	none		
Derham (C)	332	971		
5 Lowenstein (D-L)	1,139	1,139		
LENT (R-C)	none	none		
6 HALPERN (R-L)	3,475	3,472	*	*
Flynn (C)	2,110	2,675		
7 ADDABBO (D-R-L)	14,030	13,845		
Acer (C)	50	497		
8 ROSENTHAL (D-L)	8,625	4,997	14,751	10,804
DiTucci (R-C)	7,134	7,243		
9 DELANEY (D-R-C)	10,085	9,357		
Rubin (L)	none	554		
10 CELLER (D)	570	570		
Occhiogrosso (R-C)	6,397	5,075		
11 BRASCO (D)	1,300	6,617		
Sampol (C)		No Report Available		
Meyrowitz (L)	30	859		
12 CHISHOLM (D-L)	11,960	10,032		
Coleman (R)	none	none		
Shepherd (C)		No Report Available		
13 PODELL (D)	4,778	4,057		
McKenzie (R)	100	114		
Rauch (C)		No Report Available		
Dicker (L)	none	none		
14 ROONEY (D)	none	none	29,600	17,321
Jacobs (R-C)	none	1,618	*	*
Eikenberry (L)	917	1,085		
15 CAREY (D)	14,550	10,437		
Spinner (R)	none	200	*	*
Marion (C)	none	none		
Saks (L)	none	none		
16 MURPHY (D)	none	none	49,053	48,169
	(Totals given only partial breakdown)			
Smith (R-C)	none	none	12,502	6,751
McClain (L)	1,624	1,475		
17 KOCH (D-L)	none	646		
Sprague (R)	none	none	*	*
Callahan (C)	none	none		
18 RANGEL (D-R)	8,083	8,936		

	PERSONAL Receipts	PERSONAL Spending	COMMITTEE Receipts	COMMITTEE Spending
NEW YORK				
Wasiutynski (C)	none	none		
Taylor (L)	none	none		
19 ABZUG (D)	none	500		
Farber (R-L)		No Report Available		
Lodico (C)	64	64		
20 RYAN (D-L)	none	none	*	*
Goldstein (R)	none	900		
Saunders (C)	none	80		
21 BADILLO (D-L)	none	none	*	*
Smaragdas (C)	2,980	2,316		
22 SCHEUER (D-L)	5,150	5,000		
Schneck (R-C)	5	132		
23 BINGHAM (D-I)	none	none	5,412	3,742
Seeney (R)	none	none		
Kardian (C)	none	none		
24 BIAGGI (D-C)	none	3,200		
Periconi (R)	250	859	*	*
Hagan (L)	none	none		
Dretzin (D)		No Report Available		
25 PEYSER (R)	none	15,400	*	*
Greenawalt (L)	200	290		
DeVito (C)	3,881	3,878		
26 James (D)	1,704	3,595		
REID (R-L)	1,663	1,663		
Coffey (C)	2,475	3,335		
27 DOW (D-L)	none	none		
Mc Kneally (R-C)	none	none	*	*
28 Greaney (D)		No Report Available		
FISH (R)	none	none	*	*
Hoffman (C)	360	360		
29 STRATTON (D)	10,265	8,528		
Button (R-L)	none	none		
30 Pattison (D-L)	none	none		
KING (R-C)	none	none		
31 Bornstein (D-L)	2,425	3,166		
MC EWEN (R-C)	none	none		
32 Simmons (D)	4,881	8,022		
PIRNIE (R-L)	2,500	11,250	*	*
33 Bernstein (D-L)	701	701		
ROBISON (R)	6,790	16,009	*	*
34 Mc Curn (D)	none	500	*	*
TERRY (R-C)	none	950		
35 HANLEY (D)	none	500	*	*
O'Connor (R-C)	3,140	3,677	*	*
36 Pappas (D)	8,606	20,504		
HORTON (R)	none	none	*	*
Hampson (C)	25	none		
Schloss (L)	none	5		
37 Anderson (D-L)	355	585		
CONABLE (R)	18,624	18,810		
Wallis (C)	none	none		
38 Cretekos (D)	1,704	1,944		
HASTINGS (R-C)	16,425	5,781		
39 Flaherty (D-L)	34,966	45,806		
	(Only 14,966 shown in breakdown.)			
KEMP (R-C)	none	5,440	*	*
40 Cuddy (D-L)	9,254	13,302		
SMITH (R-C)	325	410		
41 DULSKI (D-L)	150	261		
Johns (R-C)	320	872		
NORTH CAROLINA				
1 JONES (D)	614	none	*	*
Everett (R)	none	17,692	*	*
Leggett (AI)	none	1,902		
2 FOUNTAIN (D)	none	545		
3 HENDERSON (D)	none	none	*	*
Howell (R)	none	none		

	PERSONAL Receipts	PERSONAL Spending	COMMITTEE Receipts	COMMITTEE Spending
NORTH CAROLINA				
4 GALIFIANAKIS (D)	none	none	46,084	63,195
Hawke (R)	none	none		
Ragsdale (Ind.)	none	none	15,469	11,587
5 White (D)	23,822	42,089		
MIZELL (R)	none	535		
6 PREYER (D)	none	1,500	*	*
Barham (R)	6,185	7,687		
Bullock (AI)	3,795	3,781		
7 LENNON (D)	2,300	2,619		
Weber (R)	1,344	3,662		
8 Blue (D)	18,616	21,951		
RUTH (R)	none	1,482	*	*
9 Bahakel (D)	none	8,020		
JONAS (R)	6,204	6,157		
10 Whitener (D)	7,072	6,833	11,979	8,238
BROYHILL (R)	none	1,560		
11 TAYLOR (D)	22,709	22,856		
Atkinson (R)	1,785	2,210		
NORTH DAKOTA				
1 Brooks (D)	9,996	9,996	*	*
ANDREWS (R)	none	83		
2 LINK (D)	205	554		
Mc Carney (R)	none	1,266	*	*
OHIO				
1 Turner (D)	14,487	15,748		
KEATING (R)	none	184	64,734	64,734
2 Springer (D)	none	none	19,456	20,046
CLANCY (R)	none	none	10,090	9,469
3 Kerr (D)	5,075	6,995		
WHALEN (R)	none	82	*	*
Butcke (AI)	130	288		
4 Laws (D)	1,294	1,525		
MC CULLOCH (R)	8,785	3,543		
5 Sherer (D)	71	73		
LATTA (R)	662	662	*	*
6 Stevens (D)	2,011	6,921		
HARSHA (R)	160	6,743		
7 Lewis (D)	4,191	4,042	*	*
BROWN (R)	none	600	*	*
8 BETTS (R)	1,000	841		
9 ASHLEY (D)	none	none		
Shapiro (R)	none	2,586	*	*
10 Arnett (D)	none	50	*	*
MILLER (R)	none	none	*	*
11 Rudd (D)	none	4,999		
STANTON (R)	none	320	*	*
12 Goodrich (D)	none	50	*	*
DEVINE (R)	none	none	*	*
13 Bartolomeo (D)	8,262	12,990		
MOSHER (R)	none	248	*	*
14 SEIBERLING (D)	none	121	*	*
Ayres (R)	none	50	*	*
15 Mc Gee (D)	none	1,048	*	*
WYLIE (R)	none	none	*	*
16 Musser (D)	none	651	*	*
BOW (R)	2,000	792		
17 Hood (D)	6,873	6,873		
ASHBROOK (R)	none	none	*	*
Simpson (AI)	360	3,477		
18 HAYS (D)	none	none		
Stewart (R)	1,525	1,479		
19 CARNEY (D)	none	none		
Dennison (R)	none	3,800	*	*
20 STANTON (D)	none	none		
Petro (R)	none	none		
OHIO				
21 STOKES (D)	none	1,500		
Mack (R)	500	2,335	*	*
22 VANIK (D)	none	none	*	*
Fink (R)	none	50		
23 Mottl (D)	200	1,200	*	*
MINSHALL (R)	none	350		
24 Ruppert (D)	7,193	2,463	*	*
POWELL (R)	none	1,327	*	*
Payton (AI)	134	1,981		
OKLAHOMA				
1 Jones (D)	4,875	5,675		
BELCHER (R)	18,250	19,552		
2 EDMONDSON (D)	none	9,200		
Humphries (R)	none	4,932		
3 ALBERT (D)	none	none		
4 STEED (D)	7,400	9,012		
Wilkinson (R)	none	769	*	*
Rawls (A)	149	780		
Kottka (Ind.)	275	757		
5 JARMAN (D)	7,190	7,765		
Campbell (R)	none	200		
6 Cassity (D)	1,293	3,469		
CAMP (R)	none	200		
OREGON				
1 Cook (D)	6,707	8,564		
WYATT (R)	77,975	84,735		
2 ULLMAN (D)	none	none		3,367
Thoren (R)	none	none	*	*
3 GREEN (D)	none	500	14,507	8,609
Dugdale (R)	11,118	11,568		
4 Weaver (D)	4,018	7,088		
DELLENBACK (R)	none	3,000	*	*
PENNSYLVANIA				
1 BARRETT (D)	6,175	7,086		
Ziccardi (R)	none	160		
Botts (AI)	17	399		
2 NIX (D)	4,785	3,267		
Taylor (R)	2,010	2,219	*	*
3 BYRNE (D)	none	none		
Pelagappi (R)	none	none	*	*
4 Eilberg (D)	none	none	*	*
Dougherty (R)	none	35	*	*
5 GREEN (D)	none	none	*	*
Ring (R)	2,105	2,080	4,956	1,433
Donahue (AI)	none	50		
6 YATRON (D)	none	125	*	*
Kitsock (R)	5,000	5,122		
Atkins (CST)	none	85		
7 Bresun (D)	561	652		
WILLIAMS (R)	none	145	*	*
8 Hennessy (D)	1,987	3,148		
BIESTER (R)	none	550	*	*
Moore (CST)	10	205		
9 Waldmann (D)	2,988	7,678		
WARE (R)	none	none	*	
Winkleman (CST)	none	146		
10 Smith (D)	2,200	6,817		
MC DADE (R)	4,055	4,055		
Depue (CST)	792	2,356		
11 FLOOD (D-R)	4,575	4,672		
Balschi (CST)	none	86		
12 Karycki (D)	1,425	1,495		
WHALLEY (R)	none	none	*	*
Ferry (AI)	79	138		
Cope (CST)	100	519		

Candidate in 2 districts - 12 and 21. Duplicate reports.

	PERSONAL		COMMITTEE	
	Receipts	Spending	Receipts	Spending

PENNSYLVANIA

	PERSONAL		COMMITTEE	
	Receipts	Spending	Receipts	Spending
13 Romano (D)	10,602	16,495		
COUGHLIN (R)	none	35	*	*
Demeno (AI)	28	1,888		
Matthews (CST)	440	980	*	*
14 MOORHEAD (D)	9,368	8,970		
Levine (R)	1,632	2,052		
Chaitin (CST)	none	50		
15 ROONEY (D)	21,108	19,136		
Roberts (R)	No Report Available			
Litz (CST)	none	185		
16 Pflum (D)	1,160	1,094		
ESHLEMAN (R)	6,676	10,172		
Willard (CST)	none	35		
17 Zurick (D)	none	4,500	*	*
SCHNEEBELI (R)	none	35	*	*
Weber (CST)	none	none		
18 Leslie (D)	1,877	1,860		
CORBETT (R)	none	none	*	*
Backmen (CST)	none	517		
19 Berger (D)	none	2,000		
GOODLING (R)	none	3,535		
Paul (CST)	none	128		
20 GAYDOS (D)	20,036	20,412		
Honeygosky (R)	775	1,020		
Staub (CST)	53	1,437		
21 DENT (D)	1,250	1,250		
Anderson (R)	1,366	1,366		
Cope (CST)	100	519	Candidate in 2 districts - 12 and 21. Duplicate reports.	
22 O'Kicki	14,923	15,355		
SAYLOR	none	6,232		
Hahn (AI)	47	94		
23 Harrington (D)	none	none	*	*
JOHNSON (R)	1,090	1,685		
24 VIGORITO (D)	150	150		
Merrick (R)	none	none	11,271	16,695
Shilling (AI)	none	none		
25 CLARK (D)	5,160	15,845		
Loth (R)	150	150		
Thornton (CST)	none	none		
26 MORGAN (D)	2,215	2,514		
Cupellia (R)	880	2,227		
Daecheck (CST)	No Report Available			
27 Walgren (D)	2,470	4,091		
FULTON (R)	7,900	8,648		
Johnston (AI)	349	731		

RHODE ISLAND

	PERSONAL		COMMITTEE	
	Receipts	Spending	Receipts	Spending
1 ST. GERMAIN (D)	none	none		
Miska (R)	none	85	*	*
Murray (PF)	896	1,397		
2 TIERNAN (D)	none	1,680		
Dimitri (R)	2,500	2,479		
O'Hara (Ind.)	1,027	1,474		

SOUTH CAROLINA

	PERSONAL		COMMITTEE	
	Receipts	Spending	Receipts	Spending
1 RIVERS (D)	3,105	3,105	*	*
2 Mc Donald (R)	none	500		
SPENCE (R)	none	532	*	*
Cole (SCI)	1,000	570		
3 DORN (D)	1,100	2,200	*	*
Ballard (R)	none	2,000		
4 MANN (D)	none	none		
5 GETTYS (D)	3,951	7,100	*	*
Phillips (R)	none	none		
Sumner (SCI)	none	none		

SOUTH CAROLINA

	PERSONAL		COMMITTEE	
	Receipts	Spending	Receipts	Spending
6 MC MILLAN (D)	14,000	21,300		
Baskin (R)	none	2,409		
Smith (SCI)	No Report Available			

SOUTH DAKOTA

	PERSONAL		COMMITTEE	
	Receipts	Spending	Receipts	Spending
1 DENHOLM (D)	none	none	*	*
Gunderson (R)	none	176		
2 ABOUREZK (D)	none	none	*	*
Brady (R)	none	1,700		

TENNESSEE

	PERSONAL		COMMITTEE	
	Receipts	Spending	Receipts	Spending
1 Shine (D)	3,595	3,273		
QUILLEN (R)	none	none	*	*
2 Cowan (D)	1,181	1,702		
DUNCAN (R)	none	none		
3 Winningham (D)	none	645	20,086	20,427
BAKER (R)	4,179	2,377		
Massey (Ind.)	No Report Available			
Shickey (Ind.)	No Report Available			
4 EVINS (D)	7,645	7,829	*	*
Boles (R)	none	none		
5 FULTON (D)	none	none		
Kelly (R)	No Report Available			
6 ANDERSON (D)	16,714	17,689		
Davies (R)	none	3,625		
7 BLANTON (D)	3,375	7,604		
Doss (R)	679	3,654		
8 JONES (D)	3,800	3,493		
9 Osborn (D)	250	457		
KUYKENDALL (R)	325	450		

TEXAS

	PERSONAL		COMMITTEE	
	Receipts	Spending	Receipts	Spending
1 PATMAN (D)	none	1,504		
Hogan (R)	711	3,802		
2 DOWDY (D)	none	none		
Hoyt (Ind.)	No Report Available			
Runnels (Ind.)	No Report Available			
Wills (Ind.)	No Report Available			
3 Mead (D)	3,196	41,695	*	*
COLLINS (R)	none	4,250	*	*
4 ROBERTS (D)	4,015	11,842		
5 CABELL (D)	3,263	3,263		
Crowley (R)	9,792	59,130		
6 TEAGUE (D)	2,300	3,442		
7 Greenwood (D)	36,461	54,343		
ARCHER (R)	none	4,250	*	*
8 ECKHARDT (D)	363	1,352		
9 BROOKS (D)	3,588	3,699		
Pressler (R)	293	581		
10 PICKLE (D)	none	none		
11 POAGE (D)	21,042	1,774	*	*
12 WRIGHT (D)	none	none		
13 PURCELL (D)	25,479	20,820		
Staley (R)	none	none	16,046	15,462
14 YOUNG (D)	2,500	none		
15 DE LA GARZA (D)	7,124	3,930		
Martinez (R)	1,050	4,340		
16 WHITE (D)	3,384	3,666		
Provencio (R)	2,805	3,677		
17 BURLESON (D)	3,335	2,647		
18 PRICE (R)	none	1,400		
19 MAHON (D)	3,825	3,155	*	*
20 GONZALEZ (D)	770	800	*	*
21 FISHER (D)	24,775	26,640		
Gill (R)	none	2,818		
22 CASEY (D)	23,813	26,022		
Busch (R)	none	775	*	*
23 KAZEN (D)	100	309		

	PERSONAL		COMMITTEE	
	Receipts	Spending	Receipts	Spending
UTAH				
1 MC KAY (D)	1,759	1,759		
Richards (R)	none	2,501	*	*
Worthington (AI)	none	225		
2 Nance (D)	none	3,602		
LLOYD (R)	2,600	3,884		
Marsh (AI)	297	313		
VERMONT				
AL O'Shea (D)	1,935	3,548		
STAFFORD (R)	none	none	*	*
MORRISSEAU (LU)	Refused to file as a protest against existing law.			
VIRGINIA				
1 DOWNING (D)	1,005	1,002		
2 Fitzpatrick (D)	none	1,262		
WHITEHURST (R)	6,671	343	*	*
3 SATTERFIELD (D)	none	none	*	*
Wilkinson (R)	8,000	8,000	*	*
4 ABBITT (D)	19,061	21,431		
Helms (R)	none	3,390		
Ragsdale (Ind.)	1,800	5,009	15,469	11,587
5 DANIEL (D)	14,724	10,129		
St. Clair (R)	3,216	3,968		
6 White (D)	1,210	2,061		
POFF (R)	12,383	11,507		
7 Williams (D)	12,000	35,278		
ROBINSON (R)	5,200	49,950	*	*
8 Stearns (D)	10,407	14,646		
SCOTT (R)	none	none	*	*
9 Buchanan (D)	none	800	*	*
WAMPLER (R)	6,735	9,399	*	*
10 Miller (D)	723	none		
BROYHILL (R)	139,470	139,714	*	*
WASHINGTON				
1 Hughes (D)	6,322	11,204		
PELLY (R)	none	425	15,170	4,538
Iverson (B)	No Report Available			
Coontz (SW)	850	850	*	*
2 MEEDS (D)	45,675	45,350		
Mc Bride (R)	781	5,312		
3 HANSEN (D)	none	none	*	*
Mc Conkey (R)	none	none	*	*
4 Mc Cormack (D)	770	1,297		
May (R)	3,950	4,500	*	*
5 FOLEY (D)	950	2,645	3,590	—
			(Udall-Foley)	
Gamble (R)	none	3,512	*	*
6 HICKS (D)	none	none	*	*
Jarstad (R)	9,961	12,463		

	PERSONAL		COMMITTEE	
	Receipts	Spending	Receipts	Spending
WASHINGTON				
Congress (SW)	883	883	*	*
7 ADAMS (D)	33,902	39,538	*	*
Lewis (R)	none	825	*	*
Block (SW)	883	883	*	*
WEST VIRGINIA				
1 MOLLOHAN (D)	1,310	3,114	13,400	13,484
Doll (R)	none	none	5,595	4,855
2 STAGGERS (D)	4,575	5,421		
Reddecliff (R)	none	1,600		
3 SLACK (D)	12,015	5,011		
Kinsolving (R)	1,538	1,935		
4 HECKLER (D)	1,210	1,606		
Shannon (R)	none	none		
5 KEE (D)	3,955	3,654	*	*
			(included in personal)	
Mc Quade (R)	7,265	9,568		
WISCONSIN				
1 ASPIN (D)	none	1,178	*	*
Schadeberg (R)	none	none		
2 KASTENMEIER (D)	890	1,545	3,360	—
Anderson (R)	none	none	*	*
Krohn (A)	240	325		
3 Short (D)	5,845	5,845		
THOMSON (R)	2,355	2,693		
4 ZABLOCKI (D)	110	1,122		
Mrozinski (R)	108	108		
Zierhut (A)	728	774		
5 REUSS (D)	none	none		
Dwyer (R)	25	25		
Denny (A)	No Report Available			
Boulton (PLS)	none	100		
6 Utech (D)	none	726		
STEIGER (R)	215	309		
Davidson (A)	1,190	1,594		
7 OBEY (D)	none	212		
Le Tendre (R)	37,812	50,312		
Wolfe (A)	94	670		
8 Cornell (D)	4,779	4,689		
BYRNES (R)	4,195	2,820		
Dery (A)	none	1,324		
9 Tabak (D)	none	none		
DAVIS (R)	470	682		
10 Thorensen (D)	37	921		
O'KONSKI (R)	none	90		
Hable (A)	none	143		
WYOMING				
AL RONCALIO (D)	1,125	1,441		
Roberts (R)	none	2,374	*	*

REPORTS BY LABOR AND MISCELLANEOUS COMMITTEES IN 1970

Following is a list of 54 labor and 89 miscellaneous groups filing reports of their financial activities during 1970 with the Clerk of the U.S. House of Representatives.

The list includes the name of the group and the location of its headquarters. The reports, unless otherwise noted, cover the period from Jan. 1, 1970 to Dec. 31, 1970. Figures are rounded off to the nearest dollar.

Note that adjusted receipts and adjusted expenditures are given for some groups. These figures represent a group's total receipts or expenditures minus funds it either received from or transferred to other nationally reporting groups.

The reporting committees are divided into two main categories—labor and miscellaneous. The miscellaneous category is subdivided into business and professional, ad hoc peace, major miscellaneous, and other miscellaneous groups.

Figures were supplied by the Citizens' Research Foundation.

Labor Groups

ABC
Active Ballot Club—Retail Clerks International Association
Washington, D.C. 20006
| Receipts | $143,501 |
| Expenditures | $188,188 |

ACW-M
Amalgamated Clothing Workers—Miscellaneous Local Joint Boards
Receipts	$ 31,918
Expenditures	$ 46,944
Adjusted Expenditures	$ 29,068

AFM
American Federation of Musicians
Newark, New Jersey 07104
| Receipts | $ 22,298 |
| Expenditures | $ 27,899 |

AMC
Amalgamated Meat Cutters and Butcher Workmen
Chicago, Illinois 60657
Receipts	$121,439
Expenditures	$172,416
Adjusted Expenditures	$105,297

APEC
Amalgamated (Clothing Workers) Political Education Committee
New York, New York 10003
Receipts	$ 62,630
Expenditures	$ 82,049
Adjusted Expenditures	$ 62,549

BBP-CF
Boilermakers-Blacksmiths Legislative Education Action Program, Campaign Assistance Fund
Kansas City, Kansas 66101
| Receipts | $ 17,942 |
| Expenditures | $ 27,100 |

BBP-EF
Boilermakers-Blacksmiths Legislative Education Action Program, Legislative Education Fund
Kansas City, Kansas 66101
Receipts	$ 65,122
Expenditures	$ 41,893
Adjusted Expenditures	$ 21,593

BCT
Building and Construction Trades Department (AFL-CIO), Political Education Fund
Washington, D. C. 20006
10/29/70 to 12/31/70
| Receipts | $ 28,820 |
| Expenditures | $ 36,684 |

BL
Brooklyn Longshoremen's Political Action and Education Fund
Brooklyn, New York 11231
9/11/70 to 12/31/70
| Receipts | none reported |
| Expenditures | $ 7,616 |

BMWE
Brotherhood of Maintenance of Way Employees Political League
Detroit, Michigan
| Receipts | $ 27,706 |
| Expenditures | $ 7,471 |

CGG
Committee for Good Government
Detroit, Michigan 48214
| Receipts | $ 77,392 |
| Expenditures | $126,538 |

CLIC
Carpenters Legislative Improvement Committee
Washington, D.C. 20001
| Receipts | $ 90,224 |
| Expenditures | $139,887 |

COPE
Committee on Political Education, AFL-CIO
Washington, D.C. 20006
Receipts	$ 859,226
Adjusted Receipts	$ 435,015*
Expenditures	$1,024,960
Adjusted Expenditures	$ 913,365

* Survey shows $424,211 in reported transfers to COPE from other labor committees. COPE did not list these transfers as receipts.

COPE-Conn.
Connecticut Committee on Political Education
Hamden, Connecticut 06518
1/1/70 to 11/4/70
Receipts	$ 16,345
Adjusted Receipts	$ 2,345
Expenditures	$ 15,941

CWA-1969*
Communications Workers of America—COPE
Washington, D.C. 20006
1/1/69 to 12/31/69 (only 1969 filing; filed 8/21/70)
| Receipts | $113,715 |
| Expenditures | $105,570 |

*These 1969 receipts and expenditures were reported in 1970, but not included in 1970 grand total.

CWA
Communications Workers of America—COPE
Washington, D.C. 20006
Receipts	$119,161
Expenditures	$167,419
Adjusted Expenditures	$145,694

DRIVE
Democrat, Republican, Independent Voter Education Committee, Brotherhood of Teamsters
Washington, D.C. 20001
| Receipts | $104,084 |
| Expenditures | $170,790 |

DRIVE-M
DRIVE Locals
Receipts	$271,871
Adjusted Receipts	$270,871
Expenditures	$341,550
Adjusted Expenditures	$277,076

EPEC
Engineers Political Education Committee
Washington, D.C. 20036
1/5/70 to 1/4/71
| Receipts | $ 6,232 |
| Expenditures | $ 1,164 |

IBEW-ICF International Brotherhood of Electrical Workers—
Individual Contributions Fund
Washington, D.C. 20005
Receipts $ 58,701
Adjusted Receipts $ 5,979
Expenditures $ 81,474

IBEW-EF International Brotherhood of Electrical Workers—
Education Fund
Washington, D.C. 20005
Receipts $ 10,600
Adjusted Receipts $ 6,100
Expenditures $ 12,250

IBF International Brotherhood of Firemen and Oilers—
Political Fund
Washington, D.C. 20002
Receipts $ 14,173
Expenditures $ 12,420

IBPAT-PF International Brotherhood of Painters and Allied
Trades, Political Action Together—Political Fund
Lafayette, Indiana 47901
1/1/70 to 3/31/70
Receipts $ 26,868
Expenditures $ 21,985

IBPAT-EF International Brotherhood of Painters and Allied
Trades, Political Action Together—Education Fund
Lafayette, Indiana 47901
1/1/70 to 3/31/70
Receipts $ 51,615
Expenditures $ 51,854

IBPSP International Brotherhood of Pulp, Sulphite and
Paper Mill Workers—Political Education Program
Fort Edward, New York 12828
Receipts $ 27,756
Expenditures $ 29,841

ICWU International Chemical Workers Union Investment
in Voter Education
Akron, Ohio 44313
Receipts $ 4,320
Expenditures $ 7,720

ILGWU-1968 International Ladies Garment Workers Union—
1968* Campaign Committee
New York, New York 10019
1/1/70 to 6/3/70 (committee closed out: 6/3/70)
Receipts $ 2,958
Expenditures $ 31,188
Adjusted Expenditures $ 7,800

*Receipts and expenditures are for 1970 even though the committee name reflects the year it originated, 1968.

ILGWU International Ladies Garment Workers Union—
1970 Campaign Committee
New York, New York 10019
4/10/70 to 12/31/70
Receipts $728,189
Adjusted Receipts $704,801
Expenditures $304,017
Adjusted Expenditures $258,627

ITU International Typographical Union Political Committee
Colorado Springs, Colorado 80901
Receipts $ 3,783
Expenditures $ 8,092
Adjusted Expenditures $ 6,200

IUD Industrial Union Department, AFL-CIO
Washington, D.C.
Receipts $ 29,688
Expenditures $ 29,776
Adjusted Expenditures $ 28,776

IUE-1969* International Union of Electrical, Radio and Machine Workers—COPE
Washington, D.C. 20036
1/1/69 to 12/31/69 (no subsequent report as of 3/1/71)
Receipts $ 49,792
Expenditures $ 50,768

*1969 receipts and expenditures reported in 1970 but not included in 1970 grand totals.

LNPL Laborers' Non-Partisan League—Contribution Fund
Washington, D.C. 20005
Receipts $ 32,496
Expenditures $ 19,867

LPL Laborers Political League
Washington, D.C. 20006
1/1/70 to 1/7/71
Receipts $150,298
Adjusted Receipts $145,298
Expenditures $145,007

MAC Maritime Action Committee
Washington, D.C. 20006
Receipts $ 83,000
Expenditures $ 95,646

MEBA No. 1 Marine Engineers Beneficial Association Political
Action Fund—District #1 (Pacific Coast)
New York, New York 10004
Receipts $126,272
Expenditures $105,023

MEBA-DF Marine Engineers Beneficial Association Defense
Fund—District #1 (Pacific Coast)
New York, New York 10004
1/1/70 to 2/28/70 (fund terminated)
Receipts 0
Expenditures $ 2,206

MEBA-RG Marine Engineers Beneficial Association Retirees
Group—District #1 (Pacific Coast)
New York, New York 10004
Receipts $224,617
Expenditures $294,313
Adjusted Expenditures $ 93,313

MEBA No. 2 Marine Engineers Beneficial Association Political
Action Fund—District #2
Brooklyn, New York 11232
Receipts $ 60,495
Expenditures $ 70,193
Adjusted Expenditures $ 69,893

MNPL-EF Machinists Non-Partisan Political League—Education Fund
Washington, D.C. 20036
Receipts $301,936
Expenditures $318,980
Adjusted Expenditures $310,708

MNPL-GF Machinists Non-Partisan Political League—General Fund
Washington, D.C. 20036
Receipts $256,872
Expenditures $327,839*
Adjusted Expenditures $260,992

*MNPL reported a figure of $404,030, but this was based on an error in the report for 9/1/70-10/16/70 in which some EF funds were added to the General Fund.

NMU National Maritime Union—Fighting Fund
New York, New York 10011
6/21/69 to 11/30/70
Receipts $187,705
Expenditures $ 27,150*

*Total expenditures not given; this figure represents contributions to congressional and senatorial candidates only.

OCAW Oil, Chemical and Atomic Workers International Union
Denver, Colorado 80201
Receipts $ 48,190
Expenditures $ 48,479
Adjusted Expenditures $ 33,010

RPEC Rural Political Education Committee
Denver, Colorado
Receipts $ 1,849
Expenditures $ 3,177

RYC Railway Clerks Political League
Washington, D.C. 20001
Receipts $ 85,861
Expenditures $ 86,449

SIU-C Seafarers International Union—COPE
Brooklyn, New York
Receipts $ 21,842
Expenditures $ 30,038

SIU-S Seafarers International Union—Political Activity Donation Committee
Brooklyn, New York
Receipts $314,754
Expenditures $422,650

SMWIA Sheet Metal Workers International Association—Political Action League
Washington, D.C. 20036
Receipts $ 30,151
Expenditures $ 26,950

TPEL Transportation Political Education League
Cleveland, Ohio 44107
Receipts $191,619
Expenditures $283,821

TWUA Textile Workers Union of America Political Fund
New York, New York 10003
Receipts $ 22,024
Adjusted Receipts $ 17,024
Expenditures $ 29,124

UAW United Auto Workers—COPE
Detroit, Michigan 48214
Receipts $476,737
Expenditures $254,945

UFT United Federation of Teachers Political Action Committee
New York, New York 10010
Receipts $ 11,846
Expenditures $ 10,664

UPG United Plant Guard Workers of America—Political Action Committee
Detroit, Michigan 48215
Receipts $ 2,228
Expenditures $ 4,163

URW United Rubber, Cork, Linoleum and Plaster Workers of America
Akron, Ohio
7/1/70 to 12/28/70
Receipts not reported
Expenditures $ 31,440*

*Amount of contributions to senatorial and congressional candidates. No other expenditures reported.

USA United Steelworkers of America—Political Action Fund
Pittsburgh, Pennsylvania 15222
Receipts $238,457
Expenditures $319,535
Adjusted Expenditures $309,535

Miscellaneous Groups

Business and Professional

ACT Agricultural Cooperative Trust
Washington, D.C. 20001
Receipts $ 10,871
Expenditures $ 6,700

ADEPT Agricultural and Dairy Education Political Trust
Springfield, Missouri 65805
7/8/70 to 12/31/70
Receipts $ 10,034
Expenditures $ 9,601

ADPAC American Dental Political Action Committee
Washington, D.C. 20016
Receipts $ 1,651
Expenditures $ 300

AIM American Insurance Men's Political Action Committee
Yankton, South Dakota
Receipts $ 6,161
Expenditures $ 3,949

AMPAC American Medical Political Action Committee
Chicago, Illinois 60611
Receipts $448,423
Expenditures $693,413

ANH American Nursing Home Political Action and Education Committee
Alexandria, Virginia
Receipts $ 28,549
Expenditures $ 19,356

BANC Bankers Action Now Committee
Columbus, Ohio 43215
7/1/70 to 10/30/70
Receipts $ 24,355
Expenditures $ 32,020
Adjusted Expenditures $ 20,270

BANKPAC Bankers Political Action Committee
East Lansing, Michigan 48823
Receipts $205,428
Adjusted Receipts $193,678
Expenditures $ 85,795

BANKPAC-WIS. Wisconsin Bankers Political Action Committee
Manawa, Wisconsin
Receipts $ 19,668
Expenditures $ 15,500
Adjusted Expenditures $ 1,500

BCC Bankers Congressional Committee
Washington, D.C. 20036
    Receipts $ 3,145
    Expenditures $ 2,410

BIPAC Business-Industry Political Action Committee
New York, New York 10022
    Receipts $302,554
    Adjusted Receipts $301,503
    Expenditures $539,157
    Adjusted Expenditures $534,157

BIPAC-NY Business-Industry Political Action Committee of New
York
New York, New York
    Receipts $ 5,000
    Expenditures $ 6,049
    Adjusted Expenditures $ 5,000

BUSPAC Business-Industry Public Affairs Committee
Washington, D.C. 20013
    Receipts $ 1,493
    Expenditures $ 2,169

CAL Committee on American Leadership
Washington, D.C. 20036
    Receipts $ 10,158
    Expenditures $ 12,059

CAP Committee for American Principles
Washington, D.C. 20036
    Receipts $ 10,230
    Expenditures $ 10,145

CAR Committee of Automotive Retailers
Washington, D.C. 20036
    Receipts $ 2,699
    Expenditures $ 6,683

CCIG Citizens Committee for Improved Government
Hamilton, Ohio 45013
    Receipts $ 4,700
    Expenditures $ 4,500

CEPAC Construction Equipment Political Action Committee
Washington, D.C. 20007
    Receipts $ 1
    Expenditures $ 293

CFA-E Committee for Action—East
Bellevue, Washington 98004
    Receipts $ 29,158
    Expenditures $ 37,791

CFA-MW Committee for Action—Midwest
Bellevue, Washington, 98004
    Receipts $ 29,615
    Expenditures $ 58,491

CFA-S Committee for Action—South
Bellevue, Washington 98004
    Receipts $ 45,368
    Expenditures $ 36,041

CFA-W Committee for Action—West
Bellevue, Washington 98004
    Receipts $ 54,922
    Expenditures $ 53,391

COMPAC Communications Political Action Committee
Washington, D.C. 20044
    Receipts $ 7,555
    Expenditures $ 10,607

CPAC Canners Public Affairs Committee
McLean, Virginia 22101
    Receipts $ 5,139
    Expenditures $ 4,707
    Adjusted Expenditures $ 4,682

EEC Employment Education Committee
Pittsburgh, Pennsylvania 15219
    Receipts $ 200
    Expenditures $ 200

EGA Effective Government Association
New York, New York 10005
    Receipts $ 19,760
    Expenditures $ 25,468

FEDPAC FED Political Action Committee
Dallas, Texas 75235
    1/1/70 to 10/31/70
    Receipts $ 4,793
    Expenditures $ 4,103

FGG Fund for Good Government
New York, New York 10015
    Receipts $ 12,139
    Expenditures $ 13,580

FP Forest Products Political Education Committee
Potomac, Maryland 20854
    Receipts $ 28,151
    Expenditures $ 26,569

FPC Food Processors Public Affairs Committee
Rochester, New York 14620
    6/1/70 to 12/31/70
    Receipts $ 2,812
    Expenditures $ 4,644

FZ Freezers Political Action Committee
Baltimore, Maryland 21223
    Receipts $ 397
    Expenditures $ 897

GIG Government Improvement Group
Washington, D.C.
    1/1/70 to 10/30/70
    Receipts $ 8,514
    Expenditures $ 15,718

HF Home Furnishings Political Committee
Washington, D.C. 20005
    Receipts $ 2,955
    Expenditures $ 2,877

INA INA Political Action Committee
Washington, D.C. 20044
    9/1/70 to 12/31/70
    Receipts $ 9,535
    Expenditures $ 9,177

LSE Lone Star Executives Voluntary Political Fund
Greenwich, Connecticut 06830
    Receipts $ 9,116
    Expenditures $ 7,200

LUPAC Life Underwriters Political Action Committee
Washington, D.C. 20036
    Receipts $ 35,351
    Expenditures $ 43,855

MDC	Motel Development Committee Washington, D.C. 20005 1/1/70 to 6/10/70			SCRAP	Scrap Political Action Committee Alexandria, Virginia 22314	
	Receipts	$ 2,865			Receipts	$ 4,350
	Expenditures	$ 2,477			Expenditures	$ 6,264

MPAC-IND. Indiana Medical Political Action Committee
Seymour, Indiana 47274

Receipts	$ 74,143
Adjusted Receipts	$ 41,623
Expenditures	$ 86,064
Adjusted Expenditures	$ 85,824

NAVA National Audio-Visual Association Inc.
Fairfax, Virginia 22030

Receipts	none reported
Expenditures	$ 770*

*Amount given to candidates; *not a total.*

NSG North Street Good Government Group
White Plains, New York 10602

Receipts	$ 7,460
Expenditures	$ 6,800
Adjusted Expenditures	$ 5,400

PACCT Political Action Committee of Cable Television
Washington, D.C. 20007

Receipts	$ 15,258
Expenditures	$ 30,002

PACE Political Action for Cooperative Effectiveness
Washington, D.C. 20006

Receipts	$ 10,161
Expenditures	$ 18,740

PACOSA Public Affairs Committee of Savings Associations
Harrisburg, Pennsylvania 17108

Receipts	$ 23,182
Expenditures	$ 16,882

PIC The Public Interest Committee
Chicago, Illinois 60654
10/1/70 to 12/31/70

Receipts	$ 9,427
Expenditures	$ 9,406

REPEC Real Estate Political Education Committee
Chicago, Illinois 60611

Receipts	$ 26,375
Expenditures	$ 17,729

RPC Restaurateurs Political Action Committee
Chicago, Illinois 60601

Receipts	$ 33,935
Expenditures	$ 71,683

SAPAC Savings Association Public Affairs Committee
Lansing, Michigan

Receipts	$ 9,892
Expenditures	$ 11,676
Adjusted Expenditures	$ 9,176

SAPEC Savings Association Political Education Committee
Washington, D.C. 20016

Receipts	$ 70,801
Adjusted Receipts	$ 66,101
Expenditures	$ 88,281

SBPAC Savings Bankers Non-Partisan Political Action Committee
New York, New York 10017

Receipts	$ 4,353
Expenditures	$ 4,272

SCRAP Scrap Political Action Committee
Alexandria, Virginia 22314

Receipts	$ 4,350
Expenditures	$ 6,264

SIC Securities Industry Campaign Committee
Washington, D.C. 20036

Receipts	$ 65,555
Expenditures	$ 59,397

SI-N.Y. Syracuse Insurance Political Action Committee
Syracuse, New York

Receipts	$ 192
Expenditures	$ 105

SMC Shoe Manufacturers Good Government Committee
St. Louis, Missouri 63105

Receipts	$ 11,850
Expenditures	$ 6,750

SPACE Trust for Special Political Agricultural Community Education
Louisville, Kentucky 40202

Receipts	$111,787
Expenditures	$123,670

TAPE Trust for Agricultural Political Education
San Antonio, Texas 78216

Receipts	$535,423
Expenditures	$368,851

TONC Truck Operators Non-Partisan Committee
Washington, D.C. 20005

Receipts	$ 36,170
Expenditures	$ 38,523

Ad Hoc Peace

AMP Another Mother for Peace
Beverly Hills, California 90210

Receipts	$ 75,533
Expenditures	$ 72,648

BLVC Boston Lawyers Vietnam Committee
Boston, Massachusetts
9/1/70 to 12/2/70

Receipts	$ 17,114
Expenditures	$ 17,114

CAF Congressional Action Fund
Washington, D.C. 20006
3/1/70 to 1/5/71

Receipts	$ 42,376
Expenditures	$ 43,750

CPCC Congressional Peace Campaign Committee
Washington, D.C. 20008
1/1/70 to 9/21/70

Receipts	$ 115
Expenditures	$ 1,348

FCF Federalist Campaign Fund
Washington, D.C. 20008

Receipts	$ 7,311
Expenditures	$ 7,311

FNP Fund for New Priorities in America
New York, New York 10017
1/1/70 to 10/20/70

Receipts	$ 51,400
Expenditures	$ 49,650

LCEW Lawyers Committee for Effective Action to End the War
New York, New York 10005
6/1/70 to 10/30/70
Receipts $ 69,854
Expenditures $ 67,971

MCPC Metamorphosis: The Committee for a Peace Congress
New York, New York 10010
1/1/70 to 11/4/70
Receipts $ 14,755
Expenditures $ 11,157

PC Peace Candidates Fund
Washington, D.C. 20013
6/4/70 to 10/23/70
Receipts $ 1,498
Expenditures $ 990

PCF Peace Commencement Fund
Boston, Massachusetts
5/15/70 to 12/31/70
Receipts $ 75,133
Expenditures $ 75,133

PED Peace Elections Desk
Chevy Chase, Maryland 20015
5/1/70 to 12/31/70
Receipts $ 1,057
Expenditures $ 1,057

PV Peace Votes
Washington, D.C. 20013
—to 12/31/70
Receipts $ 263
Expenditures $ 263

TFP Task Force for Peace
Los Angeles, California 90048
8/21670 to 12/31/70
Receipts $ 46,425
Expenditures $ 46,253

UNAF Universities National Anti-War Fund
Cambridge, Massachusetts 02139
5/1/70 to 12/31/70
Receipts $233,771
Expenditures $229,468

Major Miscellaneous

ACA Americans for Constitutional Action
West Orange, New Jersey, and Washington, D.C. 20001
Receipts $134,960
Expenditures $191,611

ACU American Conservative Union
Washington, D.C. 20003
Receipts $319,758
Expenditures $355,716

CLW Council for a Livable World
Cambridge, Massachusetts 02139
Receipts $211,055
Expenditures $214,626

CNC Christian Nationalist Crusade
Los Angeles, California 90027
Receipts $319,575
Expenditures $297,865

NCEC National Committee for an Effective Congress
New York, New York 10016
Receipts $669,736
Expenditures $695,501

UCA United Congressional Appeal
Washington, D.C. 20013
Receipts $ 87,127
Expenditures $106,235

URA United Republicans of America
Washington, D.C. 20002
Receipts $ 83,172
Expenditures $ 81,711

Other Miscellaneous

ACRE Action Committee for Rural Electrification
Washington, D.C. 20036
Receipts $101,619
Expenditures $131,068

CVF Conservative Victory Fund
Washington, D.C. 20003
4/1/70 to 12/31/70
Receipts $427,753
Expenditures $412,852

FRE-Ind. Indiana Friends of Rural Electrification
Gosport, Indiana
11/1/68 to 10/29/70
Receipts $ 17,474
Adjusted Receipts $ 16,852
Expenditures $ 17,406

LCV League of Conservation Voters
Washington, D.C. 20005
11/28/69 to 12/31/70
Receipts $ 77,108
Expenditures $ 76,011

NSRP National States Rights Party
Savannah, Georgia 31405
Receipts $ 39,433
Expenditures $ 40,298

PA Pro-America-National Association
Littlefield, Texas 79339
Receipts $ 4,908
Expenditures $ 2,640

PA-MISC. Pro-America-Various California Chapters
Various California addresses
Receipts $ 1,454
Expenditures $ 1,889
Adjusted Expenditures $ 1,515

RCA Riverside Civic Association
Chicago, Illinois 60611
Receipts $ 4,025
Expenditures $ 2,853

SWBG Southwest Better Government Committee
Phoenix, Arizona 85002
Receipts $ 5,890
Expenditures $ 4,100

TECO Telephone Education Committee Organization
Washington, D.C. 20036
Receipts $ 6,272
Expenditures $ 4,680

VBG Volunteers for Better Government
Kingsport, Tennessee 37660
4/1/70 to 12/31/70
Receipts $ 33,345
Expenditures $ 26,036

YA Young Americans Campaign Committee
Washington, D.C. 20006
Receipts $ 21,635
Expenditures $ 20,798

$1,000 CONTRIBUTORS TO POLITICAL COMMITTEES IN 1970

The following list of contributors of $1,000 or more to 36 of the largest national political committees was compiled by Congressional Quarterly from reports filed with the Clerk of the House of Representatives. The list of contributors includes individuals and law firms. The list covers the vast majority of contributors whose names were reported to the House Clerk. All data is for 1970, except where 1969 is indicated. (Key to committee abbreviations, box this page)

ALABAMA

Boykin, S. Jr., Birmingham, RNFC, $1,000; Goodrich, James, Mobile, ACU, $1,000; Miller, John C. Jr., Montgomery, DSCC, $1,000; Schuler, J., Leeds, RNFC, $1,000; Smith, W. H., Prattville, RNFC, $1,000.

ALASKA

Locher, C., Anchorage, RNFC, $1,000; Petersen, R. I., Anchorage, RNFC, $1,000; Peterson, R. L., Anchorage, RNC, $1,000; Reeve, R. C., Anchorage, RNC, $1,000; RNFC, $1,000.

ARIZONA

Benscoter, Don L., Scottsdale, RCBC, $1,000; Bentson, K. G., Phoenix, RNFC, $1,000; Burford, G. B., Lake Havasu City, RNFC, $1,000; Converse, Mr. & Mrs. E. C., Scottsdale, RNFC, $3,000, RCBC, $1,000; De Ganahl, Mr. & Mrs. Frank, Carefree, ACA, $3,000; Douglass, L. W., Tucson, DNC, $1,000; French, J. P., Scottsdale, RNC, $1,000; Gardner, Mrs. C. N., Tucson, RNC, $1,000; Goddard, Samuel P. Jr., Tucson, DNGC, $1,000; Hickox, John B., Phoenix, RCBC, $1,000.

Johnson, G. A., Phoenix, RNFC, $1,500; Kennedy, John J., Phoenix, RCBC, $1,000; Kieckhefer, Herbert M., Scottsdale, RCBC, $1,000; Kieckhefer, Mr. & Mrs. H. M., Scottsdale, RNFC, $1,000; Legg, Wayne, Phoenix, NRCC, $1,525; Leonard, Barney J., Paradise Valley, RCBC, $1,000; Lewis, Mrs. Donna Ruth, Phoenix, RCBC, $1,000; Lewis, Orme, Phoenix, RCBC, $1,000; Lincoln, Mrs. J. C., Scottsdale, RNFC, $1,000.

Louis, Dr. Herbert J., Phoenix, RCBC, $1,000; McAllister, Frances B., Flagstaff, TFP, $1,000; McNelis, Jim, Phoenix, NRCC, $2,000; Merrill, B., Phoenix, RNC, $3,000, RNFC, $3,000; RNFC, $3,000; Middleton, Frank P., Phoenix, RCBC, $1,000; O'Connor, J. H., Phoenix, RNC, $1,000; Pritzlaff, Hon. and Mrs. J. C. Jr., Phoenix, RNFC, $3,000, RCBC, $1,000; Schoenhof, E. W., Scottsdale, RCBC, $1,000; Snyder, Harold, Dardanelle, DNC, $1,000; Staggs, Ralph E., Phoenix, RCBC, $1,000; Thorne, Mrs. Jane W., Scottsdale, RCBC, $1,000; Williams, D. R. Jr., Nogales, RNFC, $1,000; Wilson, Mr. & Mrs. R. F., Tucson, RNFC, $2,000; Witcosky, John, Phoenix, NRCC, $2,000.

ARKANSAS

Carnes, Mrs. Jack, Camden, DNGC, $1,000; Lile, R. A., Little Rock, RNC, $1,000; Oswald, Harry L., N. Little Rock, DNC, $1,000; Rockefeller, Winthrop, Little Rock, RCBC, $1,000, RNFC, $1,000; Simmons, J., Hot Springs, RNFC, $1,000.

CALIFORNIA

Able, C. R., Newport Beach, RNFC, $1,000; Adams, Morgan Jr., Los Angeles, RCBC, $1,000; Alessio, John S., La Mesa, RCBC, $1,000; Alexander, L. B., Covina, RCBC, $1,000; Alles, Mrs. Gordon, San Marino, RCBC, $1,000; Ash, R. L., Beverly Hills, RNFC, $1,000; Atencio, J., APO, San Francisco, RNFC,

$1,002; Atwood, John L., Los Angeles, RCBC, $1,000; Awfs, Gerald A., San Leandro, RCBC, $1,115.64; Baden, E. M., Los Angeles, RNFC, $1,000.

Bailey, William E., San Jose, DNC, $1,000; Baldwin, J.C., Los Angeles, RNC, $1,000; Bannan, Mr. & Mrs. T. J., Lynwood, RNFC, $1,000; Battson, Mr. & Mrs. L. M., Beverly Hills,

Key to Committees

The Key listing below gives the full names of the major national committees to which individual contributions of $1,000 or more were made.

ACA	Americans for Constitutional Action
ACU	American Conservative Union
BIPAC	Business-Industry Political Action Committee
BIPAC (N.Y.)	Business-Industry Political Action Committee of New York
BUSPAC	Business-Industry Public Affairs Committee
CAP	Committee for American Principles
CCIG	Citizen's Committee for Improved Government
CFA	Committee for Action
CFT	Committee for Ten
CPS	Committee on Party Structure and Delegate Selection
CVF	Conservative Victory Fund
DNC	Democratic National Committee
DNCC	Democratic National Congressional Committee
DNGC	Democratic National Gala Committee
DNGC (Fla.)	Democratic National Gala Committee—Florida
DSCC	Democratic Senatorial Campaign Committee
DSG	Democratic Study Group 1970 Federalist Campaign Fund
FCF	Federalist Campaign Fund
FEDPAC	Federal Political Action Committee
LCEW	Lawyers Committee for Effective Action to End the War
NCEC	National Committee for an Effective Congress
NRCC	National Republican Congressional Committee
NRSC	National Republican Senatorial Committee
RCBC	Republican Congressional Boosters Committee
RCC	Republican Candidates Committee
RDC-DC	Republican Dinner Committee—District of Columbia
RDNC	Reform Democratic National Committee
RNC	Republican National Committee
RNFAC	Republican National Finance Advisory Committee
RNFC	Republican National Finance Committee
RNFOC	Republic National Finance Operations Committee
RVC	Republican Victory Committee
TFP	Task Force for Peace
'70 CF	1970 Campaign Fund
UNAF	Universities National Anti-War Fund
URA	United Republicans of America

RNFC, $1,000; Baumhefner, C. H., San Francisco, RCBC, $1,000; DSCC, $1,000; Bechtel, K. K., San Francisco, RNFC, $2,000; Bechtel, S. D. Jr., San Francisco, RNFC, $1,000; Beckman, Dr. Arnold O., Corona Del Mar, RCBC, $1,000; Bergen, E., Los Angeles, RNC, $1,000; Berke, N. R., San Francisco, RNC, $1,000; Bertea, Richard, Corona Del Mar, RCBC, $1,000.

Blomquist, Miss Agnes, Newport Beach, RCBC, $1,000; Bohannon, David D., San Mateo, RCBC, $1,000; Brainard, E. E., San Marino, RNFC, $1,000; Bramstedt, W. F., San Francisco, RCBC, $1,000; Brawner, W. P. F., San Francisco, RCBC, $1,000; Brock, Mrs. G. C., Los Angeles, RNFC, $1,000; Brock, Mrs. Margaret Martin, Los Angeles, RCBC, $1,000; Broidy, S., Los Angeles, RNFC, $1,000; Burgess, William H., Pasadena, RCBC, $1,000; Burns, Robert S., Los Angeles, RCBC, $1,000.

Cahill, John R., San Francisco, RCBC, $1,000; Cahill, J. R., San Francisco, RNFC, $1,000; Calvert, W. N., Santa Monica, RNC, $1,000; Call, Asa V., Los Angeles, RCBC, $1,000; Cameron, Mrs. William, San Francisco, RCBC, $1,000; Cantwell, Mrs. Marianne, Rancho Santa Fe, NRCC, $1,000; Cartan, Mrs. Henry, Atherton, RCBC, $1,000; Chandler, Harrison, Arcadia, RCBC, $1,000; Chandler, H., Arcadia, RNFC, $1,000; Chaney, Alger, San Francisco, RCBC, $1,000.

Clark, Mrs. Alfred B., Santa Barbara, RCBC, $1,000; Clark, Mr. & Mrs. A. B., Santa Barbara, RNFC, $1,000; Clarke, Thurmond, Corona Del Mar, RCBC, $1,000; Cody, Claude B., Danville, DNC, $1,000; Coe, H. S., San Jose, RNFC, $1,000; Coe, Mr. & Mrs. H. S., San Jose, RNC, $1,000; Coleman, W. H., Pacific Palisades, RCBC, $1,000; Cook Brothers, Industry, NRCC, $1,000; Cook, Howard F., Industry, RCBC, $1,000; Cook, J. B., Los Angeles, RNC, $1,000; Copley, James S., La Jolla, RCBC, $1,000.

Copley, J. S., La Jolla, RNFC, $1,000, ACA, $1,000, RNC, $1,000; Costello, Arthur R., Newport Beach, RCBC, $1,000; Crossett, Mrs. E. R., Pasadena, RNFC, $1,000; Cruickshank, Mrs. C. L., Carmel Valley, RNFC, $1,000; Curci, John, Newport Beach, RCBC, $1,500; Daley, Donald L., San Diego, RCBC, $1,000; Dant, Mrs. C. E., Palm Springs, RNC, $1,000; Dart, Mr. & Mrs. J. W., Los Angeles, RNC, $2,500, RNFC, $1,000; Davies, Paul L., San Jose, RCBC, $1,000; Davies, Paul L. Jr., San Francisco, RCBC, $1,000.

Davies, P. L., Sr., San Jose, RNFC, $1,000; Davis, John A., La Mesa, RCBC, $1,000, RNC, $1,000; Davis, Thomas, Beverly Hills, RCBC, $2,000; Davis, W., Beverly Hills, RNC, $1,000; Deane, Ben C., Newport Beach, RCBC, $1,000; De Angues, L., Berkeley, '70 CF, $1,000; Dobeny, William H., Beverly Hills, RCBC, $1,000; Dobey, J. K., San Francisco, DSCC, $2,000; Doheny, T. M., Beverly Hills, RNFC, $1,000; Drown, Jack, Westminster, RCBC, $1,000.

Duggan, Dan L., Los Angeles, RCBC, $1,000; Dumm, W. I. La Jolla, RNC, $1,000 Durney, W. W., Los Angeles, RNFC, $1,000; Edgerton, J. H., Los Angeles, RNC, $1,000; Evans, Barton, Culver City, RCBC, $1,000; Evans, Mrs. G. C., Los Angeles, RNFC, $1,000; Evans, Mr. & Mrs. Lee, Santa Rosa, RCBC, $1,000; Evans, T. W., Los Angeles, RNC, $1,000; Factor, John, Los Angeles, DNC, $1,000; Farr, M. S., Los Angeles, RCBC, $1,000.

Farr, Richard S., El Segundo, RCBC, $1,000; Falk, Mrs. E. M., Sepulveda, RNC, $1,000, RNFC, $1,000; Fedderson, D., Studio City, RNFC, $1,000; Ferris, A. L., Altadena, RNFC, $1,000; Field, Mr. & Mrs. C. D., San Francisco, RNC, $3,000; Field, Joseph N., Los Angeles, RCBC, $1,000, RNC, $1,100; Fischer, Mrs. M. E., Hollywood, RNFC, $1,000; Fletcher, Kim, San Diego, RCBC, $1,000; Fliermans, Mrs. M. F., Beverly Hills, RNC, $1,300; Flour, John S., Los Angeles, RCBC, $1,000.

Fluor, J. S., Santa Ana, RNC, $1,000, RNFC, $1,000; Frame, H. A., Atherton, RNFC, $1,000; Fuller, W. R., San Marino, RCBC, $1,000; Fuller, Mr. & Mrs. W. R., San Marino, RNFC, $1,000; Getty, J., Malibu, RNC, $3,000; George, Lt. Gen. H. L., Beverly Hills, RNC, $1,000; Gillies, Mr. & Mrs. B. Allison, Rancho Sante Fe, RCBC, $1,000; Gillies, Mr. & Mrs. B., Rancho Sante Fe, RNFC, $1,000; Golden, M. H., San Diego, RCBC, $1,000; Gordon, R. S., Beverly Hills, RNC, $1,000.

Gortikov, Stanley M., Woodland Hills, TFP, $1,500; Graham, Clifford C., La Jolla, RCBC, $3,000; Graham, Mr. & Mrs. C. C., La Jolla, RNC, $3,000; Graham, Dr. Ralph E., Santa Ana, RCBC, $1,000; Guggenheim, Robert, Newport Beach, RCBC, $1,000; Hamilton, H. R., Beverly Hills, RCBC, $1,000; Harris, Clinton O., Whittier, RCBC, $1,000; Harris, C. O., Whittier, RNC, $1,000; Harrison, Mrs. E. T., San Francisco, RNC, $1,000; Hartley, F. L., Los Angeles, RNFC, $1,000.

Harutunian, A., San Diego, RCBC, $1,000; Hay, C. A., Burbank, NRCC, $1,600; Hewlett, W. R., Palo Alto, RNFC, $1,000; Hixon, F. P., Pasadena, RNFC, $1,000, RNC, $1,000; Hoeft, J. E., Glendale, RCBC, $1,000; How, J. H., Burlingame, RNC, $1,000; Hughes, R. P., Anaheim, RNC, $1,000; Hume, Jacquelin H., San Francisco, RCBC, $1,000, RNC, $1,000; Jameson, Mrs. Mary Gard, Corona, RCBC, $1,000; Janss, Mrs. Edwin, Thousand Oaks, RCBC, $1,000.

Jennings, G. M., Los Angeles, RNFC, $1,000; Jewett, Geo. F. Jr., Ross, RCBC, $2,000, RNFC, $1,000; Jewett, Mr. & Mrs. G. F. Jr., Ross, RNFC, $1,000; Johnson, F., San Pedro, RNC, $1,000; Johnson, L. F., Los Angeles, RNC, $1,000; Jorgensen, K. A., Los Angeles. RNFC, $1,000; Kaiser, L. M., San Francisco, RCBC, $1,000, RCC, $2,000, RNFC, $3,000; Kalmbach, H. W., Newport Beach, RNFC, $1,000; Kerr, Robt. W., Santa Rosa, RCBC, $1,000; Ketchum, S. M., Los Angeles, RCBC, $1,000.

King, Frank L., Los Angeles, DSCC, $1,000; Kingsley, L. A., Hollywood, RNC, $1,000; Knott, Walter, Buena Park, RCBC, $3,000; Korth, H. J., Oakland, RNFC, $1,000; Krehbiel, V., Pasadena, RNC, $1,000; Krueger, R. W., Los Angeles, RNC, $1,000; Latham, Dana, Los Angeles, RCBC, $1,000; Leavey, T. E., Los Angeles, RCBC, $1,000; Lewis, Milton, Los Angeles, RCBC, $1,000; Lilienthal, Sally, San Francisco, TFP, $1,000.

Long, J. M., Oakland, RNC, $1,000; Lusk, John D., Newport Beach, RCBC, $1,000; MacLeod, John, Newport Beach, RCBC, $1,000; McBean, Peter, San Francisco, RCBC, $1,000; McBride, Mrs. E. W., Carmel, RNFC, $1,000; McCray, Maurice C., Newport Beach, RCBC, $1,000; McGowen, J. R., Long Beach, RNC, $1,000; Madison, Mr. & Mrs. Marshall P., San Francisco, RCBC, $1,000; Marble, Mrs. John M., Carmel Valley, RCBC, $1,000, RNFC, $1,000; Markham, Mrs. F. S. Balboa Island, RCBC, $1,000.

Mathis, Glenn E., El Toro, RCBC, $1,000; Maytag, Marquita, La Jolla, CVF, $2,500; Meakin, E. N., San Francisco, RNC, $1,000; Millay, George D., San Diego, RCBC, $1,000; Miller, O. N., San Francisco, RNC, $1,000; Montgomery, Mrs. V., Los Angeles, RNC, $1,000; Morison, W. W., San Francisco, RNFC, $1,000; Newman, P. Los Angeles, '70 CF, $1,000; Nichols, Mrs. J. E., Piedmont, RNC, $1,000; Nielson, S. F., San Diego, RCBC, $1,000.

Norris, Kenneth, T. Jr., San Marino, RCBC, $1,000; Norris, K. T., Sr., Los Angeles, RCBC, $1,000; O'Connor, Mrs. Thomas Ireland, Pebble Beach, RCBC, $1,000; Ousley, Earle E., Los Angeles, ACU, $1,000; Packard, Mrs. David, Los Altos Hills, RCBC, $1,000; Palevsky, Max, El Segundo, CPS, $5,000; Palmer, Mrs. Paul A., Corona Del Mar, RCBC, $1,000; Peters, Mrs. H. N., Beverly Hills, RNC, $1,000; Pike, Robert M., San Francisco, DSCC, $1,000; Pleger, Herman, San Francisco, RCBC, $1,000.

Polinsky, A. B., San Diego, DNC, $1,000; Prentice, S., San Francisco, RNFC, $1,000; Preston, John M., Hillsborough, RCBC, $1,000; Rains, Mrs. W. M., Beverly Hills, RNFC, $1,000; Reynolds, James M., Pacoima, RCBC, $1,000, RNC, $2,000; Reynolds, R. O., Los Angeles, RNC, $3,000, RCC, $3,000; Richard, T., La Jolla, RNFC, $1,000; Roberts, W. E., Redwood City, RNFC, $1,000; Roche, Theodore, Jr., Santa Barbara, RCBC, $1,000; Rogers, L., Los Angeles, RNC, $1,000.

Rogers, L., Los Angeles, RNFC, $1,000; Rose, Mr. and Mrs., D. H., San Marino, RCBC, $1,000, RNFC, $1,000; Roth, William M., San Francisco, DNGC, $1,000; Roth, Mrs. William P., Redwood City, RCBC, $1,000; Salvatori, Henry, Los Angeles, CVF, $5,000; Sanders, Edward, Los Angeles, TFP, $1,000; Schreiber, T. B., University City, RNFC, $1,000; Schulman, S., Los Angeles, RNC, $1,000; Seaver, Mr. & Mrs. Frank R., Los Angeles, RCBC $3,000, RNFC, $1,000, ACU, $1,185; Seipp, E. A., Jr., Menlo Park, RNC, $1,000.

Seipp, Edwin A. Jr., Atherton, RCBC, $1,000; Sesnon, Porter, San Francisco, RCBC, $1,000; Sheinbaum, Mr. and Mrs. Stanley K., Santa Barbara, TFP, $5,000; Sheinbaum, Mrs. Betty Warner, Santa Barbara, TFP, $1,500; Shorenstein, Walter H., San Francisco, DNC, $1,000; Shurtleff, L. L., Emeryville, RNC, $1,000; Simpson, W. A. Jr., Los Angeles, RCBC, $1,000; Singleton, H. E., Los Angeles, RNC, $1,000; Smith, H. R., San Marino, RNC, $1,000; Smith, Telford C., Millbrae, RCBC, $1,000.

Spencer, Mrs. W. M. Jr., Mill Valley, RNFC, $1,000; Sperry, Mrs. Leonard M., Los Angeles, DNC, $1,000; Spitzer, A., Los Angeles, RNFC, $1,000; Sprague, Dr. N., Los Angeles, RNC, $1,000; Stambaugh, John H., Indian Wells, RCBC, $1,000; Stanford, Dwight E., San Diego, RCBC, $1,000; Statler, E. M., Pauma Valley, RNFC, $1,000; Statler, E. M., El Cajon, RNFC, $2,000; Steele, Mrs. George C., Newport Beach, RCBC, $3,000; Steele, Richard, Newport Beach, RCBC, $1,000.

Stern, Carl W., San Francisco, TFP, $1,000; Stoller, Robert J., Pacific Palisades, DNC, $1,000; Stone, Martin, Los Angeles, TFP, $2,500; Stone, N. C., Menlo Park, RNC, $3,000; Stuart, E. H., Los Angeles, RNC, $1,000; Sturgis, George R., Newport Beach, RCBC, $1,000; Sullivan, R. Parker, Santa Monica, RCBC, $1,000; Sutro, J. A. Sr., San Francisco, RNFC; $1,000; Sutro, J., San Francisco, RCBC, $1,000; Tannehill, John Q., King City, ACU, $1,000.

Tarble, N. E., Los Angeles, RNFC, $1,000; Teetor, Donald H., Laguna Beach, RCBC, $1,000; Thomas, Charles S., Corona Del Mar, RCBC, $1,000; Thomas, George H. Jr., San Francisco, RCBC, $1,000; Thompson, H. W., Los Angeles, RNFC, $1,000; Todd, Malcolm C. M.D., Long Beach, RCBC, $1,000; Trane, Frank Hood, Balboa, RCBC, $1,000; Tremaine, Katherine W., Santa Barbara, TFP, $1,000; Trousdale, P. W., Los Angeles, RNFC, $1,000; Turner, L. A., Newport Beach, RNFC, $1,000.

Tuttle, Holmes, Los Angeles, RCBC, $1,000; Vaughn, J. V., San Marino, RNC, $1,000; Virtue, Julian A., Rolling Hills, RCBC, $1,000; Wallace, R., Carmel Valley. '70 CF, $1,000; Walter, R. H., San Diego, RNFC, $1,000; Ward, Murray, Beverly Hills, RCBC, $1,000; Washburn, Donald K., Corona Del Mar, RCBC, $3,000; Weatherford, R. V., Glendale, RNFC, $1,000; Wheeler, Mrs. C. S., Corona Del Mar, RCBC, $1,000; Wiel, Mrs. Eli H., Atherton, RCBC, $1,000.

Williams, Mrs. H. B., San Diego, RNFC, $1,000; Wilson, Charles H. Campaign Committee, Los Angeles, DSG, $1,110; Wrather, Mr. & Mrs., J. D. Jr., Beverly Hills, RNC, $4,000, RNFOC, $6,000; Zable, Walter H., San Diego, RCBC, $1,000; Zaffaroni, Alejandro, Atherton, DNGC, $1,000.

COLORADO

Arneill, Mrs. J. R., Denver, RNC, $1,000; Bunger, Mills, Wheat Ridge, DNC, $1,000; Coors, Jr., Golden, RNFC, $1,000; Dietler, C. S., Denver, RNC, $1,000, RNFC, $1,000; Donner, Mrs. R. Sr., Colorado Springs, RNC, $1,000, RNFC, $1,000; Harper, J. P., Denver, RNC, $1,000; Hondius, P., Denver, NCEC, $1,000; Lahman, Mrs. E., Longmont, RNFC, $1,000; Neilsen, A. Denver, RNC, $1,000; Pabst, H., Snowmass, RNC, $1,000, RNFC, $1,000.

CONNECTICUT

Aitken, Mr. & Mrs. R. B., Greenwich, RNFC, $1,000; Baekeland, G., Fairfield, RNFC, $1,000; Barker, R. R., New Canaan, RNFC, $1,000; Behrend, M. B., Greenwich, RNFC, $1,500; Belding, M. M., West Hartford, RNFC, $1,000; Chapin, Mrs. C. T., Old Saybrook, RNFC, $1,000; Chapman, W. L. Jr., Greenwich, RNFC, $1,000; Cooley, J. C., New Hartford, NCEC, $1,000; Deeds, Mr. & Mrs. Charles W., Farmington, RCBC, $2,000; Deeds, C. W., Farmington, RNFC, $1,000.

Deeds, C. W., Hartford, RNFC, $1,000; Deeds, Mrs. C. W., Farmington, RNFC, $1,000; Deeds, Mrs. R. B., Farmington, RNFC, $1,000; De Witt, J., Hartford, RNFC, $1,000; Flynt, H. N., Greenwich, RNFC, $1,000; Francoeur, P. M., Stamford, RNFC, $1,000; Gagarin, A., Litchfield, NCEC, $1,000; Geismar, R. L., Riverside, RNC, $1,000; Gilbert, Mrs. Benjamin, Stamford, ACU, $2,500; Goodnow, E. B., Darien, RNFC, $1,000.

Harcke, R. W., Branford, RNFC, $1,000; Harris, W. R., Salisbury, RNFC, $1,000; Hayes, C. C. Jr., Suffield, ACU, $1,000; Hermes, H., West Redding, '70 CF, $5,000; Hermes, R. A., West Redding, '70 CF, $5,000; Hillman, E. Jr., Fairfield, RNC, $1,000; Holmyard, Mrs. S., Darien, RNC, $1,000; Hoover, A., Greenwich, RNC, $1,000; Jackson, R. S., North Haven, RNFC, $1,000; Kemball-Cook, D. B., Darien, RNC, $1,000, RNFC, $1,000.

Kramer, Mrs. E., Greenwich, RNC, $1,000; List, V., Byran, '70 CF, $1,000; Lyon, F. G., Greenwich, RNC, $3,000; McBride, Mrs. E. W., Greenwich, RNC, $1,000; McCormick, Mrs. Gordon, Green Farms, RCBC, $1,000; McCurdy, R. C., Darien, RNFC, $1,000; McDonell, A., Hartford, '70 CF, $5,000; Matthies, Miss K., Seymour, RNC, $1,000; Merck, Mrs. George W., Greenwich, RCBC, $1,000, RNFC, $1,000; Miller, M. C. Fairfield, RNC, $1,000.

Moore, W. H., Greenwich, RNFC, $1,000; Morsman, J. J. Jr., Darien, RNC, $1,500, RNFC, $1,000; Mumford, M. C., Darien, RNFC, $1,000; Newington, Mr. & Mrs. John C., Greenwich, RCBC, $1,000, RNFC, $6,000; Nyselius, G., Stamford, RNFC, $1,000; Olin, S. Jr., Hartford, RNFC, $2,000; Pratt, Mr. & Mrs. George D. Jr., Bridgewater, DNC, $1,000, DNGC, $1,000, CFT, $1,200, NCEC, $25,000; Radley, Mrs. Eleanor B., Greenwich, RCBC, $1,000; Reed, Gordon W., Greenwich, RNFOC, $2,500, RNC, $2,500, RNFC, $2,500, RCBC, $1,000; Ross, Vincent C. Sr., Greenwich, RCBC, $1,000; Ruger, W. B., Southport, RNFC, $1,000; Stewart, J. H., Greenwich, RNFC, $1,000; Stollenwerck, E., Greenwich, RNFC, $1,000; Wiegand, Mr. & Mrs. E. L., Greenwich, ACA, $5,000, ACU, $1,120, RNFC, $1,000.

DELAWARE

Bolling, R. H., Jr., Greenville, RNC, $1,000, RNFC, $1,000; Bredin, J. Bruce, Greenville, RCBC, $1,000; Carpenter, E. N. II, Wilmington, RNFC, $1,000, RCBC, $1,000; Carpenter, R. R. M., Jr., Wilmington, NRSC, $2,000; Carpenter, Walter S. Jr., Wilmington, RCBC, $1,500, RNC, $1,500, RNFC, $1,000; Copeland, Lammot Du Pont, Wilmington, RCBC, $3,000; Copeland, L. Jr., Wilmington, RNC, $3,000; Copeland, Mrs. L. D., Greenville, RNC, $1,000; Dallas, Joseph A., Wilmington, RCBC, $1,000; Downs, Mr. & Mrs. R. N. III, Wilmington, RNC, $2,000.

Draper, Mrs. R. C., Montchanin, RNC, $1,000; Du Pont, Reynolds, Wilmington, RCBC, $3,000, RNC, $3,000, RNFOC, $3,000; Du Pont, Mrs. Reynolds, Greenville, RCBC, $3,000; Du Pont, S., Wilmington, RNFC, $1,000; Du Pont, Mr & Mrs. W. K., Newark, RNFC, $1,000; Edmonds, Mrs. G. P., Wilmington, RNFC, $1,000; Evans, T. B., Jr., Wilmington, RNC, $1,000; Forster, A. E., Wilmington, RNC, $1,000; Gordon, Wallace E., Greenville, RCBC, $1,000; Grasselli, Caesar A. II, Wilmington, RCBC, $1,000.

Grasselli, C. A. II, Wilmington, RNC, $1,000; Greenewalt, Mrs. Margaretta, Greenville, NRCC, $1,000, RNC, $1,000; Greenwalt, Crawford H., Wilmington, NRCC, $1,000, RCBC, $1,000, RNC, $1,000; Harrington, Charles J., Greenville, RCBC, $3,000, RCC, $3,000, RNFC, $3,000; Harrington, George S. Wilmington, RCBC, $1,000; Haskell, Hon. H. G. Jr., Wilmington, RNFC, $1,000; McCoy, C. B., Wilmington, RCBC, $1,000, RNC, $1,000; McDonald, Mr. & Mrs. Ellice Jr., Montchanin, ACA, $1,000, ACU, $3,000; May, Ernest N., Wilmington, RCBC, $2,000; May, Mrs. E. N., Wilmington, RNFC, $1,000.

Pearson, Mrs. Edith Du Pont, Montchanin, RCBC, $1,000; Raskob, William F., Wilmington, RCBC, $1,000; Reynolds, Mr. & Mrs. W. G., Greenville, RNFC, $1,000; Roe, W. G., Greenville, NCEC, $3,000; Rollins, Hon. J. W., Wilmington, RCC, $3,000, RVC, $3,000, RNFOC, $3,000, RNC, $3,000, NRCC, $3,000; Sharp, Bayard, Wilmington, RCBC, $4,000, RNC, $1,000; Sharp, Hugh R. Jr., Wilmington, RCBC, $1,000; Silliman, Mrs. H. H., Montchanin, RNFC, $1,000; Speakman, Willard A., Wilmington, RCBC, $1,000; Stradley, Wilmer, Wilmington, RCBC, $1,000; Worth, William A., Greenville, RCBC, $1,000; Worth, William A., Wilmington, RCBC, $1,000.

DISTRICT OF COLUMBIA

Adkinson, Austin, RCBC, $2,050; Anderson, D. J., RNFC, $1,000; Bason, C. B., RNC, $1,000; Bayne, Mrs. J. Breckinridge, RCBC, $1,000; Belin, Capt. P., RNFC, $1,000; Biddle, Mr. & Mrs. J., RNC, $1,000; Biggs, William R., DNC, $1,000; Bowersock, Justin D., RCBC, $1,000; Brundage, Percival F., RCBC, $1,000; Cafritz, Mrs. G. D., RNC, $1,000.

Capone, R. A., RNC, $1,000; Carothers, N. III, RNFC, $1,000; Carr, E. R., RNFC, $1,000; Carter, Clifton C., DNGC, $1,000; Clagett, C. Jr., RNC, $1,000; Corcoran, Thomas G., DNGC, $1,000; Corber, Robert J., RCBC, $1,000; Cox, Mrs. Raymond E., RCBC, $1,000; Cox, Mrs. R. E., RNFC, $1,000; Crosby, K. M., RNFC, $1,000.

Danzansky, Joseph B., DNGC, $1,000; Darling, J., RNFC, $1,000; Davidson, I., RNFC, $1,000; Davis, True, DNC, $1,000, DNGC, $1,000; Dawson, Donald S., DSCC, $2,000; Dufour, R. A., RNFC, $1,000; Du Pont, Mrs. M. M., RNFC, $1,000; Dwinell, L., RNFC, $1,000; Faricy, W. T., RNC, $1,000; Folger, John C. RCBC, $1,000.

Frank, V., '70 CF, $1,000, NCEC, $1,000; Gardner, Mrs. A., RNC, $1,000; Garrett, Mrs. George A., RCBC, $1,500; Glover, C. C., Jr., RNC, $1,000; Goodspeed, Elinor, DNC, $1,000, '70 CF, $3,000, DSG, $3,000; Gorman, J. R., RNFAC, $1,000; Gray, Gordon, RCBC, $1,000; Greenberg, Sanford D., DNC, $1,000; Greenway, G. C., RNFC, $1,000; Hagner, A. B., RNC, $1,000.

Healy, P.B., RNFC, $1,000; Hill, Arthur M., RCBC, $1,000; Hoff, Irvin A., NRCC, $3,000; Hood, E. M., RNFC, $1,000; Hunter, O. B. Jr., RNFC, $1,000; Jennings, L. A., RNC, $1,000; Kampelman, Max M., DNGC, $1,000; Kearns, Henry, RCBC, $1,000; Kearns, H., RNC, $1,000; Koch, Robert M., DNGC, $1,000.

Kogod, Robert P., DSCC, $3,000; Lankford, Thomas J., RCBC, $1,000; Lemon, James H., NRCC, $1,000; Lloyd, Mrs.

Demarest, RCBC, $1,000; Lloyd, Mrs. D., RNFC, $1,000; Lloyd, Mrs. Katharine N., RCBC, $1,000; McGranaghan, J. P., RNFC, $1,000; McKesson, J. A. III, RNFC, $1,000; Marriott, Mr. & Mrs. J. Willard, RCBC, $2,000, RNC, $2,000, RNFC, $1,000; Marriott, Mrs. Alice S., RCBC, $1,000.

Martin, Guy, RCBC, $1,000; Mellon, Paul, NRCC, $3,000, NRSC, $3,000, RNC, $3,000; Meyer, Mr. & Mrs. Charles A., RNFC, $2,000, RCBC, $1,000; Miller, F. P., NCEC, $1,000; Monk, G. E., RNC, $1,000; Moorhead, William S., DNGC, $3,000; Mountain, B. F., RNC, $1,000, RNFC, $1,000; Munson, Mr. & Mrs. Curtis B., RCBC, $1,000; Murray, Mr. & Mrs. Francis A., RCBC, $2,000, RNC, $1,000; Naden, K. D., RNFC, $1,000.

Nunn, Ira H., DNGC, $1,000; O'Connell, Joseph J., DNGC, $1,000; Olmsted, George, RCBC, $1,000; Packard, Hon. D., RNFC, $1,000; Palmer, Mrs. L. T., RNFC, $1,000; Patterson, Hon. Jefferson, RCBC, $3,000; Pfeffermann, I., '70 CF, $1,000; Porter, Paul A., DNC, $1,000; Purves, Dr. & Mrs. Pierre M., RCBC, $2,000; Rea, Henry O. Jr., DNC, $1,000.

Rea, Michael, DNGC, $2,000; Rentzel, D. W., DSCC, $1,000; Riddell, James W., DSCC, $2,000; Roberts, K., '70 CF, $1,000; Shu, Paul C., NRCC, $1,000; Silverstein, L. L., RNC, $1,000; Sisk, Roger, NRCC, $1,000; Smith, Charles E., DNGC, $1,000, DSCC, $6,000; Smith, C. R., DNC, $1,000; Smith, Robert H., DSCC, $3,000.

Stadtler, John, NRCC, $3,000; Stern, Philip M., CPS, $1,000 (1969); Stirling, David, NRSC, $1,500; Stirling, Wm. G., NRSC, $1,500; Strong, H., RNC, $3,000; Taliaferro, Henry B. Jr., DNGC, $1,000; Train, R. E., RNFC, $1,000; Traynor, Mr. & Mrs. H. S., RNFC, $1,000; Troop, Glen, DSCC, $3,000; Vice, Leslie T., RCBC, $1,000; Volpe, John A., RCBC, $1,000, RNFC, $1,000.

Volpe, Joseph Jr., DSCC, $5,000; Wagley, J. R., NCEC, $4,000; Watts, Glenn E., DNC, $1,000, DNGC, $5,000; Watts, Philip H., RCBC, $2,000; Wells, J. C., RNC, $1,000; Whalley, Hon. J., RNFC, $1,000; Wild, Claude C. Jr., NRSC, $1,000; Winsor, Curtin Jr., RCBC, $1,000; Wrather, Mrs. W. E., RNFC, $2,000; Zalles, Mrs. R. S., RNFC, $3,000.

FLORIDA

Alford, Mr. & Mrs. W. J., Naples, RNFC, $1,000; Bassett, Harry Hood, Miami Beach, RCBC, $1,000; Bassett, H. H., Miami Beach, RNC, $1,000; Berry, Loren M., Surfside, BIPAC, $3,000; Berry, Mrs. Loren M., Miami Beach, RCBC, $3,000; Buckley, P. J., Palm Beach, RCBC, $1,000; Carpenter, Wm. K., Ft. Lauderdale, RCBC, $1,000; Carpenter, W. K., Ft. Lauderdale, RNC, $1,000, ACA, $1,000; Coffin, Dexter D. Jr., Palm Beach, RCBC, $1,000; Cordiner, R. J., Clearwater, RNFC, $1,000.

Courshon & Courshon, Miami Beach, DNGC (Fla.), $1,000; Craigmyle, Ronald M., Palm Beach, RCBC, $1,000; Cummings, Dexter, Hobe Sound, RCBC, $2,000; Davie, Mr. & Mrs. Bedford, Palm Beach, RCBC, $1,000; Davis, Mrs. L. W., Jacksonville, RNC, $1,000; Duberg, Mr. & Mrs. H., Hobe Sound, RNFC, $1,000; Dyett, John H., Hobe Sound, RCBC, $1,000; Ecclestone, Mrs. E. Llwyd, North Palm Beach, RCBC, $1,000; Ecclestone, M. E. Jr., N. Palm Beach, RCBC, $1,000; Emerson, E. A., Clearwater, RNC, $1,000.

Evinrude, Mr. & Mrs. R., Jensen Beach, RNFC, $1,000; Folger, Mrs. J. Clifford, Palm Beach, RCBC, $1,000; Foskett, Walter S., Palm Beach, RCBC, $1,000; Fox, Sylvia, Miami Beach, DNGC, $1,000; Fox, S. Ft. Lauderdale, RNC, $1,000; Frank, H. J., Clearwater, DNGC (Fla.), $1,000; Friday, Elmer O. Jr., Fort Myers, DNGC, (Fla.), $1,000; Griffith, W. S., Ft. Lauderdale, RNFC, $1,000, RNC, $3,000; Gunster, J. F., Palm Beach, RNC,

$1,000; Hancock, J. B., Delray Beach, RNFC, $1,000; Hanley, Wm. L., Palm Beach, RCBC, $2,000.

Hanley, W. L., Palm Beach, RCBC, $1,000; Heede, B. M. Jr., Palm Beach, RNC, $1,500; Henderson, Mrs. L. E., Pompano Beach, RNFC, $1,000; Hoffman, Mrs. Charles L., Jacksonville, RCBC, $1,000; Holton, Addison, Hobe Sound, RCBC, $1,000; Homan, Rudolph, Naples, ACU, $1,450; Hungerford, D. E., Ft. Lauderdale, RNC, $1,000; Hunt, Robert E., Miami, DNGC, $5,000; Kelly, Mr. & Mrs. C. D., Palm Beach, RNC, $2,000; Kelley, Russell P., Palm Beach, RCBC, $1,000.

Kelley, Mrs. Solon C. Jr., Hobe Sound, RCBC, $1,000; King, W. H., Boca Raton, RNC, $1,000; Kirby, Capt. L., Hobe Sound, RNFC, $1,000; Lattner, Forrest C., Delray Beach, RCBC, $1,000; Lattner, Mr. & Mrs. F. C., Delray Beach, RNFC, $2,000, RNC, $2,000; Lau, E. B., Miami Beach, RNFC, $1,000; Light, Mrs. Rudolph A., Palm Beach, RCBC, $1,000; Lunt, S. D., Boca Raton, RNFC, $1,000; McKillips, Mr. & Mrs. James F. Jr., Miami Beach, RCBC, $1,000; Merwin, Davis Sr., Delray Beach, RCBC, $1,000.

Miller, P. E., Redington Beach, RNFC, $1,000; Nicholson, R., Tallahassee, RNFC, $1,000; O'Nett, George L., Miami, DNGC (Fla.), $1,000; Ordway, Mrs. Lucius P., Palm Beach, RCBC, $1,000; Palmer, P. A., Newport Beach, RCBC, $1,000; Pawley, Wm. D., Miami, NRCC, $1,800, RNC, $1,000; Pawley, Hon. William D., Miami, RCBC, $1,000; Phillips, William A., Palm Beach, RCBC, $1,000; Phipps, Ogden, Palm Beach, RCBC, $3,000; Plante, Mr. & Mrs. L., Oveido, RNC, $1,000.

Pollar, Lou, Miami, DNC, $1,000; Randall, Donald T., Palm Beach, RCBC, $1,000; Reed, Verner Z. Jr., Palm Beach, RCBC, $1,000; Reynolds, W. R. Jr., Palm Beach, RNC, $1,000; Richards, Bartlett, Jupiter, RCBC, $1,000; Ringhaver, L. C., Jacksonville, RNC, $1,000; Rust, Robert, Miami, CVF, $1,000; Sanford, Miss Mary Ducan, Palm Beach, RCBC, $1,000; Santell, J. J. Jr., Miami, RNFC, $1,000; Seyburn, Mrs. Wesson, Palm Beach, RCBC, $1,000.

Slemaker, Mrs. S. M., St. Petersburg, RNFC, $1,000; Stewart, Mrs. W. T., Merritt Island, RCBC, $1,000; Storer, G. B., Miami Beach, RNFC, $1,000; Sullivan, Bolton, Hobe Sound, RCBC, $1,000; Swenson, Edward F., Coral Gables, RCBC, $1,000; Tiernan, J. William, Delray Beach, RCBC, $3,000; Tiernan, Mrs. J. William, Delray Beach, RCBC, $1,000; Tonks, Raymond W., Miami, DNGC (Fla.), $1,000; Turner, R. L., Palm Beach, RNC, $1,000; Urbanek, A., Ft. Lauderdale, RNFC, $1,000; Waddell, C. Emmett, Palm Beach, RCBC, $1,000; Walsh, Mrs. Cornelius S., Palm Beach, RCBC, $1,000.

GEORGIA

Brandon, I., Atlanta, RNFC, $1,000; Callaway, Hon. H. H., Pine Mt., RNFC, $1,000; Cooper, Jerome M., Atlanta, DNC, $1,000, DNGC, $1,000; Dubrof, Jerry A., Atlanta, DNC, $1,000; Foster, R. G. Sr., Wadley, RNFC, $1,000; Foster, R. G. Jr., Wadley, RNFC, $1,000; Foster, R. G. III, Wadley, RNFC, $1,000; Fuqua, J. B., Augusta, DNGC, $1,000; Kenan, J. G., Atlanta, RNFC, $1,000; King, C. B., Albany, DNGC, $1,000.

Lane, M. B. Jr., Atlanta, RNC, $1,000; Livingston, D. R., Savannah, RNFC, $1,000; Moore, O. R., Atlanta, RNFC, $1,000; Rafshoon, Gerald M., Atlanta, DNC, $1,000; Roebling, R. C., Savannah, RNC, $1,000; Serrato, Dr. J. C. Jr., Columbus, DNGC, $1,000; Smith, H., Atlanta, RNFC, $1,000; Tarkenton, F. A., Atlanta, RNFC, $1,000; Wasden, W. A. Jr., Savannah, RNC, $1,000.

HAWAII

Black, R. E., Honolulu, RNFC, $1,000; Spalding, P. E., Ewa, RNFC, $1,000; Von Holt, H. V., Honolulu, RNFC, $1,000; Wrenn, Mr. & Mrs. H. L., Honolulu, RNC, $2,000.

IDAHO

Fery, J. B., Boise, RNFC, $1,000; Hansberger, R. V., Boise, RNFC, $1,000; Hansberger, Mrs. R. V., Boise, RNFC, $1,000.

ILLINOIS

Anderson, R. R., Chicago, RNC, $1,000; Archambault, Bennett, Chicago, RCBC, $1,000, RNFC, $1,000; Armour, Mrs. A. Watson III, Lake Forest, RCBC, $2,000; Armour, D. B., Libertyville, RNFC, $1,000; Armour, Mrs. Laurance, Lake Forest, RCBC, $1,000; Armour, Mr. & Mrs. Lester, Chicago, RCBC, $1,000; Arrington, Hon. W. R., Evanston, RNFC, $1,000; Arvey, Jacob M., Chicago, DNGC, $1,000; Barker, James M., North Brook, RCBC, $1,000; Barker, J. M., Chicago, RCBC, $1,000.

Barkes, C., Chicago, RNFC, $1,000; Belder, F. II, Lake Forest, RNC, $1,000; Benes, Miss H., Berwyn, RNC, $1,500; Bennett, A. H., Decatur, RNC, $1,000; Bent, John P., Lake Forest, RCBC, $1,000; Bent, Mrs. J. P., Lake Forest, RNC, $1,000; Brach, Mrs. F. V., Glenview, RNFC, $1,000; Burch, C. B., Winnetka, RNC, $1,000; Butler, Mrs. J. M., Winnetka, RNC, $1,000, RNFC, $1,000; Campbell, Mrs. C. M., Wilmette, RNFC, $1,000.

Cochran, J. L., Chicago, RNFC, $1,000; Cole, W. W., Chicago, RNFC, $1,000; Colwell, Mrs. P. G., Champaign, RNC, $3,000; Colwell, Mrs. P. G., Evanston, RCC, $2,000, RNFC, $3,000; Cook, Mr. & Mrs. G., Chicago, RNFC, $1,000; Cook, Mrs. G. Bradford, Chicago, RCBC, $1,000; Cook, Mrs. J. A., Lake Buff, RNFC, $1,000; Cowles, Mrs. Louise L., Lake Forest, RCBC, $3,000; Cummings, D., Chicago, RNFC, $1,000; Davis, Charles W., Chicago, DNGC, $1,000.

Deree, W. S., Chicago, RNC, $1,000; Dick, Mrs. Albert B. Jr., Lake Forest, RCBC, $1,000; Dickinson, W. R. Jr., Chicago, RNC, $1,000; Dillon, P. W., Sterling, RNFC, $1,000; Donnelley, E., Chicago, RNFC, $1,000; Donnelley, G., Chicago, RNFC, $1,500; Donnelley, Mr. & Mrs. G., Libertyville, RNFC, $1,000; Donnelley, Gaylord, Chicago, RCBC, $2,500; Douglas, J. A., Chicago, RNC, $1,000; Erickson, D., Chicago, RNFC, $1,000.

Erman, W., Chicago, RNC, $1,000; Farwell, Albert D., Chicago, RCBC, $2,000; Fennelly, J. F., Chicago, RNFC, $1,000; Florsheim, H. M., Chicago, RNFC, $1,000; Funk, E. D. Jr., Bloomington, RNFC, $1,000; Gaylord, Robert, Rockford, ACU, $1,100; Genius, R. M. Jr., Chicago, RNC, $1,000; Gibbs, Dr. Frederic A., Chicago, TFP, $2,000; Goddard, Mrs. D., Sterling, RNFC, $1,000; Graham, W. B., Morton Grove, RNC, $1,264.08.

Gunn, C. L., DeKalb, RNC, $1,000; Hales, Mrs. Burton W., Winnetka, RCBC, $1,000; Hanson, Norman R., Elmhurst, RCBC, $1,000; Harris, A. H., Springfield, RNC, $1,000; Harris, Irving B., Chicago, DNC, $1,000; Haskins, S. G., Lake Forest, NCEC, $1,000; Hay, J. T., Chicago, RNFC, $1,000; Heineman, Ben W., Chicago, DNGC, $1,000; Hemphill, James C., Chicago, RCBC, $1,000; Hemphill, J. C., Chicago, RNFC, $1,000.

Hoover, H. Earl, Glencoe, RCBC, $1,000; Hoover, Mr. & Mrs. H. E., Glencoe, RNFC, $1,000; Hossinger, R. A., Mendota, RNFC, $1,000; Howlett, Mrs. W., Winnetka, RNFC, $1,000; Howlett, W., Winnetka, RNC, $1,000; Hubacher, Frank B., Chicago, RCBC, $1,000; Hull, D. B., Winnetka, RNFC, $1,000; Irwin, G. M., Quincy, RNFC, $1,000; Jarchow, Charles C., Glenview, RCBC, $1,000; Johnson, R. E., Chicago, RNFC, $1,000.

Keck, G. E., Palatine, RNFC, $1,000; Keith, Mrs. Stanley, Chicago, RCBC, $1,000; Kemper, James Scott, Chicago, RCBC, $1,000; Kemper, Hon. J. S., Chicago, RNC, $2,000; Knight, L. B., Chicago, RNFC, $1,000; Korhumel, H. F., Lake Forest, RNC, $1,000; Krafft, Mrs. Walter A., Chicago, RCBC, $1,000; Kroc, R. A., Chicago, RNC, $1,000, RNFC, $1,000; Kroehler, K., Naperville, RNC, $1,000; Langhorne, Mrs. George, Chicago, RCBC, $1,000.

Leslie, John W., Chicago, RCBC, $3,000; Leslie, J. W., Evanston, RNC, $3,000; Livezey, Mrs. K. T., Chicago, RNFC, $1,000; Lloyd, Mr. & Mrs. G. A., Chicago, RNFC, $1,000; Lourie, Donald B., Chicago, RCBC, $1,000; Louis, Mrs. Henrietta J., Evanston, RCBC, $1,000; Louis, John J., Winnetka, RCBC, $1,000; Louis, John J. Jr., Chicago, RCBC, $1,000; Louis, Mrs. John J., Evanston, RCBC, $3,000; Louis, J. J., Wilmette, RNFC, $1,000.

Louis, Michael W., Wilmette, RCBC, $1,000; Louis, M. W., Evanston, RNFC, $1,000; Mc Cormick, Fowler, Chicago, RCBC, $1,000, RNFC, $1,000; Mc Crink, E. J., Northlake, RNC, $1,000, RNFC, $1,000; Mc Gaw, F. G., Evanston, RNC, $3,000, RCC, $3,000, RNFDC, $3,000, RNFC, $3,000; McGibbon, E. L., Chicago, RNC, $1,000; Metcalf, G. M., Chicago, RNC, $1,000; Miller, Joe D., Whaton, RCBC, $1,000; Mitchell, Wm. H., Chicago, RCBC, $1,000; Mueller, F. L., Chicago, RNFC, $1,000.

Murdough, Thomas G., Evanston, RCBC, $1,000; Nielsen, Arthur C. Sr., Chicago, NRCC, $2,000; Nielsen, Mr. & Mrs. A. C., Chicago, RNC, $5,000, ACA, $5,000; Norris, Bruce Arthur, Chicago, RCBC, $1,000, RNFC, $1,000; Norris, L. J., St. Charles, RNFC, $1,000; Notaro, M., Chicago, RNFC, $1,000; Olin, J. M., Alton, RCBC, $3,000; Otis, James Sanford, Chicago, RCBC, $3,000; Pick, A. Jr., Chicago, RNFC, $1,000; Pillsbury, Mrs. C. S., Chicago, ACU, $2,418.

Pirie, Mrs. Gordon L., Chicago, RCBC, $1,000; Potter, Mr. & Mrs. Charles S., Chicago, RCBC, $2,000; Prentice, J. R., Chicago, RNFC, $1,000; Prince, W. W., Chicago, RNC, $3,500, RCC, $2,500, RVC, $2,500, RNFC, $2,500; Prince, Mrs. W. Wood, Chicago, RNFC, $1,000; Reid, Robert H., Chicago, RCBC, $1,000; Replogle, Hon. L. I., Oak Park, RNFC, $3,000; Roberts, Shepherd McG. Sr., Winnetka, RCBC, $1,000; Rockola, David C., Chicago, RCBC, $1,000, RNFC, $1,000; Rule, J. T., Wildwood, RNFC, $1,000.

Runnells, Mrs. Clive, Lake Forest, RCBC, $2,000, RNC, $1,000; Runnells, John S., Lake Forest, RCBC, $1,000; Rust, E. B., Bloomington, RNFC, $1,000; Ryerson, Anthony M., Chicago, RCBC, $1,000; Ryerson, Edward L., Chicago, RNC, $1,000, RCBC, $1,000; Ryerson, Mrs. Donald M., Lake Forest, RCBC, $1,000; Schweppe, Dr. & Mrs. J. S., Chicago, RNC, $1,000; Scribner, G. H. Jr., Chicago, RCBC, $1,000; Searle, Mr. & Mrs. John G., Chicago, RNC, $1,000, RCBC, $6,000; Shaheen, John M., Tampico, NRCC, $3,000.

Solinsky, R. S., Chicago, RCBC, $1,000; Spencer, Mrs. William M., Chicago, RCBC, $1,000; Spindell, Robert F., Chicago, RCBC, $1,000, RNFC, $1,000; Steubner, Erwin A., Kenilworth, RCBC, $1,000; Stone, W. Clement, Chicago, RCBC, $3,000; Stuart, Hon. & Mrs. R., Chicago, RNC, $1,000, RNFC, $2,000; Stuart, Hon. & Mrs. R. Douglas, Chicago, RCBC, $1,500; Stuart, Robert D. Jr., Chicago, RCBC, $1,000, RNFC, $1,000; Swearingen, John E., Chicago, RCBC, $1,000; Swift, Mrs. P. H., Lake Bluff, RCBC, $1,000.

Taylor, E., Winnetka, RNC, $1,000; Taylor, E., Chicago, RNFC, $1,000; Terra, Daniel J., Kenilworth, RCBC, $3,000; Terra, D. J., Chicago, RNFC, $3,000; Venema, M. P., Des Plaines, RNFC, $1,000; Watson, William L., Palatine, RCBC, $1,000; Weissbourd, Bernard, Chicago, TFP, $2,000; Welles, Donald P., Lake Forest, RCBC, $1,000; West, J. M., Chicago, RNFC, $1,000; Wetmore, H. O., Chicago, RCBC, $1,000.

Whipple, Jay N., Chicago, RCBC, $1,000; White, W. P., Glencoe, RNC, $1,000; Wilkie, L., Des Plaines, RNC, $2,000, RNFC, $1,000; Williams, E., Chicago, RNFC, $1,000; Wilson, John P. Jr., Chicago, RCBC, $1,000; Wiman, Mrs. C. D., Moline, RNFC, $1,000; Witwer, S. W., Chicago, RNFC, $1,000; Wood, Arthur M., Lake Forest, RCBC, $1,000, RNC, $1,000; Woodruff, George Gould, Wayne, RCBC, $1,000; Wrigley, P. K., Chicago, RNFC, $2,000; Zweiner, K. V., Winnetka, RNFC, $1,000.

INDIANA

Ball, E. F., Muncie, RNFC, $1,000; Beardsley, Walter R., Elkhart, RCBC, $6,000; Beardsley, W. R., Elkhart, RNFC, $1,000; Carmichael, Mr. & Mrs. O. C. Jr., South Bend, RNFC, $1,000; Cohn, D. C., Bloomington, UNAF, $1,000; Fink, R. A., Auburn, RNFC, $1,000; French, E. T., Indianapolis, RNFC, $1,000; Goodrich, Pierre F., Indianapolis, ACA, $1,000; Honeywell, Mrs. Mark C., Wabash, RCBC, $1,000; Leighton, J., South Bend, RNC, $1,000.

Leighton, Judd, South Bend, RCBC, $2,000; Lilly, Mrs. Eli, Indianapolis, URA, $1,000; Little, D., Emmett, RNC, $1,000; Lynn, Mrs. Charles J., Indianapolis, RCBC, $1,500; McKinney, Frank E., Indianapolis, DNGC, $1,000; Martin, R., Elkhart, RNFC, $1,000; Miller, Mr. & Mrs. J., Columbus, RNFC, $1,000; Moxley, David, Indianapolis, RCBC, $1,000; Neff, H. A., Fort Wayne, RNFC, $1,000; Noyes, Mr. & Mrs. N. H., Indianapolis, NRCC, $5,000, RCBC, $4,000, RNC, $2,000, RNFC, $1,000; Oppenheim, J. P., N. Manchester, RNFC, $1,000; Ransburg, Harold, Indianapolis, RCBC, $4,000, RNC, $1,000, ACA, $1,000; Tarzian, Sarkes, Bloomington, RCBC, $2,000; Van Riper, Mrs. G. Jr., Indianapolis, RNC, $1,000, RNFC, $1,500; Welch, Robert V., Indianapolis, DNGC, $1,000.

IOWA

Deardorf, Mrs. J. C., Fort Dodge, RNC, $1,000; Hoenner, R. N. Sr., Keokuk, RNC, $1,000; Hoerner, R. N., Keokuk, RCBC, $1,000; Rosenfield, Joseph T., Des Moines, CPS, $1,000 (1969); Stanley, C. M., Muscatine, RNC, $1,000.

KANSAS

Asel, G., Kansas City, NCEC, $1,000; Barnett, A. D., Wichita, RNFC, $1,000; Bartlett, Mr., Wichita, ACU, $1,000; Beech, Mrs. W., Wichita, RNFC, $1,000; Brookover, E. C., Garden City, RNFC, $1,000; Cray, C. L., Atchison, RNFC, $1,000; Fegan, R. J., Junction City, RNC, $1,000; Fink, H. B., Topeka, NRCC, $2,927.40, RNFC, $918.85; Garvey, Mrs. Olive W., Wichita, RCBC, $1,016.05; Garvey, W. W., Wichita, RNC, $2,441.91, RNFC, $2,441.91, RCC, $2,441.91, RNFOC, $2,441.91.

Goppert, C. H., Prairie Village, RNC, $1,000; Hedrick, F. E., Wichita, RNFC, $1,000; Hixson, A. R. Jr., Topeka, RNC, $1,000; Michener, C. D., Lawrence, NCEC, $1,000; Phillips, Mr. & Mrs. L. E. Jr., Wichita, RNC, $1,000.

KENTUCKY

Atkins, O. E., Ashland, RNC, $1,000; Brown, John Y. Jr., Louisville, DNC, $1,000, $2,500; Gardner, Hoyt D., Louisville, RCBC, $1,000; Ireland, Miss K., Wendover, RNFC, $1,000; Jones, David A., Louisville, DNC, $1,000; Markey, Mrs. G. P., Lexington, RNFC, $1,000; May, William H., Frankfort, DNC, $1,000; Sanders, Col. H. B., Shelbyville, RNC, $1,000; Stapleton, O. Jr., Ashland, RNC, $1,000; Webb, Mrs. P. W., Paris, RNC, $3,000; Widener, P. B., Versailles, RNC, $1,000, ACA, $1,000, RNFC, $1,000.

LOUISIANA

Beaird, C. T., Shreveport, RNFC, $1,000; Boh, R. H., New Orleans, RNC, $1,000; Brown, J. Marshall, New Orleans, DNGC, $2,000; Cole, Mrs. C. G., Houma, RNC, $1,000; Deming, Dr. John W., Alexandria, RCBC, $1,000; Feazel, Cynthia D., West Monroe, DNGC, $1,000; Foster, Murphy J., Franklin, RCBC, $1,000; Funderburk, M. L., Houma, RNC, $1,000; Helis, William G. Jr., New Orleans, DNGC, $5,000; Kinsey, Norman V., Shreveport, BIPAC, $2,000.

Kinsey, N. V., Shreveport, RNFC, $1,000; Lyons, Charlton, Shreveport, NRCC, $1,000; Noe, Hon. J. A., Monroe, RNFC, $3,000; Poindexter, R. D., Shreveport, BIPAC, $2,000; Roemer, Mr. & Mrs. Charles E. II, Bossier City, DNGC, $1,000; Stern, Mrs. Edgar B., New Orleans, DNC, $1,000; Williams, L. M., New Orleans, RNFC, $1,000.

MAINE

Chadwick, Mrs. E. Jerry, Northeast Harbor, RCBC, $1,000; Hutchins, C. M., Bangor, RNC, $1,000; Petts, S. F., Kennebunkport, RNC, $1,000, RNFC, $1,000; Tate, Mrs. H. C., Blue Hill, RNC, $1,000.

MARYLAND

Arrowsmith, George H. C., Upperco, RCBC, $2,500; Arrowsmith, G. C., Upperco, RNC, $2,500; Aubinoe, Mrs. A., Bethesda, RNC, $1,000; Baker, J. D., Monkton, RNC, $1,000; Bowis, A. H., Bethesda, RNFC, $1,000; Bray, William, Carrolton, ACU, $1,000; Burke, D. W., Bethesda, RNFC, $1,000; Catto, Hon. H. E. Jr., Bethesda, RNFC, $1,000; Colligan, Mrs. F. J., Chevy Chase, RNC, $3,000, RNFC, $3,000; Ewing, F. M., Potomac, RNC, $1,000.

Fleming, D. M., Potomac, RNFC, $1,000; Franklin, John M., Cockeysville, RCBC, $1,000; Graham, J. Jr., Baltimore, RNC, $1,000; Grassmuck, G., Bethesda, RNC, $1,000; Groves, Mrs. L. Lloyd, Elkton, RCBC, $1,000; Groves, Mr. & Mrs. L. L., Elkton, RNC, $2,000, RCBC, $1,000; Hammerman, I. H. II, Baltimore, RNFC, $1,000; Hopkins, David Luke, Baltimore, RCBC, $1,000; Juliana, J. N., Rockville, RNFC, $1,000; Kogod, Mrs. Arlene, Bethesda, DSCC, $2,500.

Lankford, T. J., Potomac, RNFC, $1,000; McGovern, George, Chevy Chase, DNC, $1,000; Masson, C. A., Baltimore, RNC, $1,000; Meyer, E. III, Baltimore, NCEC, $1,500; Parks, Henry G. Jr., Baltimore, DNGC, $1,000; Pasco, N. D., Chevy Chase, RNFC, $1,000; Palavsky, Max, Baltimore, CPS, $1,000 (1969); Polinger, Milton, Chevy Chase, DSCC, $1,000; Rogers, Hon. W. P., Bethesda, RNFC, $1,000; Sherwood, Donald H., Towson, RCBC, $1,000; Smith, C. C., Silver Spring, RNC, $1,000.

Smith, Clarice R., Bethesda, DSCC, $2,500; Symington, Hon. J., Lutherville, RNC, $1,000, RCBC, $1,000; Tarr, R. H., Silver Spring, RNFC, $1,000; Voss, E. S., Monkton, URA, $5,000; Weir, O. L., Kensington, RNC, $1,000; White, Mrs. N. H. Jr., Baltimore, RNFC, $1,000; White, Mrs. R. T., Mitchellville, RNFC, $1,000; Williams, R. M., Baltimore, RNFC, $1,000.

MASSACHUSETTS

Alker, H., Newtonville, '70 CF, $1,000; Alker, H. R., Newtonville, NCEC, $1,000; Allen, Mrs. Eleanor W., Boston, RCBC, $1,000; Ames, David, North Easton, RCBC, $1,000; Ames, Mrs. David, North Easton, RCBC, $1,000; Ames, John S. Jr., Boston, RCBC, $1,000; Anderson, O. Kelley, Boston, RCBC, $1,000; Arnold, E. M., Melrose, RNC, $1,000; Arnold, Mrs. Richard, Melrose, RCBC, $1,000; Ayer, N. R., Boston, RNC, $1,000.

Blanchard, Robert, Billerica, ACU, $1,000; Boyd, Ralph G., Boston, RCBC, $1,000; Brooks, W. D. Jr., Dedham, RNFC, $1,000; Case, J. P., Boston, RNFC, $1,000; Case, Laura, Cambridge, UNAF, $1,000, '70 CF, $5,000; Chapin, Homer N., Wilbraham, RCBC, $1,000; Chapin, H. N., Springfield, RNFC, $1,000; Clapp, Eugene H. II, Boston, RCBC, $1,000; Cooper, J. L., Needham, RNFC, $1,000; Cotting, Charles E., Boston, RCBC, $1,000.

Cox, J. B., Cohasset, RNC, $1,000; Cox, Mrs. J. B., Cohasset, RNFC, $1,000; Curtis, Louis, Boston, RCBC, $1,000; Danielson, R. E., Boston, RNFC, $1,000; Demers, G. N. Jr., Cambridge, RNC, $1,000, RNFC, $1,000; Dumaine, F. C. Jr., Boston, RNC, $1,000; Faulkner, J., Brookline, '70 CF, $1,000; Gardner, G. Peabody,

Brookline, RCBC, $1,000; Gardner, G., Boston, RNFC, $1,000; Gilbert, Carl J., Dover, RCBC, $1,000.

Gilbert, Hon. Carl J., Dover, RCBC, $1,000; Goodwin, Neil, Cambridge, CFT, $1,000, NCEC, $2,000; Hagemann, H. F. Jr., Boston, RNFC, $1,000; Hall, H. S. Jr., Cambridge, RNFC, $1,000; Jenks, J. L. Jr., Winchester, RNC, $1,000; Latshaw, John H., Melrose, RCBC, $1,000; Lee, S., Boston, NCEC, $3,000; Lee, S. M., Boston, NCEC, $1,000; Lyman, R. T. Jr., Boston, RNC, $1,000; Mc Connell, William G., Winchester, RCBC, $1,000.

Mc Curdy, M., Concord, '70 CF, $1,000; Makrauer, S., Boston, RNFC, $1,000; Pappas, Hon. T. A., Boston, RNFC, $3,000; Peabody, Miss Amelia, Boston, RNC, $1,000, RNFC, $1,000, RCBC, $1,000; Philips, J. N., Boston, RNFC, $1,000; Plumley, H. L., Worcester, RNFC, $1,000; Robie, R. S., Boston, RCBC, $1,000; Rowland, B. A., Lawrence, RNC, $1,000; Simon, Mr. & Mrs. M., Boston, RNC, $1,000; Smith, R. A., Boston, RNC, $1,500.

Sprague, R. C., Williamstown, RNC, $1,000; Storer, Miss E. B., Boston, RNFC, $1,000; Taft, Mr. & Mrs. Edward A., Boston, RCBC, $1,000, RNC, $1,000; Vance, Henry T., Boston, NRCC, $2,000; Wald, George, Cambridge, UNAF, $1,000; Wallace, Mr. & Mrs. G. R., Fitchburg, RNFC, $1,000; Waring, Mr. & Mrs. Lloyd B., Boston, RNC, $4,000, RNFC, $7,000, RCC, $4,000, RCBC, $1,000; Weyerhaeuser, C. A., Milton, RNFC, $1,000; Whitney, W. E., Belmont, RNC, $1,000; Yeager, C., Attleboro, RNFC, $1,000; Yonts, Mrs. Janette R., Boston, RCBC, $1,000, RNFC, $1,000.

MICHIGAN

Beresford, Mr. and Mrs. J. A., Bloomfield Hills, RNC, $1,000; Bliss, Mrs. C. Haskell, Grosse Pointe Farms, RCBC, $1,000; Bonnar, A. W. Sr., Farmington, RNFC, $1,000; Carey, Walter F., Bloomfield Hills, NRCC, $1,000; Chambers, C., Lansing, NRCC, $1,500; Cook, P.C., Grand Rapids, RNFC, $1,000; Cousins, Mrs. A. M., Bloomfield Hills, RNFC, $1,000; Cousins, Mrs. A. Y., Bloomfield Hills, RNFC, $1,000; Crapo, W. W., Grosse Pointe, RNFC, $1,000; Cunningham, H. B., Detroit, RNC, $1,000; Cunningham, K. W., Grosse Pointe Park, RNFC, $1,000; Dunnings, Stuart J. Jr., Lansing, DNC, $1,000.

Earhart, Richard, Ann Arbor, RCBC, $1,000; Earhart, R., Ann Arbor, RNFC, $1,000; RNC, $1,000; Evans, R. B., Detroit, RNFC, $1,000; Fetzer, J. E., Kalamazoo, RNFC, $1,000; Fink, P. R., Mount Clemens, RNC, $1,000; Fisher, A. J. Jr., Grosse Pointe, RNFC, $1,000; Fisher, Mr. & Mrs. M. M., Franklin, RNFC, $3,000; Ford, Mrs. Edsel B., Grosse Pointe, RCBC, $3,000; Ford, Benson, Grosse Pointe, RCBC, $1,000; Ford, H. II, Dearborn, RNC, $3,000.

Foskett, Walter W., Palm Beach, RCBC, $1,000; Fruehauf, Mrs. H. C., Detroit, RNFC, $1,000; Gerber, D. F., Fremont, RNC, $1,000, RNFC, $1,000; Gerity, Mr. & Mrs. J., Adrian, RNC, $5,000; Gilmore, J. Jr., Kalamazoo, RNC, $1,000; Gilmore, J. S. Jr., Kalamazoo, RNFC, $1,000; Hasting, R. F., Detroit, RNC, $1,000; Howard, W. B., Mrs., Grosse Pointe, RNC, $2,000; Hutchinson, Mr. & Mrs. M. J., Alma, RNFC, $1,000, RNC, $1,000; Ivory, J. F. Sr., Union Lake, RNFC, $1,000.

Kamm, R. L., Birmingham, NCEC, $1,000; Kennedy, Mrs. J. A., Ann Arbor, RNFC, $1,000; Kyes, R. M., Bloomfield Hills, RNFC, $2,500; Kirsch, C. E., Sturgis, RNFC, $1,000; McClure, Mrs. Harold Sr., Alma, RCBC, $3,000; McClure, Mrs. Harold H. Jr., Alma, RCBC, $1,000; McClure, Harold H. Jr., Alma, RCBC, $1,000; McCuen, Charles L., Bloomfield, NRSC, $1,000; McCuen, C. L., Bloomfield Hills, RNFC, $1,000; McNaughton, Mrs. L., Grosse Pointe Farms, RNFC, $2,000.

Markman, Stephen, Oak Park, ACU, $1,000; Meader, Mr. & Mrs. E., Kalamazoo, RNFC, $3,000; Merrell, A. W., Grosse Pointe, RNC, $1,000; Pierson, H. L., Detroit, RNFC, $1,000; Power, Philip A., Plymouth, DNC, $1,000; Raphael, Dr. T., Ann Arbor, RNC, $1,000; Raphael, Mr. & Mrs. Theophile, Ann Arbor, RCBC, $1,100; Riegal, Albert, Chelsea, ACU; $1,000; Russell, G., Bloomfield Hills, RNFC, $1,000; Seyburn, Mrs. W., Grosse Pointe, RNFC, $1,000.

Shelden, Mr. & Mrs. Allan III, Detroit, RNC, $3,000, RCBC, $3,000; Slaughter, W. E., Jr., Birmingham, RNFC, $1,000; Stackpole, Mrs. S. T., Grosse Pointe Shore, RNFC, $1,000; Staebler, Neil, Ann Arbor, DNGC, $1,000; Towsley, Dr. H. A., Ann Arbor, RNC, $1,500; Towsley, Dr. M., Ann Arbor, RNC, $1,500; Upton, F. S., St. Joseph, RNFC, $1,000; Woody, W. W., Detroit, RNFC, $3,000.

MINNESOTA

Anderson, Fred C., Bayport, RCBC, $1,000; Bennett, R. H., Minneapolis, RNC, $1,000; Bennett, Russell, Minneapolis, RCBC, $1,000; Bennett, T. W., Minneapolis, RNFC, $1,000; Berger, Benjamin, Minneapolis, RCBC, $1,000; Briggs, Charles W., St. Paul, RCBC, $1,000; Bros, Raymond J., Minneapolis, RCBC, $1,000; Bros, R. J., Minneapolis, RNFC, $1,000; Chandler, Wm., St. Paul, RNFC, $1,000; Charlson, L. L., Eden Prairie, RNC, $1,000.

Christopherson, Paul, Minneapolis, RCBC, $1,000; Congdon, Mrs. Dorothy Moore, Duluth, RCBC, $1,000; Cross, B. S., Dellwood, RNFC, $1,000; Dahlberg, K. H., Wayzata, RNC, $1,000; Dayton, D. C., Minneapolis, RNC, $1,000; Donovan, R. G., Sr., St. Paul, RNFC, $1,000; Ford, Mrs. A. K., Minneapolis, RNFC, $1,000; Ford, Mrs. Emily Brazer, Minneapolis, RCBC, $1,000, RNC, $1,000, RNFC, $1,000; Hansen, I. R., West St. Paul, RNFC, $1,000; Heffelfinger, F. Peavey, Minneapolis, RCBC, $1,000; Heltzer, H., White Bear Lake, RNFC, $1,000.

Holton, Robert V., Edina, RCBC, $1,000; Hudson, Mrs. W. G., Minneapolis, RNC, $1,000; Hulings, A. D., Bayport, RNFC, $1,000; Hulings, Mr. & Mrs. A. D., Bayport, RCBC, $1,000; Jackson, Mr. & Mrs. C. C. Jr., Wayzata, RNC, $1,000; Johnston, Mrs. N. C., Duluth, ACA, $5,000; Lindsay, J. F., St. Paul, RNFC, $3,000; Little, Mr. & Mrs. P. Jr., Wayzata, RNFC, $1,000; Lund, R. T., Minneapolis, RNC, $1,000; McGough, M. J., Rush City, RCBC, $1,000; McKnight, W. L., St. Paul, RCC, $3,000, RNFC, $3,000, RCBC, $3,000.

Menk, L. W., St. Paul, RNFC, $1,000; Nyrop, Donald W., Minneapolis, DNC, $1,000; Ordway, Mrs. John G., St. Paul, RCBC, $1,000; O'Shaughnessy, I. A., St. Paul, RNFC, $1,000; Pesek, C. P., Minneapolis, RCBC, $1,000; Polk, L. F., Jr., Minneapolis, RNC, $1,000, RNFC, $1,000; Pond, H. J., Minneapolis, RNC, $1,000; Pond, R., Edina, RNC, $1,000; Rawlings, Gen. E. W., Excelsior, RCBC, $1,000; Reid, H. T., St. Paul, RNC, $1,000; Slater, L. H., St. Paul, RNC, $1,000.

Sweatt, H. W., Minneapolis, RNC, $1,000; Thatcher, Paul R., Minneapolis, DNC, $1,000; Tucker, R. H., St. Paul, RNFC, $1,000; Walker, Archie, Minneapolis, RCBC, $1,000; Weyerhaeuser, Mr. & Mrs. F. K., St. Paul, RNC, $6,000, RCBC, $1,000.

MISSISSIPPI

Erickson, E., Jackson, RNFC, $1,000; Fairchild, Wiley, Hattiesburg, DNC, $1,000; Foote, A., Laurel, RNFC, $1,000; Perry, G. D., Tunica, RNC, $1,000; Ransom, Mr. & Mrs. W., Charlevoix, RNFC, $3,000, RNC, $1,000; Roblin, John Paul, Hattiesburg, DNGC, $1,000; Watts, J. J., Meridian, RNFC, $1,000.

MISSOURI

Beaham, G. T. Jr., Kansas City, RNFC, $1,000; Buder, Mrs. O. E., Clayton, RNC, $1,000; Bussmann, H. T. Jr., St. Louis, DNGC, $1,000; Costigan, Wm. Keane, St. Louis, NRSC, $1,000; Danforth, Donald, St. Louis, RCBC, $1,000; Danforth, D., St. Louis, RNFC, $1,000; Douglas, D. W. Jr., St. Louis, RNC, $1,000; Garvey, Mr. & Mrs. James S. Kansas City, RCBC, $2,775.84; Green, E. H., Springfield, DNGC, $5,000, DNC, $5,000; Holmes, J. A., Jr., Clayton, RNC, $1,000.

Hunter, Lee, Bridgeton, RCBC, $1,000; Johnson, Oscar, St. Albans, RCBC, $1,000; Lyddon, Jack R., Kansas City, RCBC, $1,000, RNC, $1,000; Lyddon, J. R., Kansas City, RNFC, $1,000; McDonnell, J. S. III, St. Louis, RNFC, $2,000; Mendle, M., St. Louis, RNFC, $1,000; Murphy, John T., St. Louis, DNGC, $1,000; Olin, Mr. & Mrs. J. M., St. Louis, RCC, $3,000, RVC, $3,000, RNFOC, $3,000, RNC, $3,000, RNFC, $3,000; Olin, Mr. & Mrs. Spencer T., St. Louis, NRCC, $2,000, RCBC, $3,000, RNC, $1,000, RNFC, $1,000; Ploeser, Hon. W.C., St. Louis, RNFC, $1,000.

Schultz, Mr. & Mrs. O. C., St. Joseph, RNFC, $1,000; Shenker, Morris A., St. Louis, DNGC, $1,000; Soult, John P., Clayton, DNGC, $1,000; Stark, Lloyd Crow, Eolia, RCBC, $1,000; Sverdrup, Major Gen. L. J., St. Louis, RNC, $1,000, RCBC, $1,000; Webb, F. M., Clayton, RNC, $1,000, RNFC, $1,000; Weintraub, Sam, University City, DNGC, $1,000; Wells, Ben H., St. Louis, RCBC, $1,000; Wilcox, J. V., Blue Springs, RNFC, $1,000.

MONTANA

NEBRASKA

Buffet, Warren E., Omaha, CPS, $1,000 (1969); Cook, G. B., Lincoln, RNC, $1,000; Hosford, Willard D. Jr., Omaha, RCBC, $1,000; Kiewit, Peter, Omaha, RNC, $1,000; Paxton, James L. Jr., Omaha, RCBC, $1,000; Pratt, Dr. P. T., Omaha, RNC, $1,000; Skutt, V. J., Omaha, RNFC, $1,000; Stahmer, B., Omaha, RNFC, $1,000.

NEVADA

Bell, Thomas G., Las Vegas, DSCC, $1,000; Gund, George, Lee, BANC, $3,000; Henderson, G. B., Las Vegas, RNC, $3,000; Henderson, Mr. & Mrs. G. B., Las Vegas, RNFC, $3,000; Maheu, R. A., Las Vegas, RNFC, $1,000.

NEW HAMPSHIRE

Carter, E. A., Nashua, RNFC, $1,000; Stokes, A., West Chesterfield '70 CF, $3,000.

NEW JERSEY

Adleman, M., Pennsauken, RNC, $1,000, RNFC, $3,000; Alexander, Archibald S., Bernardsville, DNGC, $1,000; Bobst, Elmer H., Morris Plains, RCBC, $1,000; Bobst, E. H., Morris Plains, RNFC, $1,000; Busch, Mrs. R. W., Short Hills, RNC, $1,000; Denckla, W. D., Tenafly, NCEC, $3,000; Dorfmuller, J. S., North Bergen, RNFC, $1,000; Dorrance, John T. Jr., Camden, RCBC, $3,000; Dorrance, J. T. Jr., Camden, RNC, $3,000; Englehard, Charles W., Newark, DNGC, $5,000.

Frick, Dr. H. C. II, Alpine, RNFC, $1,000; Green, E. J., Ridgewood, NRCC, $1,000; Horr, M. E., Short Hills, RNFC, $1,000; La Barre, G. D., Hawthorne, RNFC, $1,000; Lasdon, W. S., Morris Plains, RNFC, $1,000; Moran, Robert, West Orange, DNC, $1,000; Peters, Thomas M., Morristown, ACA, $2,000, CVF, $1,000, RNFC, $1,000; Reisweber, Mrs. G. B., Montclair, RCBC, $1,000; Roebling, Mrs. M. G., Trenton, RNFC, $1,000; Romerovski, Martin, Roselle Park, DNC, $1,000.

Schluter, F. E., Princeton, RNFC, $1,000; Thomas, Mr. & Mrs. G. C. Jr., Bay Head, RNFC, $1,000, CVF, $1,000, RNFC, $1,000, URA; $1,000; Villa, A. L., Peapack, RNFC, $1,000; Wallbridge, William K., Short Hills, RCBC, $1,000, RNC, $1,000, RNFC, $1,000; Wilson, M. M., Princeton, RNC, $1,000, RNFC, $1,000.

NEW MEXICO

Easley & Reynolds, Hobbs, DNC, $100; McCune, Mr. & Mrs. Marshall L., Tesuque, RNC, $3,000, RCC, $2,500, RCBC, $2,500; Maddox, J. F., Hobbs, RNC, $1,000; Mitchell, A. K., Albert, RNC, $1,000; Sawyer, Dessie, Crossroads, DNGC, $1,000; Whitfield, W. F., Albuquerque, RNFC, $1,000.

NEW YORK

Addinsell, Harry M., New York City, RCBC, $1,000; Aldrich, Hon. Winthrop W., New York City, RCBC, $3,000; Aldrich, W. W., New York City, RNC, $3,000, RNFC, $1,000; Aldrich, Mrs. Winthrop W., New York City, RCBC, $3,000; Aldrich, Mrs. W. W., New York City, RNC, $4,000; Allen, Herbert A., New York City, DNC, $3,000; Alt, T., New York City, '70 CF, $2,000; Amory, Thomas C., New York City, RCBC, $1,000; Amory, T. C., Tuxedo Park, RNC, $1,000; Andola, Charles, Highland, RNFAC, $1,000; Anonymous, Larchmont, NCEC, $5,000.

Antell, B. W., Brooklyn, RNC, $1,000; Ascoli, M., New York City, RNC, $1,000; Astor, Mrs. Vincent, New York City, RCBC, $3,000; Atwood, Mrs. W. B., Locust Valley, Long Island, RNFC, $1,000; Ault, Mrs. Lee A., New York City, RCBC, $1,000; Axline, R. A., Long Island, RNC, $1,000; Baker, George F. Jr., New York City, RCBC, $3,000; Baker, G. F. Jr., New York City, RNC, $2,500, RNFOC, $2,500; Baldwin, Mr. & Mrs. J. F., Locust Valley, RNFC, $3,000; Barker, R. R., New York City, RNC, $1,000.

Barrett, J. E., New York City, RNFC, $1,000; Barry, Robert R., New York City, RNFAC, $2,000; Bates, T. L., New York City, RNC, $1,000; Beinecke, William S., New York City, RCBC, $1,000; Beinecke, W. S., New York City, RNFC, $1,000; Bendetsen, K. R., New York City, RNFC, $1,000; Benjamin, R, New York City, '70 CF, $1,000; Bernard, V. W., New York City, NCEC, $1,000; Bewley, George W., Lockport, RCBC, $1,000; Bingham, Mrs. Harry Payne Sr., New York City, RCBC, $1,000.

Bingham, Mr. & Mrs. H. P. Jr., New York City, RNC, $2,000; Blough, R. M., New York City, RNFC, $1,000; Bogert, Beverley A., New York City, RCBC, $1,000, RNC, $1,000; Bogert, Mr. & Mrs. H. Laurence, New York City, RCBC, $2,000, RNC, $2,000; Boscowitz, H., New York City, RNFC, $1,000; Boscowitz, Mrs. H. H., New York City, RNFC, $1,000; Bostwich, D. W., New York City, RNC, $1,000; Bourne, Miss Mary Elizabeth, New York City, RCBC, $1,000; Boutelle, F., New York City, RNC, $1,000; Bower, M., New York City, RNFC, $1,000.

Brewster, Edward C., New York City, RCBC, $1,000; Brooks, J. W., Bedford Hills, RNC, $1,000; Brown, S. W., New York City, RNFC, $1,000; Bullock, H., New York City, RNC, $1,000, RNFC, $2,000; Burden, Mr. Shirley, New York City, RCBC, $1,000; Burden, Hon. W. M., New York City, RNFC, $1,000; Burke, C., New York City, RNFC, $1,000; Callimanopulos, P. G., New York City, RNFC, $1,000; Campbell, J., New York City, RNFC, $1,000; Carnevale, D., New York City, RNC, $1,000.

Carver, H. F., Rochester, RNFC, $1,000; Casey, J. J., New York City, RNFC, $1,000; Casiano, M. A. Jr., New York City, RNC, $1,000; Chambers, R. M., New York City, RNC, $1,000; Champion, G., New York City, RNC, $2,000, RCBC, $1,000;

Chapman, A. B., New York City, RNC, $1,000; Chisholm, William H., New York City, RCBC, $1,000; Chisholm, Mrs. S. C., New York City, RNC, $1,000, RNFC, $1,000; Clark, John Balfour, New York City, RCBC, $1,000; Clark, Mrs. Van Alan, New York City, RCBC, $1,000.

Clark, Mrs. W. V., New York City, RNFC, $1,000; Clarke, Mr. & Mrs. Richard S., Bedford, RCBC, $2,000, RNC, $1,500; Clay, Gen. L. D., New York City, RNFC, $1,000; Cleveland, C. A., Bronxville, RNC, $1,000; Closson, Mrs. A., East Hampton, RNFC, $1,000; Coe, Mr. & Mrs. W. R., New York City, RNC, $3,000; Collins, L., New York City, '70 CF, $4,000; Collins, L., New York City, '70 CF, $1,000; Combe, I.D., White Plains, RNC, $1,000; Cookson, P., New York City, '70 CF, $1,000.

Cowles, G., New York City, RNFC, $1,000; Cromwell, Jarvis, New York City, RCBC, $1,000; Dalsemer, L., New York City, RNFC, $1,000; Danforth, Theodore N., Locust Valley, RCBC, $1,000; Danforth, T. N., Locust Valley, RNC, $1,000, RNFC, $1,000; Darlington, Mrs. H., New York City, RNC, $1,000; Davie, Mrs. P., New York City, RNC, $1,000; Davison, F. T., Locust Valley, RNFC, $1,000; Davison, Mrs. F. Trubee, Long Island, RCBC, $1,000; Davison, Gates, New York City, RCBC, $1,000.

Dewey, Gordon C., New York City, NRCC, $5,000; Dewey, Hon. T. F., New York City, RNFC, $1,000; Diamond, T. L., New York City, RNFC, $1,000; Dickenson, David L., Binghamton, RCBC, $1,000; Dillon, Hon. C. D., New York City, RNFC, $3,000; Doll, H., New York City, '70 CF, $1,000, DSG, $1,000; Doll, H. G., New York City, NCEC, $1,000; Donner, J. W., New York City, RNFC, $1,000; Doyle, Ned, New York City, DNGC, $1,000; Dunnington, Mrs. T., New York City, RNFC, $1,000.

Du Pont, R. S., New York City, RNFC, $1,000; Eberle, W. D., New York City, RNFC, $1,000; Eilers, L. K., Rochester, RNC, $1,000; Ehrman, F. L., New York City, RCC, $3,000, RVC, $1,000, RNC, $3,000, RNFC, $3,000; Emmons, Hamilton, Ithaca, RDNC, $1,000; Eustis, B. C., New York City, RNFC, $1,000; Finch, E. R. Jr., New York City, RNC, $1,000, RNFC, $3,000; Fitterer, J. C., Jr., New York City, RNFC, $1,000; Fitzgerald, C. L., New York City, RNFC, $1,000, RNC, $1,000; Flanigan, H. C., New York City, RNFC, $1,000.

Flanigan, Mrs. Horace C., Purchase, RCBC, $1,000; Foshay, W. W., New York City, RNC, $1,000; Freedberg, David S., New York City, DNC, $1,000; Frick, Miss H. C., Bedford, RNC, $1,000; Fromm, E., New York City, '70 CF, $3,000; Gabrielson, Hon. G. G., New York City, RNC, $1,000; Gaisman, Mr. & Mrs. H. J., Hartsdale, RNFC, $3,000; Gardner, Mrs. P. E., Westbury, RNFC, $1,000; Gary, T. S., New York City, RNFC, $1,000; Gates, Thomas S., New York City, RCBC, $1,000, RNC, $1,000; Gelb, R. L., New York City, RNFC, $1,000; Geneen, H. S., New York City, RNC, $1,000; Gerard, Col. J. W. 2nd, New York City, RNC, $1,000; Gerrity, Ed J. Jr., New York City, DNC, $2,000, RNC, $1,000; Gerry, Henry A., New York City, RCBC, $1,000.

Gibbs, Rogers, H., New York City '70 CF, $2,000; Gilbert, B. D., New York City, NRCC, $1,000; Gillett, Mrs. F. W., New York City, RNFC, $1,000; Gilmour, L. S., Long Island, RNFC, $1,000; Gilmour, L. S., New York City, RNC, $1,000; Gisel, W. G., Buffalo, RNC, $1,000; Gordon, A. F., New York City, RNC, $3,000; Gordon, A. H., New York City, RNFC, $4,000; Gordon, Miss M. A., New York City, RNFC, $1,000; Gordon, Mrs. M. R., New York City, RNFC, $3,000.

Gould, E. J., New York City, RNFC, $1,000; Grant, W. T., New York City, RNC, $1,000; Green, Mrs. A. Margaret, Armonk, ACA, $1,000; Greenwall, F. K., New York City, RCC,

$2,251, RNFC, $3,000; Greve, Mrs. W., Southampton, RNC, $1,000; Grimson, Bettina W., New York City, CPS, $3,000, CPS, $3,000 (1969); Grimson, Mrs. S. B., New York City, DNC, $1,000; Griswold, J., New York City, RNC, $1,000; Guest, W. C., New York City, RNFC, $1,000; Hadley, Mrs. M., New York City, RNFC, $1,000.

Hamilton, M., New York City, '70 CF, $1,000; Hammond, G., New York City, RNFC, $1,000; Harriman, W. Averell, New York City, DNC, $1,000; Harriman, E. Roland, New York City, NRCC, $3,000, NRSC, $3,000, RCBC, $2,000, RNC, $3,000, RNFOC, $3,000; Harris, Henry Upham, New York City, RCBC, $1,000; Hatcher, L., New York City, RNFC, $2,500; Hawk, K. G., Binghamton, RNC, $1,000; Hays, D. P., Mineola, RNC, $1,000; Hays, Daniel P., Port Washington, RCBC, $1,000; Helm, Harold H., New York City, RCBC, $1,000.

Hertlein, C., Bronxville, RNFC, $1,000; Hickok, Mr. & Mrs. C., New York City, RNFC, $1,000; Hickox, Charles V., New York City, RCBC, $1,000; Hickox, Mrs. Charles V., New York City, RCBC, $1,000; Hickok, Mr. & Mrs. C. V., New York City, RNFC, $2,000; Hiebert, Dr. J. M., New York City, RNC, $1,000; Hilson, J. S., New York City, RNC, $1,000; Himes, E., New York City, NCEC, $2,000; Hinman, E. B., New York City, RNC, $1,000; Hitchcock, Mrs. Thomas, New York City, RCBC, $1,000.

Hochschild, H., New York City, '70 CF, $1,000; Hodes, Robert B., New York City, LCEW, $1,000; Holbrook, Mr. & Mrs. G. W., Wellsville, RCBC, $1,000; Holbrook, John, New York City, RCBC, $1,000; Holm, M. C., Fayetteville, RNFC, $1,000; Hopeman, A. A. Jr., Yonkers, RNFC, $1,000; Hopeman, Mr. & Mrs. A. A. Jr., Bronxville, RCBC, $1,000; Hopeman, Mrs. Anna, Rochester, RCBC, $3,000; Hopeman, Mrs. A. M., Rochester, RNFC, $3,000; Houghton, Amory, Corning, RCBC, $1,000.

Houghton, A. Jr., Corning, RNFC, $1,000; Houghton, Mrs. A., Corning, RNFC, $1,000; Hoving, Walter, New York City, RCBC, $1,000; Howard, Mrs. Howell, New York City, RCBC, $1,000; Humes, Hon. J. P., New York City, RNFC, $3,000; Ingersoll, Mrs. Stuart H., New York City, RCBC, $3,000; Ingersoll, Mrs. S. H., New York City, RNC, $3,000; Ireland, R. L. III, New York City, RNFC, $1,000, RCBC, $1,000; Ireland, Mrs. R. L. III, New York City, RCBC, $1,000; Irwin, Hon. & Mrs. John N. II, New York City, RCBC, $1,000.

Irwin, Hon. J. N. II, New York City, RNFC, $1,000; Irwin, Mrs. J. W., New York City, RNFC, $1,000; Iselin, O., New York City, RNFC, $1,000; Ivey, J., New York City, RNC, $1,000; Jennings, Mrs. B. Brewster, Glen Head, RCBC, $1,000; Jephson, Mrs. G.S., Cazenovia, RNFC, $1,000; Jones, C. H., New York City, RNFC, $1,000; Kahn, Harry, New York City, TFP, $1,000; Kane, J.H., Garden City, RNC, $1,000; Kaplan, J.M., New York City, NCEC, $4,750.

Kappel, F. R., Bronxville, RNFC, $1,000; Keiser, D. M., New York City, RNFC, $1,000; Kenin, Herman D., New York City, DNGC, $1,000; Kennedy, D. D., Oyster Bay, Long Island, RNFC, $1,000; Kenny, C. F., Scarsdale, RNC, $1,000; Kent, R. E., New York City, RNC, $1,000; Kerbs, Mrs. J. E., New York City, RNC, $1,000; Kernan, F., New York City, RNC, $1,000; Korn, W., New York City, NCEC, $2,000; Kuehn, C. C., New York City, RNFC, $1,000.

Lamberton, James W., New York City, LCEW, $1,000; Larmon, Sigurd S., New York City, RCBC, $1,000; Larmon, S. S., New York City, RNC, $1,000; Lasdon, William S., New York City, RCBC, $1,000; Lasker, B. J., New York City, RNC, $3,000; Laughlin, Mrs. C. P., Southampton, RNFC, $1,000; Leib, George, New York City, RCBC, $1,000; Leithead, B. T., New York City, RNC, $1,000; Lever, W. B., New York City, RNFAC, $3,000; Levering, W. B., New York City, RNC, $1,000, RNFC, $1,000.

Levy, G. L., New York City, RNC, $1,000, RNFC, $1,000; Levy, S. J., Chappaqua, NCEC, $1,000; List, V., New York City, '70 CF, $1,000; Little, Edward H., New York City, RCBC, $1,000; Loomis, A. E. Jr., Oyster Bay, RCBC, $1,000; Loomis, A. L. Jr., New York City, RNFC, $3,000; Loomis, Mr. & Mrs. H., New York City, RNFC, $6,000; Loomis, Mrs. Farnsworth, New York City, RCBC, $3,000; Lufkin, D. W., New York City, RNC, $1,000; Luke, A. M., New York City, RNFC, $1,000.

Luke, D. L. III, New York City, RNC, $1,000; RNFC, $1,000; Lundell, L., New York City, RNC, $1,000; Lynch, Mrs. Edmund C., New York City, RCBC, $3,000; Lynch, Mrs. E. Jr., New York City, RNC, $1,000; McConnell, N. A., New York City, RNC, $3,000; McCormick, Mrs. Cyrus, New York City, RCBC, $1,000, RCC, $3,000; McCormick, Mrs. E. P., New York City, RNC, $1,000; McCurdy, G. J., Rochester, RNFC, $1,000; McIntosh, Allan J., New York City, RCBC, $1,000; McMullan, Mrs. Joseph, New York City, RCBC, $1,000; McVitty, E. W., New York City, DNC, $1,000, CFT, $2,000, NCEC, $6,000; Mahoney, D. J., New York City, RNC, $2,500, RNFC, $2,500; Mallory, P. R., Fishers Island, RCBC, $1,000; Mallory, Mrs. P. R., Fishers Island, RCBC, $1,000; Mallory, Philip Rogers, New York City, RCBC, $1,000; Marros, Arthur, White Plains, RCBC, $1,000; Marshall, A. D., New York City, RNC, $1,000; Mason, L. Randolph, New York City, RCBC, $1,000; Matthews, Mrs. F., Rye, RNFC, $1,000; Mayer, A., New York City, NCEC, $3,000.

Middendorf, Hon. J. II, New York City, RNC, $1,000, RCBC, $500; Milbank, J. Jr., New York City, RNC, $3,000, RCBC, $1,000; Milbank, J. Sr., New York City, RNC, $3,000; Milbank, T. F., New York City, RNC, $1,000; Milliken, Mr. & Mrs. G. H. Jr., New York City, RNFC, $3,000; Monell, E. C., New York City, RNC, $1,000; Morgan, Mrs. E. P., New York City, RNFC, $1,000; Morgan, T., Bronxville, RNC, $1,000; Morrison, Dr. & Mrs. Thomas J., New York City, RCBC, $3,000; Morse, J. H., New York City, RNFC, $1,000.

Mortimer, C. G., White Plains, RNFC, $1,000; Mosbacher, Hon. E., New York City, RNC, $1,000; Mott, Stewart, New York City, NCEC, $3,000, CPS, $1,000 (1969); Neff, Mrs. Joseph A., New York City, RCBC, $5,000; Newman, J., New York City, RNFC, $1,000; Nichols, C. W., Jr., New York City, RNC, $1,000; Newman, J., New York City, RNFC, $1,000; Noyes, J., New York City, RNC, $1,000; Noyes, Jansen, New York City, RCBC, $1,000; Norris, Mr. & Mrs. James L., New York City, RCBC, $1,000; Onassis, A., New York City, RNC, $1,000.

Overton, Mrs. Joan B., Newburgh, CFT, $1,000; Page, R. G., New York City, RNFC, $1,000; Palmer, O. C., Brooklyn, RNFC, $2,000; Pansa, Mrs. M., New York City, RNFC, $1,000; Parkinson, C. Jay, New York City, RCBC, $1,000; Parlin, Charles C., New York City, RCBC, $1,000; Paterson, Mrs. Charles, New York City, RCBC, $1,000; Patterson, H. P., New York City, RNC, $1,000, RNFC, $1,000; Payson, Mrs. C. S., New York City, RCC, $3,000, RVC, $3,000, RNC, $3,000, RNFOC, $3,000, RNFC, $3,000, RCBC, $1,000; Payson, Mr. & Mrs. C. S., New York City, RCBC, $3,000.

Peabody, Mrs. P. E., Millbrook, RNFC, $1,000; Peake, K., New York City, RNC, $1,000; Penney, Mrs. Caroline A., New York City, RCBC, $1,000; Penney, J. C., New York City, RCBC, $1,000; Perkins, Mrs. G. W., Millbrook, RNFC, $1,000; Perkins, T. L., New York City, RNFC, $1,000; Petersmeyer, C. W., New York City, RNFC, $1,000; Petrie, M. J., New York City, RNC, $1,000, RNFC, $1,000; Phipps, Lillian Bostwick, New York City, NRSC, $6,000; Phipps, Mrs. O., New York City, RCC, $3,000, RNFOC, $3,000, RNC, $3,000, RNFC, $3,000, RCBC, $3,000, RVC, $3,000.

Picker, Mr. & Mrs. H., White Plains, RNC, $6,000; Piwerka, M., New York City, NRCC, $1,000; Place, H. G., New York City, RNFC, $1,000; Powers, J. J., New York City, RNFC, $1,000; Powers, J. J. Jr., New York City, RNFC, $1,000; Purcell, R. W., New York City, RNFC, $1,000; Redmond, Mrs. R. L., Oyster Bay, RNFC, $1,000; Reed, P. D., New York City, RNFC, $1,000; Reese, W. L., Long Island, RNC, $1,000; Reese, W. M., New York City, RNFC, $1,000.

Reese, W. W., New Hamburg, RNC, $1,000; Reese, William W., New York City, RCBC, $1,000; Rentschler, Mr. & Mrs. George A., New York City, RCBC, $1,000; Riegel, John L. Hartsdale, RCBC, $1,000; Ripley, J. P., New York City, RNC, $1,000; Ripley, Joseph P., New York City, RCBC, $1,000; Rippeteau, D. D., Watertown, RNC, $1,000; Robinson, R. I., New York City, RNC, $1,000; Rockefeller, D., New York City, RNFC, $1,000; Rockefeller, J. D. III, New York City, RNFC, $1,000, RCBC, $1,000.

Rockefeller, Mrs. Mary C., New York City, RCBC, $1,000; Rockefeller, Hon. Nelson A., Albany, RCBC, $1,000; Rockefeller, R. C., New York City, RNFC, $1,000; Rockwell, Mr. & Mrs. R. C., Loudonville, RNC, $1,000; Roon, D. C., Olean, RNFC, $1,000; Rosen, V., New York City, '70 CF, $1,000; Ross, T. J. Jr., New York City, RNC, $1,000; Roth, C. H., New York City, RNFC, $1,000; Rothchild, H. M., Ossining, NCEC, $1,000; Rothschild, Mrs. W. N., New York City, RNFC, $1,000.

Routh, Joseph P., New York City, NRSC, $5,000; Rust, Adolf, Cutchozue, Long Island, CVF, $1,000; Rust, Helen, Cutchozue, Long Island, CVF, $1,000; Salomon, Richard, New York City, DNC, $1,000; Saltzman, Arnold A., New York City, DNC, $1,000; Sanders, Frank K. Jr., New York City, RCBC, $1,000; Sandler, M., New York City, RNC, $1,000; Scheuer, S. H., New York City, NCEC, $2,000; Schiff, D. T., New York City, RNFC, $1,000; Schiff, Mr. & Mrs. John M., New York City, RNC, $1,000, RNFC, $1,000, RCBC, $1,000.

Schuster, Mrs. Anne Storrs, New York City, RCBC, $1,000; Scripps, E. W. 2nd, New York City, RNC, $1,000, RNFC, $1,000; Senior, Mrs. John L., New York City, RCBC, $1,000; Shad, J. R., New York City, RNC, $1,000; Shinn, R. R., New York City, RNFC, $1,000; Siebert, E. H., New York City, NCEC, $3,000; Slaner, Alfred P., New York City, DNGC, $1,000; Slater, Ellis D., New York City, RCBC, $1,000; Slater, Mrs. Lyon, New York City, RCBC, $1,000; Sohier, Walter D., New York City, LCEW, $1,000.

Sonne, H., New York City, RNFC, $1,000; Sperry, P., New York City, '70 CF, $2,000, DSG, $1,000, NCEC, $1,000; Stein, Fred, Scarsdale, TFP, $5,000; Steinbach, M., New York City, RNFC, $1,000; Stewart P. M., New York City, RNC, $1,000; Stirling, David Jr., New York City, DSCC, $2,500; Stirling, William G., New York City, DSCC, $5,000; Stollenwerck, E., New York City, RNC, $1,000; Stone, W., New York City, RNFC, $3,000; Stover, R. C., Poughkeepsie, NCEC, $2,000.

Straus, R. I., New York City, RNC, $2,500, RNFC, $1,000; Swick, T. P., New York City, RNFC, $2,500; Taber, Ralph F., Williamsville, RCBC, $3,000; Talmage, Mrs. J. D., New York City, ACU, $1,000; Tarbox, G. S., Yonkers, RNFC, $1,000; Thayer, W. N., New York City, RNC, $1,000; Thorne, L. K. Jr., New York City, RNFC, $1,000; Tillinghast, C. C. Jr., Bronxville, RNFC, $1,000; Tittmann, E. McL., New York City, RCBC, $1,000; Tobin, J. E., New York City, NRSC, $5,000.

Todd, W. B., New York City, RNFC, $1,000; Tucker, Mrs. C., Mt. Kisco, RNFC, $1,000; Tyson, R. C., New York City, RNC, $1,000, RNFC, $1,000; Valle, L. J., Ardsley-Hudson, RNC, $1,000; Van Alan Clark, Mrs. W., New York City, RNFC, $1,000; Van Alstyne, Mr & Mrs. D., New York City,

RNFOC, $5,000; Vander Poel, W. H., New York City, NRSC, $1,800; Voorhees, E. M., New York City, RNFC, $1,000; Wadmond, L., New York City, RNFC, $1,000; Wadsworth, H. M., Liverpool, RNFC, $1,000.

Wallace, Mr. & Mrs. De Witt, Mt. Kisco, NRCC, $2,500, RNC, $2,000; RCBC, $7,000, ACA, $1,000, RNFC, $2,500, Waller, Mrs. T. M., Bedford Hills, RNFC, $1,000; Walrod, W. A., Kennedy, RNC, $1,000; Warner, J., New York City, RNC, $1,000; Warner, L. H., New York City, RNFC, $1,000; Washburn, Watson, New York City, RCBC, $1,000; Watson, Hon. Mr. & Mrs. A. K., Armonk, RNC, $5,000, RNFC, $1,000; Watts, H. M., Jr., New York City, RNC, $2,000; Webster, Bethuel M., New York City, LCEW, $1,000; Westfall, Ted B., New York City, DNC, $1,000.

Wetenhall, R. C., New York City, RNC, $1,000; Whelan, Francis X., New York City, NRCC, $2,500, NRSC, $2,500, DSCC, $2,500; Whitney, C. V., New York City, RNFC, $1,000; Whitney, Hon. John Hay, New York City, RNC, $3,000, RCBC, $1,000; Wilson, J. C., Rochester, DNGC, $1,000; Winthrop, Robert, New York City, RCBC, $1,000; Winthrop, Mrs. Robert, Long Island, RCBC, $1,000; Wise, Dr. G. S., New York City, RNFC, $1,000; Wishnick, R. I., New York City, RNFC, $1,000; Wolf, Popper, Ross, Wolf, Jones, New York City, LCEW, $1,000.

Woodward, Mrs. W. B., New York City, RNFC, $1,000; Wooley, Mrs. K., New York City, RNFC, $1,000; Wooley, M. F., New York City, RCBC, $1,000; Wright, Mrs. J. B., Hewlett, RNFC, $1,000; Wright, Mrs. John B., New York City, RCBC, $1,000; Wyman, C. A., New York City, RNC, $1,000.

NORTH CAROLINA

Andrews, General A. B., Fayetteville, RNC, $1,000; Belk, Irwin, Charlotte, DNGC, $1,000; Broyhill, J. E., Lenior, RNFC, $1,000; Bryan, Joseph M., Greensboro, DNC, $1,000; Hanes, J. G., Winston-Salem, RNFC, $1,000; Hanes, P. H., Jr., Winston-Salem, RNFC, $1,000; Jackson, H., Pinehurst, RNFC, $1,000; Kaplan, Stanley N., Charlotte, DNGC, $1,000; Monroe, N., Greensboro, RNC, $1,000, RNFC, $1,000; Morris, E. A., Greensboro, RCBC, $1,108.71.

Myers, C. F. Jr., Greensboro, RNFC, $1,000; Owen, A. K., Winston-Salem, RNFC, $1,000; Price, J., Greensboro, '70 CF, $1,000; Reese, A. H., Charlotte, RNC, $1,000; Reuter, I. J., Ashville, RNFC, $1,000; Slick, E. F., Winston-Salem, RNFC, $1,000; Tate, Mrs. H. C., Southern Pines, NRCC, $1,000; Wainwright, Stephen A., Durham, UNAF, $1,000; Walker, J. A., North Wilkesboro, RNFC, $1,000; Wright, T. H. Jr., Wilmington, RNFC, $1,000.

NORTH DAKOTA

Anderson, L. L., Fargo, RNFC, $1,000; Rouzie, John, Bowman, CFA, $4,000; Schafer, H., Bismarck, RNC, $3,000.

OHIO

Armington, R. G., Willoughby, RNFC, $1,000; Augustus, E. H., Cleveland, RNFC, $1,000; Barrett, E. S., Chillicothe, RNC, $1,000; Berry, J. W., Dayton, RNC, $1,000; Berry, Loren M., Dayton, RCBC, $3,000; Berry, Mr. & Mrs. L. M., Dayton, RNC, $5,000; Boeschenstein, Harold, Toledo, RCBC, $1,000; Boeschenstein, H., Toledo, RNC, $1,000; Bolton, Hon. F. P., Cleveland, RNFC, $2,000; Boyer, W. B., Cleveland, RNC, $1,000.

Burton, Hon. C., Cleveland, RNFC, $1,000; Claudieux, Virgil, Toledo, ACU, $1,000; Donnell, J. C. II, Findlay, RNFC, $1,000; Donnell, J. R., Findlay, RNFC, $1,000; Eaton, C., Cleveland, NCFC, $1,000; Fischer, Harry, Cincinnati, ACA, $1,000; Fox, D. L., Dayton, RNFC, $3,000; Geier, Mr. & Mrs. F. V., Cincinnati,

RNC, $2,000; Haehnle, Miss K., Cincinnati, RNFC, $1,000; Harris, C., Cleveland, NCEC, $1,000.

Hurlbert, H. H., Warren, RNFC, $1,000; Johnston, L. T., Middletown, RNFC, $1,000; Jones, Mrs. Frederick E., Columbus, RCBC, $1,000; Langley, Mrs. G. S., Dayton, RNC, $1,000; Lazarus, Mrs. F. Jr., Cincinnati, RNFC, $1,000; Lennon, F. A., Chagrin Falls, RNFC, $1,000; Levis, J. P., Toledo, RNC, $1,000; McElroy, Hon. Neil H., Cincinnati, RCBC, $1,000; MacNichol, G. P. Jr., Perrysburg, RNFC, $1,000; Metzenbaum, Howard, Cleveland, CPS, $1,000 (1969).

Morelli, N. Knute, Canal Fulton, DNGC, $1,000; Morgens, H., Cincinnati, RNFC, $1,000; Muhlhauser, Robert F., Cincinnati, ACU, $1,270; Nash, Mrs. R. P. Jr., Novelty, RNC, $1,000; Newman, F. R., Cleveland, RNFC, $2,000; Nickless, W., Upper Sandusky, RNFC, $1,000; Olsen, W. H., Elyria, RNFC, $1,000; Patton, T. F., Shaker Heights, RNC, $1,000; Paul, L. M., Indian Hill Village, RNFC, $1,000.

Polk, L. F. Sr., Dayton, RNC, $3,000; Rose, H., Cleveland, RNC, $1,000; Schmidt, J., Cleveland, ACU, $1,000; Sears, Mrs. L. M., Cleveland, RNFC, $1,500; Shafer, Mr. & Mrs. R. H., Westerville, RNFC, $3,000; Smith, K. H., Gates Mills, RNFC, $3,000, RNC, $3,000; Smith, Mrs. T. G., Gates Mills, RNC, $1,000; Smith, V. K., Wickliffe, RNC, $1,000; Stoeckle, Miss Marilyn C., Cincinnati, RCBC, $1,000; Stouffer, V. B., Cleveland, RCC, $2,000.

Stouffer, V. B., Lakewood, RNFC, $3,000; Strecher, Dr. & Mrs. R. M., Cleveland, RNFC, $1,000; Timken, Mrs. H. H., Canton, RNC, $3,000; Timken, Mrs. L. B., Cleveland, RNFC, $2,000; Timken, W. R., Cleveland, RNFC, $3,000; Tippit, C. C., Chagrin Falls, RNC, $1,000; Trubinsky, J. C., Cleveland, RNC, $1,000; Warner, Marvin L., Cincinnati, DNC, $1,100; Wean, R. J., Warren, RCBC, $1,000; Wean, Mrs. Sara R., Warren, RCBC, $1,000; Weston, R. L., Cleveland, RNFC, $1,000; White, Charles M., Cleveland, RCBC, $2,000, RNFC, $2,000; Wuliger, Ernest M., Medina, CVF, $1,000, ACU, $2,500; Young, G. H., Findlay, RNFC, $1,000.

OKLAHOMA

Bernsen, F. E., Tulsa, RNFC, $1,000; Blair, B. B., Tulsa, RNC, $2,000; Calvert, R. A. Jr., Tulsa, RCBC, $1,000; Chapman, H. A. Sr., Tulsa, RNFC, $3,000; Everest, J. I., Oklahoma City, RNC, $1,000; Glass, Mrs. J., Nowata, RNC, $1,000; Johnson, Charles E., Edmond, DNGC, $1,000; Kerr, William G., Oklahoma City, DNGC, $1,000; McCormack, H., Oklahoma City, RNC, $1,000; McCormack, W., Oklahoma City, RNFC, $1,000.

McCune, John R., Oklahoma City, ACA, $1,000; Price, Harold C., Bartlesville, DNC, $1,000; Scisson, S. E., Tulsa, RNFC, $1,000; Thomas, Mrs. R. A., Tulsa, RNFC, $1,000; Titus, C. W., Tulsa, RNC, $1,000, RNFC, $1,000; Williams, C. P., Tulsa, RNFC, $1,000; Williams, D. R. Jr., Tulsa, RNC, $1,000; Williams, J. H., Tulsa, RNFC, $1,000.

OREGON

Ausplund, Mrs. E. G., Portland, RNC, $1,000, RNFC, $1,000; Cabell, Henry F., Portland, RCBC, $1,000; Cabell, H. F., Portland, RNC, $1,000; Cake, R. H., Portland, RNFC, $1,000; Halton, E. H. Jr., Portland, CFA, $3,500; Henningsgaard, Dr. Blair, Astoria, RCBC, $1,000; Platt, Mrs. J. D., Portland, RNFC, $1,000; Sorrels, Neal E., Portland, ACU, $1,000; Sweigert, Mr. & Mrs. E., Portland, RNC, $1,000; Walker, C. T., Portland, RNFC, $1,000; Watzek, A. R., Portland, RNFC, $2,000; Wentz, L., Portland, NRSC, $2,000.

PENNSYLVANIA

Adair, Herbert J., Philadelphia, RCBC, $1,000; Amory, G. S., Ligonier, RNC, $1,000; Atwood, Mrs. J. C. Jr., Philadelphia, RNFC, $1,000; Baker, Mr. & Mrs. Michael Jr., Rochester, DNGC, $1,000, RNC, $3,000; Baldwin, F. Jr., Philadelphia, RNC, $1,000; Barr, Joe, Pittsburgh, DNGC, $1,000; Berger, Meyer, Pittsburgh, DNGC, $1,000; Berwind, C. G. Sr., Philadelphia, RNFC, $1,000; Boyer, Francis, Philadelphia, RCBC, $1,000, NRCC, $1,000; Bright, Stanley, Rosemont, RCBC, $1,000.

Brown, Richard P. Jr., Philadelphia, RCBC, $1,000; Brown, R. P. Jr., Philadelphia, RNC, $1,000; Brown, W. H., Pittsburgh, RNC, $1,000, Buck, J. Mahlon Jr., Haverford, RCBC, $1,000; Buck, William C., Villanova, RCBC, $1,000; Burpee, D., Philadelphia, RNFC, $1,000; Butcher, H. III, Philadelphia, RNC, $1,000; Calhoun, E. N., Pittsburgh, RNFC, $1,000; Campbell, W. A., Sewickley, RNFC, $1,000; Cancelliere, M. A., Pittsburgh, RNC, $1,000.

Carter, R. A., Narberth, RNFC, $1,000; Churchman, Mrs. C. B., Gladwyne, RNC, $1,000; Cole, Mr. Charles Jr., Bryn Athyn, ACU, $1,050; Cole, Mrs. Louis S. Jr., Bryn Athyn, ACA, $1,000; Colket, Tristram C., Gladwyne, RCBC, $1,000; Colket, Tristram C. Jr., Bryn Mawr, RCBC, $1,000; Corson, Mrs. Philip L., Plymouth Meeting, RCBC, $1,000; Deeter, R. O., Pittsburgh, RNFC, $1,000; Dixon, Edward F., Wilkes-Barre, DNC, $1,000; Dixon, F. E. Jr., Philadelphia, RNFC, $3,000, RCBC, $3,000.

Dogole, S. Harrison, Philadelphia, DNGC, $1,000; Donaldson, Mr. & Mrs. B., Kennett Square, RNFC, $6,000; Dunlop, Robert G., Bryn Mawr, RCBC, $1,000; Eckman, John W., Bryn Mawr, RCBC, $1,000; Foerster, Thomas J., Pittsburgh, DNGC, $1,000; Frick, Miss Helen Clay, Pittsburgh, RCBC, $3,000; Gemmill, K. W., Philadelphia, RNFC, $1,000; Gott, E. H., Pittsburgh, RNFC, $1,000; Hann, G. R., Pittsburgh, RNFC, $1,000; Hann, G. R., Sewickley, RNC, $1,000.

Harper, J. D., Pittsburgh, RNFC, $1,000; Heinz, Henry J. II, Pittsburgh, RCBC, $3,000; Henderson, G. M., Pittsburgh, RNC, $1,000; Hoyt, Mr. & Mrs. Alex Crawford, New Castle, RCBC, $1,000; Johnson, E. R., Ardmore, RNC, $1,000; Jordan, Mrs. Elizabeth K., Philadelphia, RCBC, $3,000; Junge, Mr. & Mrs. Robert S., Bryn Athyn, ACA, $1,000, ACU, $3,000; Kennedy, Marie, Philadelphia, ACU, $1,600; Kerr, W. E., Oakmont, RNC, $1,000.

Kleinhoff, W., Hatboro, RNFC, $1,000; Kling, V. G., Philadelphia, RNC, $1,000; Lavino, Edwin M., Philadelphia, RCBC, $1,000; Lavino, E. M., Philadelphia, RNFC, $1,000; Lewis, Edward J., Pittsburgh, DNC, $1,000; Love, G. H., Pittsburgh, RNC, $1,000; McCabe, Mrs. Jeanette L., Swarthmore, RCBC, $1,000; McCabe, Thomas B., Philadelphia, NRCC, $1,000, RCBC, $3,000, RNC, $2,000; McCune, Mr. & Mrs. John R., Pittsburgh, NRCC, $1,000, RNC, $1,500; Mack, Dr. C. C., Rydal, RNC, $1,000.

Meyer, M., Ardmore, RNC, $1,000; Miers, T. Jefferson, Pittsburgh, RCBC, $1,000; Morris, Charles M., Pittsburgh, DNGC, $1,000; Mudge, L. S., Pittsburgh, RNFC, $1,000; Oliver, Mr. & Mrs. John C. Jr., Pittsburgh, ACA, $1,000, ACU, $1,425; O'Neill, Mrs. Jane, Philadelphia, RCBC, $1,000; Pew, George T., Haverford, RCBC, $1,000, RNFC, $1,000; Pew, J., Philadelphia, RCC, $3,000, RNFC, $3,000; Pew, J. Heath, Philadelphia, NRCC, $3,000; Pew, J. Howard, Philadelphia, NRSC, $2,333.34, ACA, $1,000.

Pew, Estate of J. N., Philadelphia, NRCC, $1,000; Pew, Miss Mary Ethel, Philadelphia, NRCC, $3,000, NRSC, $2,333.33, RCC, $3,000, ACA, $1,000, RNFC, $3,000; Pew, Mrs. Mabel Myrin, Philadelphia, NRCC, $3,000, NRSC, $2,333.33, RCC, $3,000, ACA, $1,000, RNFC, $3,000; Pitcairn, Feodor U., Jenkintown,

RCBC, $1,000; Pitcairn, Rev. Theodore, Jenkintown, RCBC, $1,000; Price, G. A., Pittsburgh, RNC, $1,000; Rea, H. O., Pittsburgh, RNFC, $1,000; Robinson, Alex, Pittsburgh, DNGC, $1,000; Rockwell, Col. W. F., Pittsburgh, RNC, $1,000.

Rockwell, William F. Jr., Pittsburgh, RCBC, $1,000; Rockwell, W. F. Jr., Pittsburgh, RNC, $1,400; Scaife, R. M., Pittsburgh, RNFC, $3,000; Sharples, Mr. & Mrs. Philip T., Haverford, RCBC, $4,000; Sheppard, R. H., Hanover, RNFC, $1,000; Smith, Robert P., Pottstown, RCBC, $1,000; Staisey, Leonard C., Pittsburgh, DNGC, $1,000; Steinman, Mr. & Mrs. J. F., Lancaster, RNFC, $2,000; Steinman, John F., Pequa, RCBC, $1,000; Sullivan, Mr. & Mrs. B. R., Laughlintown, RNFC, $1,000.

Thacher, Mrs. Thomas D., Philadelphia, RCBC, $1,000; Toland, Mrs. Owen J., Wynnewood, RCBC, $1,000; Underwood, J. G., Harrisburg, RNC, $1,000, RNFC, $1,000; Van Alen, William L., Philadelphia, RCBC, $1,000; Warden, Clarence A. Jr., Wynnewood, RCBC, $1,000, RNFC, $1,000; Ware, Hon. J. H., Oxford, RNFC, $1,000; Weiss, M., Philadelphia, '70 CF, $3,000; Whitaker, U. A., Harrisburg, RNC, $1,000, RNFC, $1,000; Widener, George D., Philadelphia, RCBC, $2,000; Wilmerding, Mrs. David R., Berwyn, RCBC, $1,000; Zimmerman, E. W., Harrisburg, RNFC, $1,000.

RHODE ISLAND

Anderson, O. V., Providence, RNFC, $1,000; Case, A. B., Providence, RNFC, $1,000; Chace, A. B., Providence, RNC, $1,000; Davie, Mrs. Preston, Newport, RCBC, $1,000; Dresser, Robert B., Providence, CVF, $2,000, ACA, $2,000; Goddard, Robert H. I. Jr., Providence, RCBC, $1,000; Marston, Hunter L., Watch Hill, RCBC, $1,500; Metcalf, Mrs. Houghton P. Exeter, RCBC, $1,000; Morgan, R. T., North Kingstown, RNFC, $1,000; Wrenn, G. L. II, Watch Hill, RNC, $1,000.

SOUTH CAROLINA

Ballenger, C. P. Jr., Greenville, RNFC, $1,000; Cassels, W. T., Columbia, RNC, $1,000; Edens, J., Columbia, RNC, $1,000; Milliken, R., Spartanburg, RNC, $1,000; Williams, Greenville, ACU, $1,000.

SOUTH DAKOTA

TENNESSEE

Bush, Jack T., Danbridge, RCBC, $1,000; Crichton, R. M., Nashville, RNC, $1,000; Dobbs, J. H., Memphis, RNFC, $3,000; Dudley, Hon. G. Jr., Nashville, RNFC, $1,000; Farris, Frank M. Jr., Nashville, RCBC, $1,000; Hannon, W. M., Nashville, RCBC, $1,000; Ingram, E. Bronson, Nashville, RCBC, $1,000; Ingram, E. B., Nashville, RNC, $1,000; Ingram, Mrs. O. H., Nashville, RNFC, $1,000, RCBC, $3,000; Maddox, D. W., Nashville, RCBC, $1,000.

Massey, Jack C., Nashville, RCBC, $3,000, RNFC, $3,000; Nelson, E. G., Nashville, RNC, $1,000; Nunnally, J. D., Memphis, RNC, $1,000; Potter, Mrs. J., Nashville, RCC, $3,000, RVC, $3,000, RNFC, $3,000; Potter, Mrs. Valere Blair, Nashville, RCBC, $1,000; Smith, W. E., Memphis, RNFC, $1,000; Stewart, James W., Nashville, RCBC, $1,000; Wilson, Anne Potter, Nashville, RCBC, $1,000; Wilson, Mr. & Mrs. David K., Nashville, RCC, $6,000, RVC, $6,000, RNFC, $6,000, RCBC, $1,000.

TEXAS

Agnich, F. J., Dallas, RNFC, $1,000; Anderson, Thomas D., Houston, RCBC, $1,000; Armstrong, Maj. T. R., Armstrong, RNFC, $1,000; Bel Fay, Albert, Houston, RCBC, $1,000; Bowdle, Mrs. M., Wichita Falls, RNFC, $1,000; Bracewell, S., Houston, CFA, $1,000; Brandt, Mildred, Dallas, DSCC, $1,000; Briggs, R., San Antonio, RNC, $1,000; Brown, B. L., Dallas, NRCC, $2,000,

NRSC, $5,000 (with C. J. Benner, CITIGO); Brown, Mr. & Mrs. E. W. Jr., Orange, RNFC, $3,000; Bullock, Thomas A., Houston, DNC, $1,000.

Butler, J. R., Houston, RNFC, $1,000; Cahill, John J., Houston, ACU, $1,000; Carrillo, Ramiro, Benavides, DNGC, $1,000; Catto, H. E. Jr., San Antonio, RNC, $1,000; Claxton, B., Houston, RNFC, $1,000; Clemens, E. W., San Antonio, RNC, $1,000, RNFC, $1,000; Clement, Mrs. J. H., Kingsville, RNFC, $1,000; Conner, W. C., Ft. Worth, RNC, $1,000; Corley, O. P., Dallas, RNC, $1,000; Cox, G. C., Houston, CFA, $1,297.

Crawford, O. R. Sr., Jasper, RNC, $1,000; Cullen, Roy H., Houston, RCBC, $1,000; Decker, W. M., Amarillo, DNC, $1,000; Dunlap, R. C. Jr., Dallas, RNC, $1,000; Dyche, W. E. Jr., Houston, RNC, $1,000, RNFC, $1,000; Elkins, J. A. Jr., Houston, DNC, $1,000; Elliott, J. E., Austin, RCBC, $1,000; RNC, $1,000; Farah, W. F., El Paso, RNFC, $1,000; Farish, W. S. Sr., Houston, RNFC, $1,000; Fay, Mrs. Albert, Houston, RCBC, $1,000.

Fish, Mrs. B. N., Houston, RNFC, $1,000; Fogelson, E. E., Dallas, RNFC, $1,000; Forbes, Douglas W., Dallas, RCBC, $1,000; Forbes, D. W., Dallas, RNC, $1,000; Frensley, H. J., Houston, CFA, $1,000; Garvey, Mr. & Mrs. J. S., Fort Worth, RNFC, $5,547.05; Garwood, St. John, Jr., Houston, RCBC, $1,000; Good, E. B., Houston, CFA, $1,000; Gueymard, A. G., Houston, RNFC, $1,000; Haggerty, P. E., Dallas, RNC, $3,000.

Halbouty, M. T., Houston, RNFC, $1,000; Harrell, F. B., Dallas, CFA, $1,000; Harvey, M. J., Tyler, RNC, $1,000; Harvey, M. J. Jr., Dallas, RNC, $2,000, RNFC, $3,000; Haynes, W. R., Houston, RNC, $1,000; Holliday, Mr. & Mrs. R. M., Houston, RNFC, $1,000; Hudnall, J. S., Tyler, NRSC, $1,000; Hurd, J. G., Laredo, RNFC, $1,000; Johnson, B. K., San Antonio, RNC, $1,000; Jonsson, Hon. J., Dallas, RNFC, $1,000.

Kaggerty, P. E., Dallas, RNFC, $1,000; Kampmann, Flora C., San Antonio, NRSC, $3,000, RCBC, $3,000; Kampmann, Mrs. I. S. Jr., San Antonio, RNFC, $1,000; Ling, Joseph, Dallas, DNC, $1,000; Lynch, J. F., Houston, RNC, $1,000; Lytle, F., Arkansas Pass, RNFC, $1,000; McDermott, R., Houston, RNFC, $3,000; McElvaney, E., Dallas, RNC, $1,000, RCBC, $1,000; McLean, Mrs. M., San Antonio, RNFC, $1,000; Maguire, Cary M., Dallas, RNC, $1,000, RNFC, $1,000, RCBC, $1,000; Manning, W. K., Dallas, RCBC, $1,000.

Marshall, Douglas B., Houston, RCBC, $3,000; Masterson, Mr. & Mrs. H., Houston, RNFC, $1,000; Meyer, P. J. Sr., Waco, RNC, $1,000; Mischer, W. M., Houston, CFA, $1,000; Mosbacher, R., Houston, RNFC, $1,000; Mundy, A. J. Jr., Houston, CFA, $1,198; Oliver, W. B., Dallas, RNFC, $1,000; Padon, William B., Houston, RCBC, $1,000; Parten, J., Houston, '70 CF, $1,000; Patman, C., Ganado, DNC, $1,000.

Pew, J. W., Dallas, RNC, $1,000; Pitts, Phelps & White, Beaumont, DNC, $1,000; Rentzel, D. W., Dallas, DNGC, $1,000; Rhea, Mr. & Mrs. J. W. Jr., Dallas, RNFC, $1,000; Robertson, Corbin J., Houston, DNC, $1,000; Russell, W. L., Houston, RNFC, $1,000; Sanchez, Henry Jr., Brownsville, DNGC, $1,000; Scott, W. E. Jr., Houston, RNFC, $1,000; Sharp, Dudley C., Houston, RCBC, $4,000; Shouse, Earl E., Houston, DNC, $1,000.

Siewert, C. L., Lubbock, RNFC, $1,000; Slick, W., Dallas, '70 CF, $1,000; Steele, T. F., Houston, CFA, $1,500; Tapp, R. S., Lubbock, RNC, $1,000; Terry, H. L., Houston, RNC, $1,000; Thayer, W., Dallas, RNFC, $1,000; Thomas, Max L., Dallas, DNC, $1,200; Vaughan, B. F. Jr., Corpus Christi, RNFC, $1,000; Wagner, Mrs. J. P., Helotes, RNFC, $1,000; Wells, B., Houston, CFA, $1,000.

Wiess, Mrs. Harry C., Houston, RCBC, $3,000; Woodfin, M. L., Houston, CFA, $1,198; Wynne, T. L., Dallas, RNFC,

$1,000; Young, S. D., El Paso, RNFC, $1,000; Zachry, H. B., San Antonio, RNFC, $1,000, RNC, $1,000.

UTAH

VERMONT

Borish, E., W. Brattleboro, DSG, $1,000; Borish, M., W. Brattleboro, '70 CF, $2,000; Borish, M. E., W. Brattleboro, NCEC; $1,000; Foster, G. N., Manchester, RNC, $1,000.

VIRGINIA

Bain, R., Arlington, RNC, $1,000; Bregman, Stanley, Alexandria, DSCC, $2,000; Brown, S. T., Roanoke, RNFC, $1,000; Cobb, Wm. L., Arlington, RCBC, $1,000; Coleman, J. S., The Plains, RNFC, $1,000; Collier, R. A., Alexandria, RNC, $1,000, RNFC, $1,000; Corber, R. J., Arlington, RNC, $1,000; Deluca, J. F., Falls Church, RNC, $1,000; Gottwald, F. D. Jr., Richmond, RNC, $1,000; Graves, Capt. & Mrs. Edwin D., Warrenton, RCBC, $1,000; Haid, Joseph W., Teays, ACU, $1,000.

Hoffman, A. L., Norfolk, RNFC, $1,000; Jordan, D. L., Roanoke, RNC, $1,000; Lewis, J. F. Jr., Charlottesville, RNC, $1,000; Lewis, Mr. & Mrs. L. Jr., Richmond, RNFC, $6,000; Loomis, Henry, Middleburg, RCBC, $1,000; Mars, Mr. & Mrs. F. E., The Plains, RNFC, $3,000; Massey, I., Richmond, RNC, $1,000; Mountain, Barry, Annandale, RCBC, $1,000; Olsson, Mr. & Mrs. S. J., West Point, RNFC, $1,000; Opstad, D. O., Great Falls, RNFC, $1,000.

Poillon, Col. & Mrs., Alexandria, RNFC, $1,000; Potter, I. Lee, Arlington, RCBC, $1,000; Pratt, J. L., Fredericksburg, RNC, $1,000; Randolph, Mrs. A. C., Upperville, RNFC, $1,000; Robins, E. Claiborne, Richmond, BIPAC, $3,000; Roper, J. L. II, Norfolk, RNC, $1,000; Scott, Mrs. M. D., Montpelier Station, RNFC, $1,000; Truchio, Patrick Jr., Alexandria, NRCC, $1,000; Via, Mrs. M. B., Roanoke, RNC, $1,000; White, Don, Fairfax, NRCC, $1,400, NRSC, $500; Wiley, Mrs. J. L., The Plains, RNFC, $2,000; Worthington, George Jr., Charlottesville, ACU, $1,000.

WASHINGTON

Brady, Hugh P., Seattle, RCBC, $1,000; Buchanan, T. N., Seattle, RCBC, $1,000, CFA, $1,000; Bullitt, S., Seattle, NCEC; $1,000; Cannon, J. E., Seattle, RNC, $1,000; Clapp, Norton, Seattle, RCBC, $3,000; Clapp, Mrs. Norton, Seattle, RCBC, $1,000; Clapp, N., Tacoma, RNFC, $1,000; Clise, A. H., Seattle, RCBC, $1,000, RNFC, $1,000; Cowles, W. H., Spokane, RNC, $1,000, RCBC, $1,000; Duecy, George P., Everett, RCBC, $1,000.

Elmore, L. V., Hoquiam, RNFC, $1,000; Eriekson, C., Seattle, NRCC, $4,000; Fuller, Dr. R. E., Seattle, RNC, $1,000; Gaiser, Mrs. D. W., Spokane, RNC, $1,000, RNFC, $1,000; Gonyea, D. A., Tacoma, RCBC, $1,000, RNC, $1,000; Johnson, J. W., Spokane, RNFC, $1,000; Lindberg, W. Hilding, Tacoma, RCBC, $1,000; Link, A. H., Seattle, RCBC, $1,000; Loomis, W. F., Seattle, RCBC, $1,000; MacDonald, D. K., Seattle, RCBC, $1,000.

Moody, Anson B., Everett, RCBC, $1,000; Murdock, M. J., Vancouver, RNFC, $1,000; O'Donnell, Flora M., Seattle, NRCC, $1,000; Orell, B. L., Tacoma, RNC, $1,000; Plgott, C. M., Renton, RNC, $1,000; Reed, William G., Seattle, RCBC, $1,000, RNFC, $1,000; Scott, John L., Seattle, RCBC, $1,000; Tenzler, H. E., Tacoma, RCBC, $3,000; Titcomb, F. R., Tacoma, RNFC, $1,000;

Wallerstein, G., Seattle, NCEC; $1,000; Weyerhaeuser, C. Davis, Tacoma, RCBC, $1,000; Wilson, Harry L., Seattle, RCBC, $1,000.

WEST VIRGINIA

Edwards, J. F., Chester, RNC, $1,000; Hubbard, David, Wellsburg, ACU, $1,055; Long, Miss Hilda, Huntington, DNC, $1,000; Wilson, Sam B., Mundsville, ACU, $1,000.

WISCONSIN

Amann, Paul M. & Mrs., Milwaukee, DNC, $1,000; Baldwin, Emily, Wisconsin Rapids, NRCC, $4,000; Baldwin, Mrs. Henry, Wisconsin Rapids, RCBC, $3,000; Brode, W. H., Milwaukee, NRCC, $1,000; Buchanan, William E., Menasha, RCBC, $1,000; Cofrin, J. P., Green Bay, RNFC, $1,000; Coughlin, C. L., Milwaukee, RNFC, $1,000; Eberbach, Mrs. C. W., Milwaukee, RNC, $1,000; Emch, H. H., Milwaukee, RNFC, $1,000; Falk, Louis W., Milwaukee, CVF, $1,000.

Feldstein, William J., Milwaukee, DNC, $1,000; Gallun, Edwin A., Milwaukee, CVF, $1,000, ACU, $1,200; Harnischfeger, W., Milwaukee, RNC, $1,000, RNFC, $1,000; Johnson, H., Racine, RNC, $3,000, RNFC, $1,000; Johnson, H. F., Racine, RCBC, $1,000; Johnson, Roy W., Milwaukee, RCBC, $1,000; Johnson, R. W., Milwaukee, RNFC, $1,000; Johnson, Samuel C., Racine, RCBC, $1,000; Johnson, S. C., Racine, RNC, $1,000, RNFC, $1,000; Kieckhefer, Mrs. M. B., Milwaukee, RNFC, $1,000.

Kritzik, Robert, Milwaukee, DNC, $1,000; Lindsay, Mrs. Thomas C., Harland, RCBC, $1,000; Lindsey, Walter S., Milwaukee, RCBC, $1,000; Mayer, O. G. Jr., Madison, RNFC, $1,000; Pabst, D., Oconomowoc, RNFC, $1,000; Schroeder, Mrs. John E., Milwaukee, RCBC, $1,000; Schwartz, B. L., Milwaukee, RNC, $1,000; Siebert, R. L., Wauwatosa, RCBC, $1,000, RNC, $1,000; Slocum, Mrs. A. Lester, Milwaukee, RCBC, $1,000; Smith, Lloyd B., Milwaukee, RCBC, $1,000.

Steiger, Mr. & Mrs. Carl E., Oshkosh, RCBC, $1,000; Stevenson, R. S., Elm Grove, RNFC, $1,000; Stone, Mr. & Mrs. S., Milwaukee, RNC, $1,000; Stratton, John F., Milwaukee, RCBC, $1,000; Trane, Mrs. Helen Hood, La Crosse, RCBC, $1,000; Uihlein, F. W., Milwaukee, RNFC, $1,000; Vogel, Mrs. Charles P., Milwaukee, RCBC, $1,000; Vogel, William D., Milwaukee, RCBC, $1,000; Wood, S. J., Beloit, RNFC, $1,000.

WYOMING

Bentzen, L. W., Sheridan, RNFC, $1,000; Stroock, T., Casper, RNC, $1,000.

GUAM, PUERTO RICO & VIRGIN ISLANDS

Camacho, J. G., Agana, Guam, RNC, $1,000; Ferre, Hon. L. A., San Juan, Puerto Rico, RNFC, $1,000; Merrill, Mrs. K. A., St. Croix, Virgin Islands, RNFC, $1,000; Phelan, F. J. Jr., Agana, Guam, RNFC, $1,000.

FOREIGN COUNTRIES

Culbertson, C. D., Cuernavaca, Mexico, RNC, $1,000; Diamantis, C., Piraeus, Greece, RNC, $3,000, RNFC, $3,000, RCC, $3,000, RNFOC, $1,000; Geier, P. E., Rome, Italy, RNC, $1,000; Humes, Hon. J. P., Vienna, Austria, RNC, $3,000; Jackman, C. M., Paris, France, RNFC, $2,000; Munson, Mr. & Mrs. C. B., Edmonton, Alberta, Canada, RNC, $2,000; Peck, Mrs. J., Dublin, Ireland, RNFC, $1,000.